Intercities

TOPOGRAPHICS

in the same series

Intercities

Stefan Hertmans

REAKTION BOOKS

Published by Reaktion Books Ltd
79 Farringdon Road, London EC1M 3JU, UK

www.reaktionbooks.co.uk

First published 2001

English-language translation copyright © Paul Vincent
The translation of this book is funded by the Flemish Foundation for
Literature – Vlaams Fonds voor de Letteren.

Printed and bound in Great Britain by
Biddles Ltd, Guildford and King's Lynn

British Library Cataloguing in Publication Data

Hertmans, Stefan
    Intercities. – (Topographics)
    1.Cities and towns – History 2.City and town life
    I. Title
    307.7'6

ISBN 1 86189 093 1

Contents

As if everyone, all over the world, had his daily visually artistic task: the task of being an image for others.
PETER HANDKE

The contemporary knows nothing.
VICTOR KLEMPERER

Check-In

The most ambitious novel on the modern city opens with the greatest zoom-in in world literature. The narrator of *The Man without Qualities* homes in on the city of Vienna as if from the height of a satellite, from a 'depression over the Atlantic':

> It was travelling eastwards, towards an area of high pressure over Russia and still showed no tendency to move northwards around it . . . The vapour in the atmosphere was at its highest tension and the moisture in the air was at its lowest. In short, to use an expression that describes the facts pretty satisfactorily, even though it is somewhat old-fashioned: it was a fine August day in the year 1913. Motor-cars came shooting out of deep, narrow streets into the shallows of bright squares. Dark patches of pedestrian bustle formed into cloudy streams.

In a single camera movement, Robert Musil, the author of these masterly opening lines from *The Man without Qualities*, has hit on a perfect *Wiener Mélange* of what was current in his day: the vision of a scientifically trained mind (the city of Mauthner and Ernst Mach), intellectual distance (Schönberg and Webern), a gift for observation that points across the frontiers to a future sensibility (the critical spirit of Karl Kraus), the talent for approaching things from a new and open perspective (Wittgenstein), but at the same time with a power of observation that places the trivia of everyday life – or rather plunges, submerges them – in a planetary framework, the sense that Vienna was a cosmopolis, a city for and of the contemporary world. Yet immediately after this spectacular beginning, in which as it were a huge curtain is drawn aside before our reading eyes, we zoom in on a minor event that becomes exemplary for the city he wants to show us: a traffic accident that is described with considerable irony and confronts us with some of the future protagonists, who, and this is telling, are involved only as spectators. It is an opening that is still impossible to avoid, unequalled even by the style with which seventeen years later the great American modernist, John Dos Passos, opened his formidable trilogy on the American city, *U.S.A. The 42nd Parallel* begins as follows:

> The young man walks fast by himself through the crowd that thins into the night streets; feet are tired from hours of walking; eyes greedy for warm curve of faces, answering flicker of eyes, the set of a head, the lift of a shoulder, the way hands spread and clench; blood tingles with wants; mind is a still beehive of hopes buzzing and singing; muscles ache for the knowledge of jobs, for the roadmender's pick and shovel work, the fisherman's knack with a hook . . . The young man walks by himself searching through the crowd with greedy eyes, greedy ears taut to hear, by himself, alone.

The reader is already almost certain: this character comes from the provinces. The way in which he drinks things in is characterized by naïve astonishment, and his admiration for the old craftsmanship betrays his rural nostalgia. In itself not a bad point of view: the provincial lacks the habit of taking things for granted, he has the openness of the immigrant, a perspective that makes him hear and look more acutely. This opening, though, despite the exhaustively spectacular modern narrative techniques used later in the novel, seems fairly conventional in comparison with Musil's magisterial first chords. Dos Passos's man goes through the city on foot. He is already a part of a film sequence that we are drawn into at the pace of the main character as he walks on. Proust also ventured out into Paris on foot, if necessary moving around at a comfortable jog in an open coach along the avenues around the Bois de Boulogne; moreover, the city glides into his novel as it were unobtrusively, with its flashbacks and flash-forwards, via a number of Monsieur

8

Swann's exploits. James Joyce, in his turn, roams the streets of Trieste like a Homeric exile with the mental street plan of Dublin in the back of his mind. But Robert Musil seems every inch a modern passenger gliding towards the city in a Boeing 747. The difference is that here the anatomist, the scientist with the literary microscope, is arriving – the man who can immediately observe the dying of a fly on a window-pane as he fastens his seat belt for the landing and the stewardess reminds him with a smile to fold away his table.

A contemporary variant of this zooming-in onto the chaotic, potentially catastrophic nature of life in the big city is offered by Thomas Pynchon in the opening passage of *Gravity's Rainbow*:

> A screaming comes across the sky. It has happened before, but there is nothing to compare it to now. It is too late. The Evacuation still proceeds, but it's all theatre. There are no lights inside the cars. No light anywhere. Above him lift girders as old as an iron queen, and glass somewhere far above that would let the light of day through. But it's night.

This last remark will become sufficiently clear later in the book. And here Musil is overtaken on the right. Whereas he described the city mainly by day, for Pynchon city life has become mainly a nocturnal, almost surreal theatrical event: Only the nearer faces are visible at all, and at that only as half-silvered images in a viewfinder, green-stained VIP faces remembered behind bullet-proof windows speeding through the city . . .

In *American Psycho*, Brett Easton Ellis makes the entry into the city of New York an immediate descent into Dante's Inferno:

> ABANDON HOPE ALL YE WHO ENTER HERE is scrawled in blood red lettering on the side of the Chemical Bank near the corner of Eleventh and First and is in print large enough to be seen from the backseat of the cab as it lurches forward in the traffic leaving Wall Street . . .

Of course the city is all those things at once – entrance and exit, the hell of the smoking city buses that glide past the docks, the long trail of cars inching past the first great blocks of houses in the direction of the centre just after dawn, the grubby paradise of a room glowing in pale sunlight where two forbidden lovers steal an hour of happiness, the vomiting boy behind a pitta bar at four in the morning, the reflection in shop windows so that there's no escape from one's own deliberateness, the porter who twists his ankle at the back of an hotel, the joggers along the dusty avenues of the park, the drunk old man with the umpteenth glass that he's sipped down, the strolling junkies, the hurried bullet-head with his eternal Samsonite, the young woman with a bored face pushing a baby carriage across the zebra crossing, the vegetable sellers already clearing up towards noon, a flash of light in an opening window, or the only vaguely visible, partly mangled body under a tram that has stopped just too late. From the perspective of the airbus circling over the city, it is all invisible, at most a few moving dots, beetle-like things scuttling around at ground level.

'Individuals come and go, the tram rails remain,' says Willem Koerse in his book *The Limitless City*. Yet a deep humanitarian significance remains attached to the concept of the city, which must never be lost sight of. The city is the territory of human communication in its most advanced form.

For Baudelaire in the mid-nineteenth century the city was the territory-less arena where human relations were no longer conducted on the basis of ownership of property or age-old customs like family rights, patriarchy and marrying off, but on the basis of a general rootlessness. The city is everyone's because it belongs to no one in particular. That is why social and erotic relationships are possible virtually without consequences other than psychological ones, why the city allows anonymity and becomes the cradle of a more open, more democratic morality. That accelerates evolution and emancipation on a grand scale. What Rousseau in his *Emile* still described as the decadence of the city, is evaluated in a radically positive way scarcely a century later by Baudelaire. What Rousseau presented in *Le contrat social* as the prerogative of the four estates, namely that they must be based on a broadly accepted general will, Baudelaire saw developing in the immediacy of contacts in the metropolis of Paris, so deplored by the romantic Rousseau. Baudelaire's vision of the city was to prove prophetic, in the first place for the emancipation of social and sexual relations. 'Marry or keep your hands off' was the motto of the villages in the countryside, since sexual relations quite simply had consequences for inheritance and for the division of land and property. In the city, this underlying contract has vanished; the social contract of the city refers only to the here and now. In the twentieth century, these ideas were taken to the extreme by Andy Warhol who, with his Factory and its accompanying jet-set image, emphasized the theatrical nature of urban societies, first and foremost New York. This theatricality, however, need not be taken in a negative sense; the city is a contemporary catwalk, the place where people become aware of many things that are bound to be subjected to merciless analysis by the surrounding eyes. Things that would never have been noticed in this way in the peace of a country village. The crisis of personality is the filter through which provincials arriving in the city have to pass in order to take on a character they must design for themselves. This means that the city remains the focus of cultural narcissism, but this self-consciousness is in turn invariably characterized by a complete absence of 'fundamentalist' ideas about enrootedness, native soil or origin. The self-realization of individuals in big cities does not take place according to traditional values, but through an emancipatory struggle for freedom.

It is probably no coincidence that in recent years a number of intellectuals, including Salman Rushdie and Jacques Derrida, have committed themselves to creating so-called 'cities of refuge', that is, an internationally based network of autonomously operating, hospitable cities where refugees and asylum seekers of all kinds, whose legal appeals have run their course, could find sanctuary. In this way, the city would again fulfil the pioneering role in the area of international relations assigned to it by Baudelaire: of being in the vanguard in the normalization of relations that in other parts of the world do not go smoothly. The concept of a city of refuge derives from what Derrida calls 'the duty of hospitality'. In order to give that legal form, it would be necessary to appeal to an old idea which in the twentieth century had faded into the background: that of urban sovereignty. In other words, such safe havens would be able to acquire an operational autonomy comparable with that of an ancient polis and the traditional city states. In this connection, Derrida speaks of cosmopolitics: no longer the nation states, but the cities would have to take the lead in the concrete tackling of urgent social problems. As nation states are no longer prepared to give a general humanitarian guarantee of the right of asylum or have become too unwieldy politically, there is perhaps a new role for cities, which should no longer be, as Koen Brams puts it in an introduction to a text by Derrida, 'the slavish icons of the nation states' that they were in the nineteenth century:

> If it is still meaningful and relevant to speak about such things as the city and urban identity, the question arises whether cities can rise above nation states, or whether they can liberate themselves from them within limits to be defined in more detail, in a new sense of the word *free cities* where hospitality and sanctuary are concerned . . . National sovereignty cannot and must not any longer be the ultimate principle of safe havens. Is that possible anyway? (from the address given by Derrida at the First Conference on Cities of Refuge, Strasbourg, March 1996)

Now that there is speculation, in numerous apocalyptic-looking strip cartoons, about cities that have developed in recent times being engulfed in an urban jungle, we see that there is another approach crystallizing which tries to give expression in an almost ecological way to the diversity of cultural points of view, the specific value of the city for demo-

12

cracy, open social psychology. The city as a microcosm of human action, balancing between apocalyptic visions of doom, suburban ghettos on the one hand and all too quaintly restored squares, monuments and small-scale district projects on the other. What our culture really is, is scattered over as many places as there are cities. *Eraserhead* and the old Slovenian woman whom I saw begging in Trieste, are two sides of the same coin, however different other urban experiences may be.

There are enough descriptions of exotic-looking cities, and anyone wanting to go to Punta Arenas, Dakkar, Baku or Anchorage will, if necessary, see surprising variants of a social culture that has become almost cosmopolitan, with all the attendant advantages and disadvantages. Mexico City, Paris and Singapore are struggling with variants of the same problems. But it's just as true that we only have to go round the corner in our own city, to see evidence all around us of a recent past. It's just that it always presents itself in unexpected forms.

Sydney: Parallel Worlds

It is as if for centuries a substance has flowed from the human eye that affects and changes the world, a glue that binds places and things. That substance doesn't really exist, things are not joined together into a meaningful whole by any glue. And yet it is our eyes that bind things together, that give them a place in the whole; a look that hesitates between understanding and incomprehension, as if we intuitively want to assign things a place in an otherwise chaotic world by the simple fact that we see them; though without necessarily having the guarantee that we can actually place them.

However, the human eye certainly does put the whole world into a meaningful context: all urban and rural landscapes have been formed, determined and constructed by concepts from geometry and perspective. Nothing is simply there. What we see is always determined by what others before us have seen in it. We, who stand there and look on, as the popular Dutch song says, link things when we see them; not a single landscape in which man has intervened escapes this linking look, which connects things, glues them back together again and interprets them as a coherent whole – a bridge, a tunnel, a tower, a bend in a road – as if we are forming sentences, 'making syntax' of the discrete things around us. The open places in urban land-scapes are the most far-reaching example of this binding, this assigning-of-a-place by the human eye: we immediately fill the emptiness with the meaning of a square. These open places suggest spatial continuity without our actually seeing it or being able to say much about it, but which we nevertheless recognize immediately and intuitively as a common experience.

Seen in this way, the desolate plain around the Berlin

Potzdamer Platz before 1990 wasn't simply an empty site, but a scar full of meaning, a story about war and cities, and what might seem empty was immediately glued together by the eye into an historical site in which each thistle shooting up could acquire a meaning of its own.

In the film *Der Himmel über Berlin*, the old Homer, a leather cap with earflaps on his wrinkled head, stumbles across the immense fallow field through the overgrown grass:

> I can't find Potzdamer Platz! No, here I thought . . . No, that's not it! Potzdamer Platz, surely that's where Café Josti . . . So this can't be Potzdamer Platz! And no one to ask . . . It was a district full of fun! Trams, buses with horses and two cars . . . Tell me, Muse, of the poor immortal precentor . . .

This twentieth-century Homer staggers past rubbish through the grass that has grown grey with urban dust and slowly the vanished square looms up in the mind of the viewer. As he talks of them blindly, the things rise up and walk in the midst of old paper, condoms and greasy chip papers, between the garbage and the signs of a space left to its own devices. The fallow field again becomes a square, the bell of the tram rings, the coffee in Café Josti regains its aroma and the first cars draw

What a pleasant neighbourhood!

up. Time's arrow is reversed for a while. Then the old man sinks into a dilapidated sofa and gets his breath back as he sadly meditates. In the background, we see the ugly improvised pedestrian bridge that, in the meantime, has disappeared.

The Campo dei Miracoli in Pisa, the Piazza dell'Unità d'Italia in the glittering bay of Trieste, the canal basin like a square of water in front of San Giorgio Maggiore in Venice, the vague (disquieting) open space in front of the Kremlin or behind the Hermitage in St Petersburg, the unforgettable bleakness around the Brandenburg Gate in Berlin, the ancient emptiness of the great Roman sites; but also the new emptinesses deliberately filled by architecture with nothing but the potential of the human eye, the deserts of suburbs. This eye immediately fills with memory and makes the new into something that can be understood in a different story. Take Sydney harbour, with its twentieth-century version of what Venice must once have been, in which the famous shell-shaped Opera House contrasts with the tall metal bridge, the park with its white ibises and corellas, and the quay with the metro line above it – all these things that were placed in a different perspective by the intervention of that most recent building, the Opera House. Such open spaces are linked together by the subtle adhesive of the human eye, which sticks contrasting elements together; even through the arbitrariness of pleasant diversion, they interact and complement each other, in turn forming the glue through which the eye goes exploring and assigns a place to the skyline, the water, the arc of the iron bridge or the kissing couples, the same the world over, in the warm dusk by the railing of a ferry boat that is just leaving.

The human eye knows about proportions and plays with them consciously but, at the same time, absent-mindedly, looking with a detached emptiness that prevents the viewer from being pinned down by a single object or focus.

The same emptiness that activates the glue of the eye assails you all the time in Australia. It begins the moment you start flying over the outback for hour after hour, the monotonous landscape intersected by heat and vague dream lines, the empty heart of this continent, like a huge deserted square around which the cities have assembled like buildings and through which the central emptiness acquires a meaning that cannot be found anywhere else; for example, this meaning remains noticeably absent when you fly over the Siberian steppes – here there is no longer any boundary, only centripetal emptiness, far below zero.

On Circular Quay, the bow-shaped quay around which Sydney's waterfront square lies, a *Writers Walk* has been set up – about 40 brass plates with quotations from authors like D. H. Lawrence, Robert Hughes, Eleanor Dark and Charles Darwin, David Malouf, Jack London, Rudyard Kipling, Mark Twain and Arthur Conan Doyle. They are all quotations which in a strangely varied way evoke a fascination with what has been forgotten, hidden under the shuffling feet of laughing tourists who, without one look at the plates, are far beyond the Oyster Bar on their way to something undefined, which they hope to find in Botany Bay.

'Silence ruled this land,' it says on Eleanor Dark's plate. 'Out of silence mystery comes, and magic, and the delicate awareness of unreasoning things.' (from *The Timeless Land*, 1941)

The rollerbladers whizz across the words.

Would Australians have done anything differently if their country had not been settled as the jail of the infinite space? Certainly they would. They would have remembered more of their own history. (from Robert Hughes, *The Fatal Shore*, 1987)

Nearby sits an Aborigine, dressed up and decorated with what was once a unique heritage but has now degenerated into its own exotic form of kitsch, playing his sonorous didgeridoo. Fascinated by the primeval power of this spectacle, the rhythm and the sound, more and more clusters of people stop. Then the man, who is at least six feet tall, takes the instrument out of his mouth, and with a smoky voice says in broad Australian, 'Well, if ya like ta hear what I play, why don't ya put some money in here?' He points contemptuously at the bowl by one of his knees and goes on playing. The primeval sound that left his listeners free to think their own thoughts has suddenly acquired a voice straight out of a soap opera, but with a tone that frightens the anonymous public to death, a direct challenge to its non-committal attitude. This is more than a walker out in search of the exotic can bear. Immediately the ogling group disperses, the man is alone again and behind their backs the monotonous ancient rhythm begins again – as the fascinating bad conscience of the exotic dream.

D. H. Lawrence, Charles Darwin, Robert Hughes and so many others whose names have been put on round brass plates in the paving of the promenade around Sydney Bay, have all described this experience of a fathomless space-time in Australia, fascinated by the constantly threatening disintegration of the meaningful context in a terrifying emptiness that Westerners find difficult to comprehend; something that forces them to confront an exotic existentialism, which for them is only bearable or comprehensible in its theoretical intellectual European form – namely the idea that existence is no more than a temporary abode, simply enduring for a while in a space and time, so that no form of meaning can become visible – even though the palms wave as they do in the adverts, the sea otters sleep on the beach and the gaudiest birds are twittering like crazy in the wonderful, prehistoric-looking trees.

For, ultimately, it is not a matter of the emptiness of the comfortably absent-minded look with which the trained tourist is by now familiar: not about the look that shoots away across the Bay of Trieste or the chessboard of marble buildings in Pisa. It is about the gigantic emptiness that nudges you in the back, the emptiness which from the centre of this hot continent has, as it were, banished the cities to the coasts: in the heart of this vast land there is something that the coast still cannot cope

18

with, something that promises no solutions, only frustration.

Here Alain Corbin's 'longing for the coast' is not an urge towards a salutary final destination where a primeval catharsis can be found, but an attempt to escape an inland underworld – as if one has to escape the pressure of the look that the continent radiates from Ayer's Rock and Alice Springs like a magic, evil heat, by almost jumping into the water of the endless-seeming ocean.

This impression of an Australian interior as a bad conscience is given sustenance in no small measure when one learns about the unbelievably irresponsible and cynical atomic tests that were carried out here by the British in the 1950s, and that have made the great Aboriginal areas, which were considered sacred land, inaccessible for a relative eternity: it is as if a curse emanates from the song lines which have since then been drawn across this area – the old courses can be seen in the Tandanya Museum in Adelaide, alongside shocking photos of the havoc.

The Aussies know about this pressure, which they carry within like an almost repressed sense of guilt. It means, among other things, that through the well-meaning and compensatory concern for the declining aboriginal culture, this society remains inexorably bound by a colonial feeling of guilt, which is precisely what it is trying to escape from: as if in the emptiness of the outback there is a huge glowing mirror into which no one can bear to look. They once came ashore here as forced labourers with the guilt of criminals, acquired in the old world, and gradually they have incurred another guilt, that of a new world, that of the subsequent colonialism and its genocide. The Aussies have become trapped between these two forms of guilt, a bourgeois, European and somewhat rancorous heritage on the one hand and on the other, a primeval, planetary guilt in respect of the genocide on which present-day Australian vitalism is founded. It makes certain conversations not exactly easy to conduct, for no apparent reason – the motor racing in Melbourne, the taste of the wonderful barramundi fish, the simple mention of the name of Bruce Chatwin, the argument can suddenly flare up, feelings are hurt, a dreadfully civilized, Victorian irritation with Europe comes to the surface, although everyone here does their level best to create the impression that you have come to the best of all possible worlds (which, all things considered, is indeed your basic impression). Later, when you leave here, it retains a little of its truth, you have become addicted to that sucking feeling of space in your back – the country and the bush – and on the other hand a paradise in front of you: six thousand kilometres of scarcely polluted sea almost as far as the South Pole, empty and pure, full of white, leaping fish in the silent heat, while your compass has gone haywire. The sensation of a child.

Thus, for Australian culture, in a spatial sense, the world of the Aboriginal has become the 'cursed and precious' part of the subconscious, just like the Native-American space, in a historical sense, has become for present-day Americans: the suppressed Other in themselves, the unknown Other who keeps the longing for identity in a constant crisis and inflames it.

In his second great novel, *Lila*, Robert Pirsig developed a very infectious and ironic thesis, which boils down to the notion that the whole attitude of the low-voiced, cool big-city dweller of the present-day States in fact expresses the repressed, massacred Sioux Indian, in spite of himself. The first pioneers copied this obviously un-European way of talking and giving oneself a mythical attitude unconsciously from the Native Americans, whose self-control had made a great impression on them: the murdered victim, as Noble Savage, corresponded to the dream image of the romantic Great Other in their own soul and arises with each word like the ghost of suppressed guilt. So, without knowing it, all the cool-talking, American men who, in all circumstances affirm the masculinity of their low male voice, keep the Other murdered as a result of keeping their settlement alive. More than that, it is this status of the unconscious that has made the paradigm of that self-control into an American delight that is impossible to eradicate: anyone who is unable to display low-voiced coolness awakens the suspicion of not really being American (it is no coincidence that all Nazis who feature in American films have high, shrill voices: this is associated with the hysterical European, who has not been initiated by the experience of 'authenticity', which the murdered Native American is – he lacks as it were this 'initiation into natural but lost space').

This explains the shrewd and sovereign impression that Mickey Rourke makes by whispering in his role as the Motor Cycle Boy in the film *Rumble Fish*: he rejects the cultural totemic cannibalism of the Real American Man, just as Marlon Brando does with his hoarse voice that always seems to announce disaster. These figures become charismatic and elusive because they seem to stand above the code of the 'spontaneous' male signal of the low voice, they are therefore 'unnatural' and hence have a different, elusive authority: because they remain cool in all circumstances, the Native American speaks with a disturbed, hoarse and almost obsessive belly voice in a strange attitude – *out of key*, but still recognizable. A figure is only really unforgivable when he doesn't preserve this Sioux coolness: then he instantly appears to lose all sex appeal (a requirement and quality of masculinity which is not really a major priority – to take a random example – in Italian or French films).

What, I wondered, speculating with a friend under the palms on Circular Quay, could have crept into the behaviour of post-war Germans from the murdered Jews? Their frustrated way of talking about the impossibility of poetry and philosophy? Their difficult relationship with psychoanalysis, the most Jewish of all theories? 'The tourist, in his exalted reflection, is always a pig with no conscience,' said my travelling companion, M., and he laughed and raised his glass to me, with his greedy top lip deep in the light Australian Chardonnay.

That evening, we were to hear Beethoven's *Fidelio* in the famous Sydney Opera House – the liberation of the slaves, that allusion to the French Revolution, became in this case a rather too pathetically coloured emphatic metaphor for former eighteenth-century convicts and galley slaves who were sent to Australia, convicts who, through the liberation scene in *Fidelio*, are finally admitted to the legal, real world from which they were previously banished. A 'real world' which here, Down Under, 'was released from its dungeon'. The atmosphere in the auditorium was excited and relaxed on that warm summer evening in February, as if something were being celebrated which must not be expressed: that all Aussies recognize something of themselves in the idealist who throws open the prison doors and sets everyone free. French revolutionary ideas in Australian form. In night-time Sydney, the skyline glows enchantingly while the ferry boats bob up and down by the quay, and you really have the feeling of being present in a kind of up-and-coming twentieth-century Venice, at the beginning of its heyday, and that all others who come after us will be condemned to look back helplessly and walk through the museum of this life as it was, as we have to with the old, first Venice. For here the world is still naïve, vital and new, and blood and silence still beckon around every corner. The partly suppressed and partly mythologized history of the distant motherland, has faded in the images of an endless new country. Any arbitrary street can suddenly open out onto the terrible emptiness of a space without history. That is why people are still heroic and confused here, capable of anything and open to anything that occurs, however much was lost in those suppressed black predecessors who now just sit dozing and begging on the pavement, daubed with long-lost signs on their fat, dark skins, the painted didgeridoo in one hand. The Great Other in themselves sits looking at the white occupiers haughtily and accusingly with ancient wisdom and begs for a dollar or a cigarette. After a while, you begin experiencing that silent presence as mentally unbearable. When you talk to Australians about it, they answer with a shrug of the shoulders. 'Look mate, they don' wanna work, ya see?' Or you're given the obligatory story that they have set fire to the houses newly built for them. If you reply that this strikes you as quite understandable, the conversation is immediately over.

Perhaps something of their victims always passes into the attitude of peoples, of the vanished weaker ones on whom they have fed, of the vampirism through which their health was strengthened. Perhaps European peoples have absorbed something of the gypsy, something of the Sephardic Jew, something of every vanished nomad, as an unconscious confession of guilt, something that betrays them, a fragment of memory, of whose origin they are no longer aware. Psychoanalytical demons in demography. As if it were a cannibalistic ritual: the souls of the oppressed, the vanished fellow-countrymen, the nomads and the pariahs, have to be consumed in order to give strength to the vital, the strongest, the murderer with the exalted look in his eyes, who with devotion and forgetfulness concentrates on the future of his own children and who is convinced that he is acting according to the laws of an ancient system which therefore finds a degree of justification in itself.

This certainly applies to the Aussies and the Aborigines: the suppressed culture manifests itself via the unconscious, via the so-called 'spontaneous' attitudes of nonchalance – a form of mild *laisser-aller*, linked to an intense moral awareness, a constant concern that actually contains empathy through fear – fear and fascination for that Other, which one carries in oneself as a result of dwelling on and occupying the Other's land and space.

'In general', says Kierkegaard, 'one could say that imperfection in man is that one can only acquire what one desires through its antipode.'

Speculations about these dream images of nationality that have been absorbed in the Australian identity are still very topical. One beautiful afternoon, as I am travelling by car to a wine-growing valley north of Adelaide, the topic of conversation is the question of whether there is a clear Irish presence in any part of Australia. The writer, David Malouf, says that he knows that 38 per cent of Queensland was once Catholic, which might point to Irish settlement. The area around Adelaide (it turns out that even an Australian child can see this) is predominantly Scottish. And, indeed, as soon as you drive into the valleys, there are hosts of names beginning with *Mc* on the advertising hoardings. Scots who grow wonderful Chardonnay and Sauvignon – 'if that is the result of the Australian blend, then the convicts did not toil wholly in vain,' says someone on the back seat with a laugh. Under the deafening screeching of the corellas, who are hidden mainly in the prehistoric-looking eucalyptus trees from which great strips of bark hang and sway in the warm wind, we next speculate whether there is still any perceptible difference between the areas populated originally by convicts and areas populated by 'ordinary emigrants'. Difficult questions, on which a non-Aussie should observe a cautious silence. It is therefore completely wrong in the eyes of the Australian if you believe you have to bring up quotations by Robert Hughes or Bruce Chatwin: these are greeted with sneering or head-shaking corrections. It is the fault of these two writers, an older man tells me later with a British Islander's doggedness, that the world understands nothing about the Australian identity.

So, on Hindley Street in the entertainment area of Adelaide, the skinny louts with their British pallor walk on if they're suddenly faced with a drunken Aborigine who gives a perfect imitation of the nasal sound of Bob Dylan and stands there pounding a fifth-hand guitar; the reflections seem to circle round each other here without historical consciousness, separated from a chronology vibrating in a present which everyone, for convenience's sake, summarizes with the humming, mystical name 'Australia'.

No less than 60 per cent of the population is made up of immigrants from after the Second World War. It is hard to fathom the extent to which demographic fantasy is reflected in this. Now and then something comes up which indicates wandering planetary ghosts. The whole affair around the blonde, innocent-looking writer, Helen Demidenko, a student at the University of Brisbane, for example, is telling in this respect. In 1994, she published *The Hand that Signed the Paper*, a book in which she tells the story of a number of Ukrainian men who turn into camp thugs in Treblinka. These men had only one aim in mind: to avenge their families, who had been decimated by massacres. These peasant families were systematically starved to death, so the story goes, by rich Bolshevik Jews who were sent by Stalin to break the resistance of the Ukrainian people. The two men, Vitaly and Evheny, commit the most dreadful murders in the camps in the conviction that they are labouring for a noble end: the restoration of justice. The book is gruesome, meticulous and written with a chilling penetration. This led to the award of the most important literary prizes. Helen Demidenko maintained in every interview that the controversial thesis in her novel was inspired by the stories that she had heard from her Ukrainian father, and that she wanted to pass on these stories. All Australia took part in a debate that gradually became heated about the supposed existence or otherwise of anti-Semitism in the book, until the most inconceivable bombshell exploded: Helen Demidenko wasn't a Ukrainian immigrant at all; her parents were ordinary emigrant Britons and her real name was Helen Darville. Not only had she invented the whole story, she had also invented her identity and, moreover, had committed demonstrable plagiarism and compiled many quotations without quotation marks. It is difficult to describe how deeply something like this must have shocked the Australian imagination; with its British, rather Victorian and almost ecological idea of how public morality must be protected; it was actually as if this society, which still experiences itself as a community of pioneers, felt the ground shifting under its feet. The unhistorical, purely fictive space which was here filled with a basically European problem, permeated with history and atrocity, suddenly burst like a balloon in the blue Australian sky: it was just another story! Critics on all sides now tried to analyse the book as a novel, as fiction, but were forced to the conclusion that this had become impossible. Public disgust with this mythomaniac liar resulted. Yet Helen Darville, whoever she may be and whatever her intentions, demonstrated something that was dangerous and yet fascinating for the whole of Australia: the emptiness in which the images of history float. Not only do they consequently become just stories, they are also public property that can be appropriated by anyone and simply passed off as true. In this way, European reflections grow into obsessions that have a life of their own. Perhaps it is because of this 'free-floating intelligence' that the Australian community has become so panicky in its morality: planting beacons in no-man's-land is a task that demands self-made standards and boundaries, and accordingly they are preoccupied with these every day, often with great integrity, and just as often in a terribly fussy way.

But authenticity, if that can ever be found, is substance without substance, what can only be seen when one isn't looking for it. Here too, we're threatened by a trap in the ground on which we're walking: the belief in the 'spontaneous' as authenticity, the absolute belief in the possibility of ever speaking the truth without violating it in some other respect.

The only population group that appears to be very little troubled by all this is the Italians, who constitute a large proportion of Australian immigrants – their assertive identity, which with every order of *scampi fritti* gives them the feeling that they are still labouring on the Sistine Chapel, makes them largely insensitive to the frustrations and the subtle moral torments of the English-speaking community. They are not bothered by modern political correctness, which often brings the Aussies' urge to freedom based on collectively discussed moral judgements, close to neo-Victorianism. Nor are they tortured by the need to affirm Australian culture in the face of such centres as London or New York; they have no urge at all to compete with Europe, for the simple reason that Rome and Milan remain the centre of the world, even though they live their whole lives on the 'periphery', as the fateful phantasm of Australia is called.

Owing to this dash of unmistakable frivolity, Australia quite frequently makes the impression that it has produced an American version of the Swiss experience. This is because everything in Australia, including the big cities, is provincial, but not in a negative way – no, it is rather the best of provincialism that has been transported to the huge modern urban centres, the open feeling of receptivity and naïvety that is a precondition for the creation of new ways of living, a mild blend of provincialism and urbanization.

However, it is of course not at all certain whether conditions will remain so idyllic under all circumstances. You notice that the Swiss experience – this relief at suddenly finding yourself surrounded by pure air and unprejudiced sincerity instead of the crowded, hectically opinionated country where you yourself live – invariably starts to grate after two weeks, at most: then the vagueness you were hoping for turns to dreadful familiarity, and you are forced to recognize with a kind of humiliation that you were simply hoping to escape from your own prejudices. It's the moment when in Switzerland you become irritated by Swiss 'modern' wooden sculptures, which are even more simplistic than those of Henry Moore, in France by the eternal Provençal gouaches with a purple or yellow van Gogh wash, in Austria by the Viennese kitsch castles of Hundertwasser, or in Australia by the artefacts with remnants of song lines as motifs, second-rate exaltation of the 'authentic'. No, it is not this type of provincialism that produces interesting art, and yet a spark of it is needed to achieve something creative and not to make one choke on the barren blasé-ness of many European big-city dwellers.

On a map of the world that I bought on my first day in Sydney, the world is depicted upside down – that is, with Siberia, Canada and Greenland at the bottom, and with Cape Town, Tierra del Fuego and Adelaide at the top. This map is called Down Under, and carries a text that emphasizes once again that there is no logical or cartographic argument against turning the map of the world on its head. With some amusement I realized, staring in fascination at this map in the shop window of a marvellous wooden, nineteenth-century shop, not only that this version could be justified and true but that I immediately found it more appealing, indeed even more harmonious, without immediately being able to think of a reason why – apart from the particularly striking fact that in this arrangement of the world, Australia came to be pontifically in the centre.

As I sat looking at this wonder of the world with a glass of Australian Sauvignon in the pizza parlour next to the shop, a large blonde came to serve me. She was a little like Helen Demidenko, I thought, but much prettier. We got talking, and I found to my astonishment that she was Norwegian, had only been here for a few months and was definitely intending to stick around for a few more years. From North Pole thinking to South Pole thinking – this great leap across the planet, which we can now make in a single day, produced in this woman a strange lightness, a kind of sensibility that Milan Kundera has described in an indecisive community in Central Europe, but which here attached itself to the feeling for the spacious, the open. Australia has indeed developed its own existentialism for the feeling of vagueness: 'I don't know what I want to do, but I know I want this feeling.'

This dazzlingly beautiful Norwegian girl, sweating and flushed and running to and fro with lasagnas, pizzas and pastas floated around in this strange, frivolous fluid of vague life in the water of Sydney Harbour like a glitterball, a circumstance which meant that she was well on her way to becoming a real Aussie. With an equally great feeling of naturalness, she plonked down large bottles of Victoria bitter next to the oven-baked Italian dishes and swayed off with her wonderful body back to the kitchen, giving the swing doors a routine push with her hips. I looked back at the map with Sydney on top and Oslo at the bottom, and the feeling of relief stayed with me all through that February evening – a warm late summer evening with lots of sauntering, laughing people under the palms by the ibises on the quay, while the tall blocks of flats loomed up almost translucent behind a metro line running high above in the emptiness.

The following day I go on a long walk through the bush

with M. The sun is again blazing high in the northern sky, we are looking for a spring indicated by flaking wooden arrows and cannot find it. Again and again, the sandy path makes an unexpected wide turn in the ear-shattering silence; again and again, we see an endlessly undulating plain with waving eucalyptus. Sweat is dripping in our eyes as we pause for breath under a grass tree, a large kind of alligator is suddenly sitting there staring at us majestically, timeless and imposing like the snake that stared at D. H. Lawrence by the spring in Taormina: 'being earth-brown, earth-golden from the burning bowels of the earth'. It sits there for a while, blinking every ten seconds with its great round eyelids. Effortlessly and lightly it slips away in the heat. We surmise that Botany Bay is in the distance, but it is almost a day's walk to the sea. The silent expanse fades in our heads to a point where we forget everything. Finally, after ten kilometres, soaked with sweat and faces sunburnt, we turn back, get blisters on our feet, start talking nonsense and get the giggles, lose the way, are dying of thirst, feel our legs going soft and arrive exhausted at a deserted terminus, where a train gleams motionless in what is otherwise a bare and empty landscape. Back in Sydney Central Station, we have the feeling of having suddenly caught a glimpse of something that quickly disappeared from our consciousness. As we got drunk that evening on the wonderful Australian wine on the quay with the quotations in the pavement, I vaguely remembered that only a few days before, at midnight European time, I had seen the sun rising over the South China Sea, after taking off in Singapore. Just below us lay the Indonesian archipelago, which the Dutch writer Multatuli had called 'the emerald girdle', but which by now shows a forest of blocks of flats, floating in light, intoxicating mists. Two hours later, Darwin already lay behind us and we were heading out over the endless plains that so obsessed Bruce Chatwin. In retrospect, Alma Ata, Tashkent, Baku, Ekatarinenburg and Islamabad are cities that seem close to Europe, in a quickly vanishing short night between the northern and southern hemispheres.

The unreal comfort of technology means we can only really travel in a dream. Only if the aeroplane had to make an emergency landing in this burning emptiness would real travel begin and fear start to teach us something of what it must have once been like for Captain Cook and Laperouse: a conquest of emptiness, which had to be reshaped by the human eye of the colonizer, at the cost of everything else, the elusive something that disappeared at lightning speed like a lizard scooting away under the hot rock; the superficiality of an eye that will remain blind to what it ignores and suppresses, and what it will later absorb as a memory of what has been forgotten, of repression and dream. Walking past the pizza parlour a few days later, I notice that the Norwegian girl is not there. 'She's gone, she wants to see the outback,' says the Italian, sitting outside on his chair looking at a huge cruise ship just mooring behind the Museum of Modern Art. There, by the entrance to the Museum, gigantic and frivolous in the fresh morning breeze, stands Jeff Koons's ridiculous lapdog, built of flowers and bushes, almost twenty metres high. M. and I, slightly hung-over as we are, decide to go and pee on this canine mountain of flowers, which seems to be turning people into idiots. 'Man', says M. laughing, 'this is going to cost a fortune, that animal is insured for an unimaginable sum and there are hordes of tourists around it with an equal number of cameras.' On the quay, a stream of people is already leaving the big white cruise ship, others are sitting on benches, walking along the paths and heading for the spacious entrance of the Museum. Everywhere tourists are standing gaping at the huge dog. We walk round it, step into the lowest bushes by its tail and let rip, sweating and hiccuping with laughter as we see each other standing there like that. We button our flies and step back onto the path. Only an ibis and a stray dog have seen us.

Do parallel worlds exist after all?

Tübingen: Gothic Graffiti

You need to have wandered through the surroundings of the small, rather narrow-minded southern German town of Tübingen to realize how much this deceptively happy, pure image of German nature and small town togetherness turned the poet Friedrich Hölderlin into an overwrought, raging human being – how this proximity of great clarity sucked him in, bewitched him with the mystery of appearance, this image of a possible, utopian world, which derived its structure from the late-medieval market day.

The whole atmosphere of the old-fashioned and easy-going university, the misty closeness of forests on the hills (apparently idyllic when seen from the town walls), the pure woodland air that penetrates into the narrowest streets in the early morning, the strange rural silence by the Neckar, even at midday – as close as this to the old town centre you can be as hushed and isolated as if you were in the middle of a forest. All this gives the illusion that what Proust called the lost period of paradisial experience can be held on to, can be extended into our age, in which you can still cover the last stretch to this rural town in a rather rickety stopping train from Stuttgart, amid woods with sandy paths that flash by like so many invitations to step out of your life and to start something else, something absurd and because of that, compelling and grotesque.

In combination with the great philosophical ambition that Hölderlin developed in the period of his friendship with his fellow-student Hegel – for whom life was also governed by an equally overwrought longing for a metaphysical experience of History and the comprehension of it – this led to a fatal cocktail: it is undoubtedly partly this provincial, flaunted

Gemütlichkeit that drove Hölderlin mad because it promised something that did not exist – deep closeness in an otherwise philosophically unfathomable world. Add to that the obsession (popular in those days) of 'Greek Noble Simplicity', as served up by the great archaeologist Winckelmann, who saddled the Germans with the *we-are-the-Greeks-of-Europe* virus – and everything is in place for an inhuman enlargement of this image of the pure, trustworthy, close world, fatally enough, however, combined with the impossibility of personal happiness. This produces the philosophical and, at the same time infantile, hope of being able to fathom what the essence may be of this ever-elusive paradisial image. What follows is the expansion of this superhuman Greek illusion that also made Nietzsche regularly change tack – and Hölderlin's Tübingen, dozing warmly in its afternoon air of distant woods and the slow-flowing water of the Neckar, becomes a diabolical arcadia that screams with the rage and disgust at everything that is German, of someone like Werner Schwab (because that is how I sometimes imagine the twentieth-century version of Hölderlin).

And so I suddenly see Hölderlin here by the Neckar, sitting dozing next to me with his broken spirit, unappreciated by Goethe, abandoned by Schelling, rather embittered but with a great, prophetic sense of his own rightness in his head and heart as yet unnoticed by anyone, with grubby dirt under his abnormally long fingernails (with which he scratched, until they bled, the official and nurse who took him to the asylum in a coach), his thin dishevelled hair, the smell of a man who no longer likes washing. This, the body odour of the filthy madman, and I, who would like to hug him pathetically and too late, to alleviate the fever in his head for a moment. Just as pathetic, I admit. Whether he was a Noble Pretender or actually what we today would call a psychiatric patient, is of absolutely no importance. Anyone who pretends to be mad for 35 years, is seriously disturbed, damaged or hurt. When I try to picture him so concretely, I'm more amazed at the way in which he made the wrong choice – namely by trying in his great hymns and elegies to understand where this omnipresent German bourgeois and perceptibly threatening purity comes from. (The light of Provence had a comparable effect on van Gogh; the melancholic tries to understand the origin of this overpowering effect of the *visible* and makes a fatally wrong choice: that is, not to submit to it mindlessly, but to ask every painful question as to why the experience of this surprising feeling recedes the moment you try to grasp it – a mistake that stems from the fact that people with a tendency towards neurosis cannot accept that the pleasant side-effects of landscape and climate have no higher meaning.)

This is just what makes life impossible, and the blue, the pure morning, the woods, the river, the wonderful and at the same time vaguely disconcerting intimacy of the ancient German Baroque market, the fruit stalls and the sloping streets become a nightmare, the defeat of human understanding emanating from the hills in the distance: unassailability – yes, this discovery can gradually crush the mind.

I sat for a number of hours alone and undisturbed in the upper room of Hölderlin's Tower, which has since become poisoned by tourist–pilgrims. It is ten years ago since I stood here for the first time with A., in love, and having found my way here almost by chance, one summer's day. The concept of the 'false spring', which I was later to work into a story, in a book of which as yet I had no inkling, came into my mind a little later on in the market square. I remember talking to her about it as we walked arm in arm. I only remember that moment now, in the market, returning here at night, ten years later, and with the memory of the expression 'false spring', the smell of her hair returned to my nose. That's how absurdly memories work. Now, however, I was drunk and tired, had finished a long conversation with the Jewish female concierge of the Hölderlin Tower – about Hölderlin and his father – and on the other side of the market place, glowing in the night like a cardboard Baroque stage set, saw the poet G. approaching like a figure from a Brecht opera. 'Hello, pal', he said cordially, taking me by the arm with his inimitable, rather absent-minded friendliness, and resuming the stream of German historical and ideological reflections that he had begun that morning at breakfast – I don't know anyone else who can talk about Germany in such a compelling way, with all its bitterness and sweetness. Later we stood together by the wall of the Hölderlin Tower with the graffiti on it, making jokes about it.

That morning in the tower, in the white silence, I had looked out of the window for a long time, hearing nothing but the paddling of ducks in the Neckar and the oars of a rowing boat somewhere on the other bank. The smell of blue irises and water, a piping blackbird nearby, and the day so terribly bright that everything grows black before my eyes. I realize with a start that here I would very quickly become a different person, perhaps an outcast, maybe a criminal. That oppressive purity leaves one no option of taking flight into any kind of irony, one must make a stand. Either you sink into the friendliness of oblivion, calling out 'Grüssgott, ganz schön ja' 50 times a day until your dotage, and looking at the innocent weighing of fruit in the hand by men and women without sensuality, passively endure the bloody stinking tepid warmth by the stalls selling pork, or else you've got to become an eccentric, fight to pre-serve the balance in yourself against this murderous security, to keep your head above water and resist the deeply pathological image of this pure German world: a world that is elusive, free and completely 'unintellectual', is simply there, and evokes images of an incomprehensible clarity in the mind without giving anything in return – particularly no place where those images can root themselves. Perhaps, even at that time, the reflective Hölderlin stood alone in the community, dreadfully lonely as a patient, and the Beautiful and the Secret soon became a torture. The smells of the midday meal are then quite enough for an attack of despair before rushing outside retching and fighting to get one's breath back, with one's eyes full of water, the stupidly floating ducks waggling about in the

34

current beneath a weeping willow. 'How are you, Mr Hölderlin?' 'Yes, yes, I'm OK, I'll come in in a moment.' But in the evening they didn't see him again, no one saw him again that evening, and not until the following morning is he found sitting on the bench just outside the kitchen, blinking his sick eyes at the German, monotonously glaring white light.

The obsession consequently soon focuses on the opposite: what in the poem 'Der Sommer', Hölderlin was to call the Unhidden – the word which was to obsess Heidegger so much that he was to make a caricature of it. The Unhidden – what emanates openly from all things and faces: the fact that the beauty of the day is a crazy side-effect of something indifferent, as a result of which it is immediately transformed into something unbearable.

Here, in the little museum, I look for a long time at the almost illegible, passionate handwriting in which Hölderlin scribbled down this serene poem, not at all masterful but helpless, agitated and hasty; how these lines written down in spidery characters contrast with the openness of the great idea of summer that is developed in the poem – and here also I see the still, silent evidence of everything I feel but cannot prove. The 'silent purity' has always found its way onto paper as if in a feverish attack, a convulsion of consciousness, because Something, It, or whatever it is, had showed itself for a moment in all its peace; while it was also bewitching; and the experience of it is unbearable, it is scribbled down with a sharp pen that almost tears the paper, reminding one of the long dirty fingernails with which the great poet scratched his nurse like a cat, while the coach bumped over the cobbles, a straitjacket was hastily put on him, and someone forced him back onto the red seat, the screaming hysterical eccentric, a cruel and shameful spectacle, wobbling through the narrow streets of the town, the town that collectively shrugs its shoulders when this offensive figure passes – 'it's that madman again' – and eats the roast meat, the potatoes boiled to a pulp and the greens mashed into a mess in a hot, rapacious peace.

I go down to the water and look up at his window. It is above the room laid out as a museum, itself a perfectly ordinary twentieth-century residence: in addition, the corny tower with its romantic spire looks nothing like the hexagonal, rather squat bay window which passed as the now famous tower in Hölderlin's day. It is impossible to find a real trace of it; only in the setting, the décor, the unchanged water, may something still flow that he also saw: the two swans under the weeping willow and a boat drifting past, the shimmer of green-and-blue flickering light, the perfume of a garden sloping down to the river with the heavy scent of lilacs mixed with the German cooking smells of roasting pork around midday, the spire of the Stiftskirche above a roof, under it a gable with blossoming wisteria with its overpowering aroma, while you walk up narrow stairways, set out like alleyways; and coolness and warmth again take on a smell of their own. In the guest book, behind glass, I see the names of later poets, André du Bouchet and Paul Celan. In 1970, that is, not long before his own deliberate death, Celan was here, also saw this, and he did something that I find unusual for someone so modest; he signed the register, and he must have been fully aware of this – he who, like no other, combined the obscurity of Hölderlin with the notion of unfathomable light in his strange poems written only for himself. Or let's say, only for the other in himself – that's how they're written.

Tübingen, January

Eyes talked into
Blindness.
Their –'an enigma is
the purely
originated' – , their
memory of Hölderlin towers afloat, circled
by whirring gulls.

Visits of drowned joiners to
These
Submerging words:

36

Should,
Should a man,
Should a man come into the world, today, with
the shining beard of the
patriarchs: he could,
if he spoke of this
time, he
could
only babble and babble
over, over
againagain.
'Pallaksch. Pallaksch.'

(From *Poems of Paul Celan*, 1988)

Well, what can you say about a country town which 50 years after the war sinks into the ordinary weekday silence of the night? That you can hear the ghosts and the stones lamenting together? Much too easy, the empathy of a cultural tourist who harms no one and hence does no one any good. And it is completely impossible to judge or condemn writers in wartime.

Later in that German summer night, I am still permeated with the morning light in the tower by the river, with all the missed opportunities that dominate that museum like the smell of a corpse, the smell of this sleeping poet in his great, long night. In the first part of his life: the stupidity of his great wisdom, and in the second part: the great existential wisdom of his madness. And I am homesick for those hours in the tower, great bright openness of the morning, which I had rediscovered – although there is nothing left of him there, because everything that was once experience grows into a form of tourism and even vampirism. But, for a moment, I came close to something else in myself, a caricature of myself when I was twenty, and I looked at it in astonishment. I was speechless: things have become too complicated between me and myself.

But my memory, that tries to be his, precisely reaches forward, to his end. (Peter Härtling, *Hölderlin*)

The following day I make the magnificent train journey along the Rhine from Mainz to Koblenz. The day seems to have high vaults above it, endless light, I have Buxtehude on my Walkman: 'Nichts, nichts, nichts – nichts soll uns scheiden.' The Rhine winds its way between the magnificent hills, the train slaloms slowly and majestically through a landscape saturated with ominous beauty and history, the Rhine barges seem to float just above the wide flowing water, the towns with their provincial platforms glide past, after each bend the landscape opens with a new, breathtaking German doom. In Sankt Goar, it takes hold of me completely: for a moment it really is the sixteenth century, it is two o'clock on a sunny afternoon, the sky is high and things are within reach in dazzling light. I see this Baroque Germany of Buxtehude and Bach, sober and celestial and threatening and terrible, a country where a village festival, a chorale with a mystical feel and an execution on the marketplace flow effortlessly into each other; I see a woman straight out of a canvas by Cranach but she is wearing an *Ossies* scarf, I see slopes covered in vineyards around the castles on the summits and the trivial things of life here by the bank, a backwash, a man with a boat, a BMW with a fishing rod sticking out of it, the shaking and splashing of a dog just emerging from the water. However, a moment later, I see just as clearly, somewhere in the twentieth century, in the station of this innocent-looking Sankt Goar, brown-eyed deportees standing waiting for a train without windows, and in between, I also mean in the centuries in between, I see *him* walking somewhere there lost in a windless valley with a confusion of deciduous and coniferous trees, one of those woods of which Milan Kundera would say that they evoke only suspicions of torture camps and nothing at all of German nature. Yes, it's him, a little bent and freaked out, *der arme Hölderlin, der war net verrückt* – the simpleton was far from mad, it says on the Hölderlin Tower in Tübingen in, sure enough, *Gothic* graffiti, as the poet G. observes, shaking his head and grinning sadly before we walk on into the night.

When late in the evening I get off the train in the prosaic, polluted city where I live, it strikes me already as a kind of attack of madness, this longing to get close to an early nineteenth-century German poet who had the secret of something that I obviously wanted to steal from him. The taxi driver tells me there has been a great pile-up that afternoon on the big ring-road around the town, with several vehicles crashing into each other and a lorry with some poisonous substance or other overturned near the old covered animal market, which is now, despite a few feeble protests, being demolished – it is raining and the car stinks of cigarettes and alcohol. On the car radio, I hear a German voice telling me about concentration camps that have been discovered on Serbian territory. The newsreader translates the report and then suddenly through the windscreen wipers I see the narrow streets of the district where I live looming up, the ordinary things, grey and desolate, lacking the enchantment of the Neckar. Only a few windows emerge vaguely from the endless chilly gusts of rain drifting over that filthy salt ditch, the North Sea; everything is meaningless and gaunt with nothing to lift the spirits and yet, lo and behold, this absence of anything uplifting I suddenly find terribly uplifting.

Trieste: Lonely In-Between

James Joyce went whoring here while his partner was about to give birth, but *Ulysses* would have been unthinkable without his difficult years here; a little way away, Rainer Maria Rilke walked and waited for a sign from the angels who would dictate to him the beginning of his *Duino Elegies*; Umberto Saba ran a second-hand bookshop on the Via San Niccolo that still contains a miniature paradise for the bibliophile; the great archaeologist Winckelmann was murdered here in obscure circumstances, according to some people by a male prostitute who wanted to steal some valuable old coins from him; the short-lived Scipio Slataper wrote a romantic and unforgettable book here in which he evokes his childhood in the Karst mountains: 'In the dawn glow I was reborn. I don't know how. The sky was clear and I saw below me the beautiful white city and the ploughed earth'; and Italo Svevo, who was describing an old-fashioned train journey from Milan, was just about to write the name of the city of his destination when his pen stopped for ever: *Trieste*.

I myself had hoped to arrive here on a boat from Venice, but it left from somewhere outside the town and didn't really go to Trieste, but finished up in the vicinity of Koper, hence almost in Croatia, and I did not have that much time to get here; the train that runs round the bay was not available either because of a general strike. So I rented a car with a female photographer who, in the course of a few hours, seemed to have become an old friend, and finally reached the hotel where I stayed a few years ago and had longed to return: Albergo al Teatro. From the windows of this stately old-fashioned house, you can see a section of the Piazza dell'Unità d'Italia and beyond it, the sea.

Just beside the hotel, across a narrow street, is my favourite coffee bar, whose irresistible smell of roasted coffee mixed with sweet pastries and the light sea breeze has always remained in my memory. It has a terrace where, after office hours, Italian girls sit posing and chatting with boys in their invariably squeaky new shoes.

This is the second time that I have seen Trieste. The first time, I came out of curiosity – roused by what I had read about writers for whom the city had become indelible. This second time, I have come to find for myself the experience that they underwent: isolation – the sense of being somewhere on the edge of Europe, though you are unmistakably also in an abandoned centre: mild, reassuring isolation such as you can only find in somewhat forgotten border areas. Here, though everything is close,yet it seems very far away. Trieste is one of the last stops before the 'other' Europe begins. Perhaps that is why it affirms its Italian consciousness so clearly: because this dual character is not at all evident. Trieste was conquered by the Doges of Venice, the Habsburg dynasty, 'he Germans, the Italians and then was claimed again by Tito; after the Second World War, it was a free zone for a time under the supervision of the British and Americans, and has only been an Italian city since 1948. In 1963, it became the capital of the region Friuli-Venezia-Giulia. And recently, the infamous Serbian general Mladič in his bloody heyday uttered the threat that Trieste would become a Serbian-dominated city. The city seems to have been spared this latter crazy scenario for the time being.

At any rate, because of this vulnerable position, Trieste retains a concentration of historical consciousness. But the 'other', in this case the Slovenian and the Croatian, wafts over you constantly from the nearby border – on a Sunday afternoon in a dusty street, for example, or at the grey bus stop with the buses to Pula, Opatija and Rijeka: a suspicion of dry grass and sparse woods, of rocky vegetation, of small villages with yellow-and-red trees on a square in October. To the south, lies the Croatian Pula, which to Joyce, when he was forced to give

English lessons there, seemed like a sort of southern Siberia, but on closer inspection is a picturesque Mediterranean Croatian town with a wonderful amphitheatre and cosy streets. To the east, lie the Slovenian hills and lonely farm houses, and a little further on, about a hundred kilometres away, the capital Ljubljana, the former Laibach (where the cult group of the same name comes from), a kind of Habsburg Baroque *bonbonnière*. To the north, where the Karst begins, lies Gorizia, in a landscape of spectacularly hollowed-out limestone with huge limestone caves, which reminded Rilke of the entrance to the underworld, where Orpheus goes in search of Eurydice. And to the west, the ever-changing light above the unusually flat Adriatic bay with Venice far beyond the horizon. Because of its location, Trieste has a kind of subtle blend of the alien and the familiar.

I do not find it difficult to be alone in Trieste. I feel like a cat that has found a perfect vantage point. But I had forgotten one thing, how intensely this little Vienna focuses on the Adriatic, on the *Molo* where people are constantly walking, talking, sunning themselves, fishing or kissing, watching or sleeping on the lukewarm stones. In the mornings, a real *Triestino* sits chattering in a crowded and noisy bar with his espresso, but in the afternoon you see him lost in himself, sitting staring at one of the many bronze mooring posts, with a mixture of scepticism and contentment. Perhaps that is an explanation for the relaxed feeling that prevails here. It is as if the inhabitants take this openness back into the busy heart of the city with them and, as a result, are proof against the pandemonium that they themselves cause. Because, despite the bustle, I've never felt stress or annoyance in Trieste – as happens to me sooner or later in all other Italian cities. As if coming to watch a show, Triestini of all ages flock together, bomber jackets next to Versace suits, old-fashioned summer dresses next to leather trousers, walking stick next to buggy. They are drawn towards the end of the pier and there, by a few steps which lead down to the still sea, become strangely immobile, as if standing in adoration of what they have seen thousands of times before: the old customhouse, a couple of sailing boats in an unreal light, the distant ocean-going ships waiting to enter the harbour, the far-away grey strip of pollution that on clear days is vaguely visible above the Italian peninsula, while above their heads, the sun of Istria burns, still as warm as summer at the end of October when in northern Europe the pouring rain descends on the endless traffic jams. Perhaps that is why they are such self-conscious Italians: they look from a distance towards the country that binds them, the culture for which they finally opted after separation from the Habsburg Empire – as if sitting on a distant bench, where they are happier than the throng on the noisy square of the nation itself. It is as though they are staring out over a huge square, because the water level is so high and so flat that it looks like an endless piazza of liquid paving stones from which something transcendent is trying to rise; light from below meets the light from above and lifts everyone up in a ritual that begins afresh every day.

This also makes Triestini different. It is obvious that they are staunch nationalists – the city has fought hard enough to be able to be a part of Italy. But somewhere there is something milder, calmer in this way of living on the edge. Near the sober inner harbour on the Canal Grande stands an Orthodox Russian church with blue onion-shaped domes and elaborate gold within. On the Ponterosso, one of the many addresses where Joyce stayed, there is also a daily vegetable and fruit market, and much of what has ripened in the remote rural orchards of Slovenia is sold here in broad Trieste dialect. On the car radio you hear sing-song Slavonic (as if everything had been sweetness and light for centuries) and the typical post-communist Wurlitzer tunes, rather gormless, alternating with awkward, clumsy rock music that has taken its cue from Laibach. This colourful exoticism of another Europe gives one the feeling that Trieste is after all closer to Vienna than Rome. Consequently it should not surprise one that the slogan 'Nord Libero' crops up now and then in graffiti: not so much inspired by the Milanese fanaticism of the Lega Nord, but because

Rome, despite irredentism (the movement for annexation by Italy), has always seemed a ghostly abstraction from this still half-Habsburg outpost. Those without Italian often get further here with a bit of German than with English. As late as 1920, Rilke talked of an 'Austrian coastal area' when he talked of the Bay of Trieste, and Joyce headed every letter: 'Trieste, Austria'.

This Viennese atmosphere is still present in the rather snooty, celebrated Caffè degli Specchi on the Piazza dell'Unità d'Italia. But it is just as much there in the little coffee bar Piazzagrande, in the rather un-Italian lusciousness of the pastries and the quality of the *capazzo* – as a *cappuccino* is called here – or in the shining parquet floors and double-room doors in the hotel.

Claudio Magris is fond of recounting the following anecdote. Biagio Marin, the great poet from Grado (a coastal town more or less on the border between the Gulf of Venice and the Gulf of Trieste), was studying at the University of Vienna. When Italy became involved in the First World War, Marin asked for an interview with the Dean of the University, with the intention of announcing his departure. By joining the Italian Army, he told the Dean, he hoped to contribute his mite to the destruction of the Habsburg monarchy. To his astonishment the Dean said goodbye to him in an extremely correct way and wished him good luck in faultless Italian. But scarcely had Marin put on his uniform when an Italian officer began roaring at him. Marin replied indignantly that as a citizen of the dual monarchy he was not accustomed to being addressed in such a way and that under no circumstances would he tolerate this kind of treatment. (Harald Haslmayr)

There is no more pleasant city for testing whether you can deal with loneliness. Yet from eleven o'clock in the evening, something completely desolate comes over the place, something provincial that could just as well be criminal. At eight o'clock at night, the streets are literally bubbling with ambience but when I wander through the city four hours later I can quite well imagine how Winckelmann was murdered here alone in the dark, the man who very symbolically died half way between Vienna and Rome. And when I think of Winckelmann,

44

I think not of Pompeii or Athens, and still less of the 'noble simplicity and silent greatness', but of that other, more obscure Trieste: the old, typically Italian and dilapidated upper town on the side of the hill, with its narrow streets around the foot of the cathedral of San Giusto, seedy cafes and poor-looking houses, ruins and archaeological stones – the area where Joyce hung around after midnight before stumbling back toward morning blind drunk, scraping his backside against the houses to find his way ('arsing along', as he called it), to his crowded apartment, where his children were crying and his wife was going through the roof. During the day, the upper city is a wonderful place where there is always a gentle breeze playing, a vantage point from where you can see the whole bay; the brothels of the past have disappeared but in some streets you can still see the drainage channels that must have been a kind of motorway of infections. Before you can get to the old cathedral, you have to make a stiff climb through the abandoned streets, dominated by a Roman arch supposedly built by Richard the Lionheart, when he passed through these regions with his hoard of Christian mosquitoes, on his way to their absurd claim: their so-called right to Jerusalem, Yerushalayim, a Semitic city in the heart of the Islamic world. And yet that Arco di Riccardo is an innocent-looking thing, by the curve in the street where I imagine myself sitting, well over 80, toothless and relieved of all pleasures and burdens, nodding in the sun, next to three other old men, who when I pass them do their best to look like living soapstone miniatures. The women who cross your path at night with a great clicking of heels look back at you with a mixture of transparent pride and hidden insecurity. I get a little drunk in a restaurant smelling of drainpipes, fiddle around with a sketch in a notebook, and a little later am standing on the quay smoking a cigarette. The moon, which I saw three-quarters full the day before yesterday above the church of the Frari in Venice, vague in the autumn mists of the salt lagoon, this evening I see full above the old quarter of Trieste as if above a primitive settlement, while in the distance below, the last traffic races off along the bay. In the evenings, Trieste borders a warm and precious nothingness that betrays its presence only by its soft lapping against the great boulders of the Molo Audace.

> As for the murder: it's not impossible that the victim had a presentiment and expectation of it without trying to avoid it. Allowing oneself to be robbed and murdered: what better way was there to appease in oneself the feeling of having betrayed one's class and the obligations of one's sex? The knife in the hand of the murderer is something like the crown on shame. (Dominique Fernandez, in *Signor Giovanni*)

This extract is from a story about the murder of Winckelmann based on archival records of the trial. But the novella can also be read as a kind of palimpsest on Thomas Mann's *Death in Venice*. The reflection of two towns opposite each other in two stories about two poisoned and fatal loves; perhaps that is what the walker can feel here at night: the near-interchangeability of a light, Italian love with an inexplicable fear of dying. Or is this the cocktail found in all ports?

The odd calm of the sea at Trieste has been observed over the centuries – 'That is how I saw the sea for the first time,' writes the German poet, von Platen: 'deathly still and motionless, not even stirred by a breeze'. Franz Grillparzer observes, 'I could never have imagined that the sea was so *beautiful*, so indescribably beautiful . . . In fact the sea at Trieste doesn't even have a really *imposing* aspect.' It was the calm and the intimacy emanating from this huge expanse of water that struck him. Adalbert Stifter too, who stood on this quay, writes that he '(has) also spent many hours by the sea, and I couldn't get enough of looking at it – I could never have suspected that the sea can be so enchanting.'

These and other considerations can be found in the book *Ah! Trieste*, edited by Bas Lubberhuizen. It has even been translated into Italian and was given the subtitle *Sguardi stupiti dal Nord Europa* – something like the 'astonished looks of Northern

Europe'. Or how the Triestini like to see themselves, as the vain object in the mirror of our astonished glances. But it is not an incidental tirade: Trieste has only become what it is now through being seen from outside. For centuries, this serene spot simmered in the sun before it was carried along in the current of Habsburg politics. For centuries, Slovenians, Germans, Croatians, Italians, Englishmen and Austrians had been coming to this city, but only when an unambiguous Habsburg identity was imposed on it did it react with an all-absorbing 'Italianization' that issued in the period of irredentism. The melting pot continued to exist, but from the modern period on it was a question of metropolitan self-consciousness, while previously it had been a question of things which were self-evident in a place which seemed more nowhere than some-where, to paraphrase the Viennese writer Hermann Bahr.

Without his experiences in Trieste, Joyce would undoubtedly not have started thinking in such a cosmopolitan way. He became acquainted there with a great, polyglot tradition that proudly displays its openness. He was to do precisely the same in the book he wrote after *Ulysses*.

It is no coincidence that the cultural and literary self-consciousness of this city began only in the twentieth century. Before that, Trieste bathed in the almost blissful stupor of a sunny terminus – the furthest point of a great northern empire governed from Vienna. An empire in which, despite the efforts to make it into a second capital, it remained not much more than a both serene and indefinable extremity. In this way, the Viennese came to regard Trieste as a Habsburg port because, from their perspective, it seemed to be an 'a-national' city, writes Claudio Magris. This duality still shows clearly to any-body who looks at it, even from a distance of a few seconds: above lies the old Italian city with its sunny roofs made of long round tiles and thick old walls, below a Habsburg nineteenth-century city reminiscent of similar urban projects from the eighteenth and nineteenth centuries, with here and there a touch of Milan. The old upper town is the city of semi-classical

Italian poets like Giosue Carducci (whose exalted text about the sea is written on a memorial plaque at the archaeological museum) but the lower town is the cradle for the nervous intelligentsia of modern literature. Once the city joins Italy, it has to turn towards a southern culture that it has as it were to remember like an archaeology of its own place; thus, as Claudio Magris says, an identity is born that expresses itself mainly through the *negation* of a traditional identity. From then on, Trieste knows mainly what it does *not* want to be, what it *no longer* is, what it is not *yet*; and in that undefined space, authors like Saba, Slataper, Svevo, the exile Joyce – and later Magris himself – wrote. It took modernism, with its grand bourgeois lifestyle, to turn Trieste into a cultural city because the problem of an indefinable identity arose there, as an echo of Musil's *Man without Qualities* – a problem that in all cultural cities in the world was the basis of a critical literary consciousness. It is no accident, says Magris, that the literary history of this city – awakening from its untimely dream – begins with a novel entitled *As a Man Grows Older* (written by Svevo in 1898): the cultural identity of Trieste begins with the negation of an old silent tradition, a long dream time, which now and then re-emerges in flashes in the vagueness of a moment's silence between two salvos of traffic on the Corso. The simultaneous birth of the '*italianità*' of Trieste brought astonishment at its own elusiveness. Without the Italian mirror, this form of polyglot self-consciousness would never have shone so brightly. That was its base for a literary culture. In fact, in Trieste Italianness means most of all *not* being an average Italian, while fully embracing Italian culture. If, for example, an Italian from Milan or Rome comes too close, then quick as a flash the inhabitant of Trieste appeals to his Habsburg background or to his links with the peoples of Istria – that is, Croatians and Slovenians. But confronted with any Slovenian or Croatian, he manifests himself as someone who is linked with Rome and Milan. The fate and work of the Slav Scipio Slataper were an eloquent example of this intermediate cultural position. The average inhabitant of

Trieste therefore seems to be mainly someone who does not want to be like others.

> Everyone lived there not according to his nature or in reality but in the idea that he formed of himself, on the basis of literature, which in that way gained a kind of edifying existential value. Italian-ness, the idea itself and the battle for that idea, became a culture. (from Claudio Magris and Angelo Ara, *Trieste: Un identità di frontiera*, 1982)

According to Magris, the Slovenian element – which for a long time 'threatened' the city because of its claims on the culture produced there, was a catalyst for precisely the opposite effect: Italianization. Irredentism, the movement that tried to link up with the great Italian tradition, was stirred up by an anti-Slovenian component no less provocative for being secret: the aim was to keep the city out of the hands of Slav culture, rather than out of those of the dominant Vienna. The collapse of Habsburg centralism at the beginning of the twentieth century made the Triestini realize that there were few options if they were not to be 'engulfed' in Slovenian aspirations of a mainly agrarian culture that, in its turn, had its eye on a great port. Magris goes so far as to maintain that irredentism only appealed to an intellectual minority, while the anti-Slovenian element could rely on a broad popular reflex: indirectly, therefore, it was the modest aspirations of Ljubljana to have a base in a sea-port, which is supposed to have driven Trieste into the arms of Rome . . . around 1910, Trieste was the city with the highest number of Slovenian inhabitants, even more than the capital Ljubljana.

For Scipio Slataper, the author of Slav origin writing in Italian, the city had an historic duty to guarantee these three civilized cultures – Austro-Habsburg, Italian and Slovenian – and to keep them alive. In this way, this innocent-looking, slightly run-down port city would have become an historic crossroads of the three fundamental European cultures: the Germanic, the Romance and the Slav. He reproaches the city bitterly for its lack of cultural awareness on this point. In 1914, of all years, Slataper had conceived the plan of launching a Trieste magazine with the title, *Europa*. Needless to say, the plan failed. Slataper died not long afterwards as a young soldier somewhere in the hills of the Karst, in a European war.

The following day, I wandered rather aimlessly through the city. In all the bookshops there were scores of copies on display of the new Trieste best-seller: *Itinerari Triestini: James Joyce*, a book with maps, addresses, anecdotes for the Joyce pilgrimage, compiled by the resident duty Joycean, Renzo Crivelli. For everyone here could tell you there is at least as much Trieste as Dublin in *Ulysses*. *Zois*, as the people of Trieste call him, has long since become Zeus himself, and I imagine him one fine day hearing himself called that for the first time and having the inspiration for a book in which such a Greek god wanders round the city as drunk as he himself did every day. Or how about turning him into a Greek hero? Odysseus perhaps? At any rate, Zois got on very well with all the sailors in the brothels and learnt the coarsest expressions from them – all of which stood him in very good stead later. In the Umberto Saba book-shop, the pleasant bookseller teaches me a number of Trieste expressions – the dialect here forms the ultimate proof of the individuality of urban culture – which are a little less coarse. In exchange, I teach him to pronounce the name of the Amster-dam publishers Bas Lubberhuizen, an almost impossible task, but he has the book on his city compiled by Lubberhuizen on the shelves (and even the Italian translation) so he tries stubbornly to pronounce the Dutch sound 'ui'. Finally he bursts out laughing, shaking his head at the stupidity of Dutch. A little later, he shows me the bookshop's *pièce de résistance*: a complete hand-written, three-volume edition of the poems of Saba. I am allowed to leaf through the relic for about half an hour and study it. It was also here in this city that Joyce briefly fell under the spell of another flamboyant North-Italian (actually born in Alexandria), Tommaso Marinetti, originator of the fascist theory of beauty. In 1918, now living in Zurich, Joyce asked his friend Frank Budgen whether he perhaps found the Cyclops episode in *Ulysses* 'futuristic'. Budgen's reply has been lost to history but when Joyce moved to Paris for good, the books of Marinetti at any rate stayed behind in his apartment in Trieste.

What he did take with him from Trieste, among other things, was the notorious Nausicaa passage (episode 13) from *Ulysses*, the scene in which Bloom allows himself to be seduced by the beauty of a handicapped girl, Gerty MacDowell, whom he watches from a distance. No wonder this scene on a northern beach exudes a rather southern atmosphere, and not so much an Irish one: Joyce wrote it while he was sitting in the vicinity of the Molo looking out over the Adriatic.

One afternoon I am sitting on the Molo next to two young women looking out over the sea, in the white afternoon light. We are suddenly ordered to leave by soldiers: the whole Molo is being cleared for a military *esercizio*. A little later the fire engine trundles slowly and rather ridiculously onto the pier. The young Triestini look on contemptuously, the older ones rather proudly. After half an hour, a small yellow helicopter lands, the carabinieri rush towards it, there is a flutter of gesticulation and the insect disappears again over the sea. The point of the manoeuvre escapes me completely. The Triestini immediately reoccupy the pier as if nothing had happened. Meanwhile I, who am trying fruitlessly to stop smoking, have cadged cigarettes from the girls and we have got into conversation. They are studying here and have been taught by the current most famous resident of their city, Claudio Magris. He has been driving them crazy with stories about Sephardic Jews in the eighteenth century, and they've decided to travel eastwards very shortly, in the direction of Romania and Bulgaria. When they invite me for a drink with them in the evening, I think rather guiltily of my promise to remain in quarantine, but come on, talking to the natives is *part* of the quarantine, I think. They take me to a crowded café where Dire Straits is blasting out at gale force. After the past three reflective days, I get a rush of adrenaline in my veins and it's already a lot more difficult to imagine what I thought was so marvellous about that solitude. But when I finally get up at about one-thirty after a mix of consciousness-expanding substances, take my leave as politely as I can and walk back alone through the streets to the Molo, I feel a slight inner exaltation. The silence on the quay wipes everything away, and I sleep dreamlessly until morning. But the following day, I'm pleased at any rate that there is so much oxygen and silence available on the Molo – to ease my pounding headache a little.

And then suddenly, quite unexpectedly, there is a moving re-encounter. On the Piazza dell'Unità, I recognize with a jolt the old Slovenian woman selling little flowers. So she's still here, years later, unchangingly gloomy, smelling of poverty and dry herbs from Istria. The bunches that she holds up rather entreatingly to the passers-by, who are almost knocking her over, contain only wild flowers from the arid Karst, which she may always pick on her way here. Suddenly she is a symbol for me, a sign of the small, obstinate everyday detail, herself a herb on the arid stone, of which Slataper said that a single stalk can contain the whole of life because it pulls itself up from the dry nothingness of the rocks. This beggar shows the face of a suppressed cultural segment of this city and its history – the old link with the Karst. In her sing-song Slovenian, she mumbles, saunters impatiently backwards and forwards, and in the evening exhausted and with scarcely ten thousand lire profit, she drops her arms and disappears. Not even five bunches a day; what she does with the remaining faded flowers, I don't know but the following morning she is already turning her slow pleading pirouettes between the tarted-up girls, the men in their fashionable suits, who bump into her with their Samsonite briefcases – a small sooty ghost from the past, a last witness of the old Slovenian dream: of being at home here, of counting for something here, of being able to return home here with the wind and the herbs of the hills of the interior still in

The so-called Rilke path near Trieste; photo by the author.

one's clothes and hair, an interior on which Trieste has turned its back to stare ecstatically at the sea.

> The born Mediterraneans have also belonged more to the city than to the state or the nation. For them cities were the state and the nation and a little more besides. The city-dwellers preferred to be patricians rather than republicans. (Croatian writer Predrag Matvejevic, in a book on the Mediterranean)

The next day I go on one of the loveliest walks that you can take on the whole of the Adriatic riviera. From Sistiana, a coastal town about ten kilometres outside Trieste, runs the so-called Rilke path, an idyllic route past rocks, caves and marvellous vistas, which emerges in the vicinity of the castle of Duino. It is said that it was here that Rilke, who regularly walked this path, had the first impulses that would later result in the first two *Duino Elegies*. The fact that from this most marvellous spot I can see the first distant mountains of Croatia and, in deep peace, under an overwhelming summery autumn sunshine can see one of the countries where the most gruesome war of the second half of this century has just taken place – this cannot be a coincidence. This jolt, on this path that seems to lead to heaven, perhaps says all there is to say about the impossibility of ever again feeling, smelling, seeing as was possible at the beginning of the twentieth century. A jogging girl, who doesn't give two hoots about Rilke, runs past me with her hair dancing along behind her; in the distance I can hear a digger pounding old tarmac. Out-of-season Duino is a backward hole, crushed by the arrogance of that bulwark of the old aristocracy above it. In the season, young Slovenian machos come to ogle the Italian girls who lie sunning themselves on the rocks or gather around the secondhand BMW and show off their sunglasses. When I want to take a bus back in the late afternoon, the timetable turns out to be totally inaccurate. After waiting for hours, trying to hitch-hike and then giving up and walking a little, I take a rickety bus to the Karst caves of Opicina, a ride through wine villages that look almost Provençal, close to and across the Slovenian border, and from there a touching old tram goes back to Piazza Oberdan, where the evening rush hour almost bursts your eardrums.

On the last evening I get a touch of the *cafard* after all. I go for a meal in a grubby restaurant in a narrow little street in the area behind the big piazza. I am the only customer. I am given equally grubby food, with a wonderful bottle of Lambrusco. I fall into a state of slight, perfectly balanced intoxication.

As *secondo piatto*, I am given something *speziale per me*, with so many red peppers in it that it takes my breath away. Burned by the late October sun, accompanied by an over-loud bad copy of Sting ('On and on the rain will fall/Like tears from the sun/How fragile we are'), I'm also given a free glass of *prosecco*, a dessert *con afrodisiaco* (yes, I really must go home now) and in the upper town sit down on a bench by the cathedral looking at the floating lights on the sea while a bunch of adolescent lovers sit fumbling rather clumsily on a cold bench in the dark.

When I am about to take the train to Venice the following day there is again *un sciopero* – a strike, that is. I rent a car in great haste, am immediately caught up in a demonstration of

54

Trieste schoolchildren and the ensuing traffic chaos, finally drive back via Duino, with an Italian version of house music on the radio and the roof open to let in the sun. Hours later, in the eternal Belgian driving rain, to the sickening stench of fatty sausages, mindless muzac and an Eastern Bloc-like polluted wretchedness in *Bruuksèl Santral*, I find out that the train announced is late and then into the bargain is suddenly leaving from another platform. I head in the wrong direction to cold blank stares from my fellow passengers, leafing through their scrunched-up Flemish newspapers for the twentieth time. This, I suddenly think, is ten times more lonely than I have ever been in the most remote spot in the Karst.

Dresden

Cities situated on rivers demonstrate the reason for their location in the most natural way; they have no need to offer the visitor anything because as soon as that visitor, emerging from streets that gave no hint, comes across a quay and there absorbs a light that is unexpectedly generous like some promise of a distance within reach, it is obvious that this is an ideal site, which once, even without a city, was a good place to be; a spot on the bank, just before a great bend for example, downstream, so that it was easy to get away, to transport things too heavy for horses and carts.

London on the Thames, Frankfurt on the Main, New York on the Hudson, Paris on the Seine, Liverpool on the Mersey, Vienna, Budapest and Ruschuk on the Danube, New Orleans on the Mississippi, Prague on the Moldau, Lisbon on the Tagus, Lyons on the Rhône and Florence on the Arno, all these cities lie squeezed round the river like a hand, they have enfolded the river in their bosom and as a result have streets everywhere that offer unexpected openness in the sense of enclosure. On the other hand, there are also cities that have clustered along the river but as it were lie and scratch their backs against it: Antwerp on the Scheldt, Liège on the Meuse, Rotterdam on the Maas, Nijmegen on the Waal. But cities where the river forms the heart of urban life have an artery flowing through their hectic bustle that brings oxygen, vistas, a source of world awareness and history, an ever-present possibility of escape – a reassuring thought for both the traveller and the stay-at-home.

Dresden is on the Elbe – an idyllic river, relaxing and clear, slow-flowing and rather majestic in its broad bed. On the low banks, deep below the famous Augustus Bridge, are the *Elb-*

auen – low-lying meadows with the specific biosphere of wet grassland. This river is not caught between two stone quays, it can swell and recede with the season to its heart's content. Room has been made for it. It is over half a kilometre from bank to bank. In this way, a great, open expanse of water – indeed a rural and park-like atmosphere – is created in the heart of the city. In the centre of Dresden you can walk through a great meadow by the side of the water, while above you and past you the city traffic continues on its way. In the distance, you can see the majestic buildings surrounded by ample greenery. This does not exactly correspond to the image that the average Westerner has had of Dresden since 13 February 1945: a dark, bombed-out city, an inferno of rubble and dust, rows and rows of empty, destroyed houses; the image that featured on the cover of Harry Mulisch's novel, *The Stone Bridal Bed*. This was Dresden: a charred spot in the world, a suppurating scar, destroyed wilfully and pointlessly by the English out of revenge – Britain's very own version of Hiroshima and Nagasaki. But Dresden is also the place where Germans lived, and hence for Westerners it was more a symbol of the absurdity of Nazism itself. Without Hitler, Dresden would still be the 'Florence on the Elbe' that it had been in the Habsburg period, which was also the great Saxon era.

This is still a difficult topic of conversation with people from the area. If they regard the ruins of what was once the most beautiful Baroque church in Europe, the Frauenkirche, as a monument that with a few pathetic remaining remnants is a protest against the English, they run the risk of being taken as nostalgically conservative Germans. To regard these ruins as an indictment of Nazism itself would mean that the Germans of today would have to admit that their country fought against itself, that Dresden became the victim of an enemy within, and that real Germany hence won out over Hitler. This debate was actually conducted in the press, not *à propos* of Dresden, but it could serve as a model for it: why shouldn't the Germans of today say that they won the Second World War? Not in the traditional sense, in which people refer dismissively to the *Wirtschaftswunder*, the compensation for war damage and that kind of thing – no, Germany defeated Hitler, together with the rest of Europe. If one follows that line of reasoning, the ruins of Dresden are indeed an indictment of Nazism and not of the English raids. But at the same time these are banal speculations, because all the ruins in the world are of course a permanent indictment of the insuppressible urge to destruction that from time to time sweeps through even the most 'civilized' society. Once a stick has been found to beat the dog with, it seems there are no holds barred. The crusaders who saw the wonderful lifestyle of Constantinople did what they had to do. Smash it to pieces. In the great orthodox churches they stood knee-deep in the blood of civilized, over-cultivated city dwellers. A summer's day in 1203, the sun blazed in the sky and the birds sang in the gardens.

Only two years ago, Dubrovnik – that marvellous Mediterranean town – was almost wiped off the map by young boys without any historical sense. Not having any historical awareness also means not having any emotional response to an architectural work of art. Destroying cities, an activity that finds its inspiration and model in the biblical story of Sodom and Gomorrah, is the ultimate, apocalyptic dream of power, the most libidinous form of submission to unbridled brute lust and at the same time the greatest humiliation of the enemy. His jewel of culture and society is torn from his neck. Destroying cities has an element of divine punishment, the image of the pillar of salt and the flames on the skyline – in a modern version, the image of Hiroshima and Nagasaki. The city destroyers who took off from England in their bomber jackets that night, were seen by the whole English nation as Avengers in the service of Justice, whatever that may be. That very same night, they landed safely back on English soil, took off their helmets and shook the hand of their commanding officer. *Well done, Jack.* A few German intellectuals later told the story of how they saw the city disintegrating. The writer Gerhard Hauptmann, a master of pathos treated rather ungraciously by Thomas Mann (who portrays him in *The Magic Mountain* as the waffling Pieter Peeperkorn), humanist, beauty freak, a typical Goethian, Apollinian German, wept bitterly and said that he envied all his old, dead friends that they had not had to experience this. For him, it must have been something like seeing Venice smashed to rubble. He died that same year. It is said that he died of destruction of Dresden. Many of the intellectuals who have spent almost their whole life in the GDR remember the downfall of Dresden from seeing it as children. They remember the light in the distance, a red glow against the night sky, or, in the suburbs, the spitting of the gorse and the stench of burning human flesh. Dresden burned like hell. The Versailles-like courtyards, the Baroque jewels of churches, but mainly the houses in which people were roasted alive, people who were not necessarily all accomplices in the war. But that's war. It is not that I disagree with Daniel Goldhagen in his view that the whole German nation must have been in a strange kind of complicity with the deportation of the Jews, but it is of course equally true that anybody who walks through any German city, immediately feels that there is a cultural world which is much older and much more interesting than all those things that we associate so easily with Germany. But even then, it of course remains the fatherland of the most typical of all Germans, Johann Faust. The testimonies of Germans who with shame and emotion shook hands with a Jew in the street during the war – a gesture that carried the death penalty – are legion.

This old world of Saxon refinement and grace had little to do with the Berlin spectres which Hitler sent coursing through the world – an unbalanced creep from a backwater in Austria, a provincial who in the big city was fatefully pushed over the edge; it happens quite often, but not with such catastrophic consequences. The German world is, however, unfortunately still a world that could always, as George Steiner has said repeatedly, combine the beating to death of a Jewish girl with the playing of 'Für Elise'. Anyone who finds himself in Weimar, scarcely 100 kilometres from Dresden, can go and view the writer's pavilion of the Olympian Peace of Goethe, in the peaceful municipal park on the River Ilm. But when he takes the city bus a little later, he can see that there is a line to Buchenwald. Just ten kilometres or so away. Weimar is a complete idyll, intellectually provincial and charming, suffocatingly friendly. Ten kilometres away from Goethe's house, part of the German nation – and the best part, as Nietzsche, branded an anti-Semite by some people, said long ago – was burnt to a cinder. Günther Andersch called it fratricide. Nazism was, as I heard it called recently in a documentary on television, completely unfeeling, and at the same time under the spell of the most dreadful sentiments. The gruesomeness of the negative enlightenment, about which Adorno wrote some years later.

Dresden must have been a paradisial spot in earlier centuries, carefully chosen by the Princes of Saxony: the early evening breeze wafts across the spring blossom in the Elbe meadows, and on the tall banks where the ambitious 'Italianate' buildings of the Saxon Baroque rise up, you smell the fresh rebirth of the water. In *The Stone Bridal Bed*, Harry Mulisch also has his protagonist Norman Corinth experience this astonishment:

> [The house] looked at immeasurable space. Into the green depths of trees, along villas of which only one, hollow and staring, was inhabited, but only by the air, a road meandered down to a faraway iron bridge, under which, between wide pastures, lay the river. On the other side of the Elbe, in the valley, lay all that was left of the town . . .

The tourists who walk through Dresden are amazed at how much is actually left. The 'blue miracle' is still there, the ethereal steel bridge across the river; the great complex of buildings, the Zwinger, is still there like a rather careless variation of greater buildings like Versailles. The famous Augustus Bridge is still there, the eighteenth-century gardens with their geometrical patterns are still there, the old opera house by the famous architect Semper is still there! Look! Only when they are disabused by an inhabitant of the city do the scales fall from their eyes: all this was flattened and later reconstructed piece by piece by the GDR. Suddenly the enthusiastic tourists who felt they could live in peace with the war, a comfortable 50 years after the event, are again dumbstruck: so all this, this classicist garden, the water in the fountain, the Orangerie and the Duchess's garden, the historical dwarves on the spires, the staircases . . . all this Baroque building, this is all the work of the peasants' and workers' state?! Certainly it is. There are photos of people clearing rubble with their hands, like the ones of Berliners propping up leaning walls with scorched beams and cleaning stones, counting them and laying them in piles; or lugging twisted tram rails about; and there are a striking number of women among them, with calf-length skirts, hair in curlers and white bobby socks on their feet, the fashion of the time. One can be amazed at the fact that a workers' state with such strong, anti-élitist principles put so much of its scant resources into the restoration of this Baroque display of elitist luxury. But beneath all historical altruism lurks another story. This is Saxony, and the historical roots of the area were symbolized by the pearl in the crown of the East, this city which must have been more beautiful and more pleasant than nearby Prague – in and through these summerhouses and architectural perspectives. The dream of Honecker was in a deeper sense certainly reconcilable with those of his Saxon ancestors, just as that of Mitterand was best equated with that of a modern pharaoh, and that of Ceauşescu with that of the Emperor Nero. When one has finally recovered from the shock that the remains are not remains but reconstructions of remains, one begins to understand something of the wound of Dresden. This Dresden, this city where of all places, Schiller wrote his famous 'Ode to Joy'. The new guides to Dresden, printed in Munich, do everything they can to emphasize this aspect and finally make people forget the wounds.

Further into town everything becomes clear; very few of those marvellous Saxon blocks of flats are left standing, the city seems like a mouth with all its teeth knocked out, where the dentures sometimes stick out like shocking reminders: the ugly Prager Strasse, for example, or the constructivist GDR buildings which spoil the skyline, the tourist says with contempt. Forgetting for a moment that Rotterdam and Cologne have exactly the same kinds of districts.

I am more and more amazed at the fact that the most famous Dutch novel set in Dresden, *The Stone Bridal Bed*, showed so little of the double face of the city: its past as a Baroque monument on a splendid wide river. Only now, I realize, because we are so much further on, is it possible to redirect our gaze at the Elbe. Mulisch's Dresden has no river, no openness. It is only an inferno ('a city of white fear on a river of magnesium, surrounded by twilit rows of hills,' he has Norman Corinth say in his aeroplane). Everything that I can still see of the 'original' Dresden, no longer existed then – that is, 'not yet'. That is the paradoxical truth. In *The Stone Bridal Bed*, the past of this city, which I can now see, was still in the future . . .

In the restored Academy for Fine Arts are perhaps the clearest symbols of the complicated relationship that the residents have with their city. Now tons of West German marks are being poured over the eastern part of the country, the catching up process cannot go fast enough. The humble restoration work of the GDR period pales a little by comparison, with its green copper cupolas on the Zwinger as an emergency solution. For look, the angels are now glinting here and there in gold leaf. The goddess Nike is once again triumphant over the 'lemon squeezer', as the dome of the Academy building is called. But for the time being, the glittering gold, fairy-tale specimens are still shoulder to shoulder with black sooty extras, which still hold the memory. Anyone wanting to see this, must hurry. Every day a little more gold buries the *dramatis personae* of memory and the sky above Dresden again shines ominously brightly, but it remains a painful matter for anyone blessed with a memory. The Angel, all too familiar from the gruesome photograph, still stands stooped over the city. A black, scorched witness – or simply covered with soot from the exhaust of carbon monoxide originating from the Trabant cars and brown coal belching from chimneys? The British journalist, Anton Gill, who crossed Eastern Europe just after the *Wende*, would have us believe that the soot originates from the diabolical night of 13 February 1945. History is tricky. But still. No one has yet dared touch this archetypal figure, this Hiroshima-German Angel. It is a symbol of the other, of history and its loss, not about its gains that all the schoolbooks blab about.

Yes, Dresden must have been heaven on earth. Wars with Poland won, political and cultural triumphs celebrated, somewhat like a young brother of the great Habsburg example of Vienna. And actually more tasteful, more full of *joie de vivre* and charm. Above all, on a more human scale. The Elbe is far more idyllic than the Danube. From the higher terraces, the Saxon princes looked down at the river below, the reassuring wide curve into Bohemia, and about twenty kilometres further upstream, the Wettiner, as they were called, built a further summer chateau, also unashamedly geared to the enjoyment of exclusive privilege. Sailing into the Czech Republic down the Elbe is an enchanting journey, my guide assures me, as her great grey eyes slip into the distance. She is still young, teaches at the University of Leipzig, but she too can only start shaking her head in certain streets in Dresden, remembering the Sundays at her grandmother's in the tranquillity of the GDR. Later she stands with me in a bookshop and shows me the black-and-white photographs that document the reconstruction from the first rubble clearers onwards. Her father is a famous writer from the former GDR, but she prefers not to talk about that. Too complicated for foreigners.

The level on which the splendid buildings of the Saxon princes were built in Dresden demonstrates perfectly the extent to which these people had different brains and eyes than their contemporaries and subjects: they wanted to look with the cultural eyes of a greater Europe, and they deliberately sought visual delight, full of contemplation of perspective – they were already the voyeurs of their own history. These princes regarded the world as a pleasant spectacle, and they had this spectacle shamelessly, hedonistically orchestrated – a face-lift for a world vision. The assertive gentlemen of the Berlin dollars are certainly intending to restore this history.

The great Central European obsession with putting the Medici in the shade was shared by the Saxon princes with the Habsburgs. In Dresden too you can still find buildings – the Schloss, for example – which are still built in complete accordance with the model of the early-Renaissance Florentine palaces . . . great, crudely hewn blocks of stone, massive walls, and the first barred window only at the height of about three metres, so that the passer-by always feels small and intimidated. But the later conceptions – the lighter, more accessible and magnificent world of the eighteenth-century Baroque – break open that early contempt for the world and show an alternative for the higher classes: looking in order to be seen, and thereby orchestrating the world even more intensely. For not only the landscape and the view, but also the ogling spectators have now become part of the décor. These conceptions, held on the strings of astonishment and manipulated as pleasant, living paraphernalia, need spectating staff for whom aristocratic *ennui* is best kept at bay through the mirror of the goggling masses.

At some time in the eighteenth century, the nephew of the great Venetian painter Canaletto arrived in this city. This Bernardo Bellotto, who soon shamelessly assumed the name of his famous uncle and hence also went through life known as Canaletto, thereby usurped the fame of the painter who immortalized Venice in the *vedute*, the vistas with complex and multiple perspective. For me, the first Canaletto, whose actual name was Antonio Canal, has always been something of the Vivaldi of painting: clear, abundant, transparent and deceptive in his lightness. Like Vivaldi, that other great Venetian, Canaletto was

Bernado Bellotto (called 'Canaletto'), *The Neumarkt in Dresden from the Jüdenhof*, 1749, oil on canvas. Staatliche Kunstsammlungen, Dresden.

someone who tried to record the sentiments of a city at the peak of its fame. Openness, a regression into intimacy, grand gestures, vague melancholy. A broad sweep and yet an eye for rhythm and detail. Canaletto made not only Venice immortal through his vistas. He did the same for London. And for those who do not know how the nephew hid under his uncle's wing,

65

the temptation is to think of Dresden as the third city. In the local museum, there are a few of the town views of the Saxon Canaletto (the Italians added the telling *detto*, the *so-called* Canaletto) – these town views were spared in the great bombing because they had been evacuated long before. Now they are back, but the day that I am in Dresden the museum is closed. I resolve to go through the rooms before the train leaves the next day, if only for half an hour. The following morning something holds me back, I'm not really sure what. I also feel sluggish and in no state to start running back and forth so hectically. In any case, I sit too long at the breakfast table with my companion from the University of Leipzig and get her to tell me more about the city. I leave with a kind of feeling of guilt. The Mitropa train passes the legendary Schulpforta, the boarding school that Nietzsche attended. The church spire of the boarding school lies amid the rural calm of an almost imperceptible village sunk into the landscape. Nietzsche, the wanderer. So it was here, in this landscape ghosting past the window: his first romantic poems, his Schumann-like compositions, the *Sturm und Drang* of the man who was to settle accounts with Hegel's Germany and who, of all people, was to be used as a vehicle by those who manipulated history so shamelessly. But by now, the Schulpforta has already slid past the window of the Mitropa train and the conductor is tugging at my sleeve.

More than a month later, when I am about to type out my travel notes in an old property in the Vaucluse, I cannot get into my work in this house, which is still full of dust from all kinds of restoration work. It looks rather like the aftermath of a minor bombardment: demolished beams everywhere, dust that forces its way into the tiniest folds of the tiniest things, old-fashioned utensils thrown down higgledy-piggledy, curtains hanging half off their rails and doors that won't close properly or open again. Finally, I reluctantly clear out a back room crammed with dusty oak beams, old furniture and all kinds of rubbish, sand and scrub the old red tiles till they regain their colour, clean the windows – the dazzling sunlight shines in and colours the red almost orange. I wipe dust from the walls and, in doing so, have to take off the wall a framed picture that must have been hanging here for decades. It is a view of the church of Giovanni e Paolo in Venice, by Canaletto. It may have been cut out of a book and lovingly framed by the previous occupant, a dreamer of a man who for scores of summers sat reading on the terrace before he went blind. In the inimitable handwriting of old people who learned to write before the Second World War, he has noted on the cardboard at the back: *Canaletto, 1697–1768, Parois de l'Eglise St Jean–St Paul – Venise.* And then added underneath: *Musée de Dresde.* The Venetian Canaletto, but in the museum of the city where the second lived and worked.

So here, in this old room, in an old village that itself hides mediaeval Jewish ruins under rampant thyme and palms, the things I had to do come together. I put a couple of Vivaldi's 400 *concerti* into the Discman and sit down, with the dusty white picture behind glass in my hands. When I brush my hand across it, I seem to take away the dust of time. The corner formed by these buildings in Venice, the light, the little bridge that I know so well – here it is. Royal-blue curtains billow out through the open door of the church as if the wind were coming from the church and trying to emerge into the streets, in the abundant light that makes everything glitter. The music of Vivaldi, composed a few hundred metres from this church, resounds deep in my ears. I can almost hear the lapping of the water in the canals of Venice. The original of this painting hangs in Dresden, I missed it there and I find it here, as if it were being flung in my face.

It is no coincidence that Dresden possesses paintings by this Venetian painter. Because I now know what attracts me so in Dresden: the light there has the same unexpected contrasts as in Venice – the same alternation of opening and narrowing of space. This similarity did not escape the second, Detto Canaletto. His *vedute* of Dresden, permeated with Venetian light and the power of concentrated observation, form the most dramatic pendant to the scorched buildings that we know, to the black Angel on the dome above the destroyed city. If you look out over the city from the Zwinger now, the constructivist and already greying buildings that tower above everything are a terrible irritant. Being a tourist means always falling for the enchantment of kitsch and longing for the pure look, relinquishing part of your critical awareness, so alert at home, because the unknown forces you back into reflexes that you thought you had overcome. The inhabitants shrug their shoulders and inform you rather matter-of-factly of the function of the building you abominate, as if trying to say: well, we have to live, don't we?

We have to live. If necessary with a dusty little reproduction on the wall. Canaletto, whom I once thought a naïve painter (when I naïvely raved about Picasso at university), did something inimitable with Venice, and his nephew repeated that with Dresden. The enchantment of the town views of the first Canaletto is inextricably bound up with the way in which he prepared his panoramic compositions. No human being is capable of seeing a city as Canaletto did. He was the inventor of the human wide-angle lens. A friend once explained to me how that worked. In order to achieve the wide-angle effect, Canaletto made at least four sketches of the place he wanted to represent. He stood right in front of the view of the city and drew it. Then, a few days later, he positioned himself somewhere on a first floor, looked at the same view and drew what he saw. He often did that again by first drawing to the right of the image and then a little to the left. Then he combined these views for the final painting, opened up the space and in so doing, gave colour and light and an illusion of manageability that still fascinates us. It is hard to take your eyes off Canaletto's town views. They radiate an unusual delight in the visible, everywhere there are white dots of paint to be seen which indicate glow and reflection, a play of highlights, a deepening of the sense of space, as if this man were constantly astonished at the miracles that looking and seeing actually are. He realized that this was a matter of experience, a game with points of view and perspectives. In this way, he captured more of the experience of living things than the naturalists could ever do in later centuries.

Canaletto's nephew produced equally brilliant views of Dresden, although they lack the sublime touch of his great model. Living in this Saxon city in its eighteenth-century lustre must have been a feast of architecture and light for him.

Detto Canaletto also painted the Frauenkirche – a jewel box, a church with an improbably compact shape, a lump of architectural symbolism, a triumph of Protestant life that, as with Bach, continued to draw endless inspiration from the clash between inner richness and a penchant for mathematical sobriety – call it a longing for a moral art, in and through the play of shapes which constantly transcended this morality itself. The fact that the Frauenkirche was bombed flat cannot be regarded by anyone as anything but a gruesome deed of the most appalling cultural vandalism. The black remains that are still standing are reminiscent of another gruesome image – the Votivkirche in Berlin. Some people, referring to the horrors of the Nazi régime, still dismiss any pain at these devastations with the argument that they thoroughly deserved it. But this is the same kind of reasoning as believing that the grandparents of a murderer should be tortured to death at the age of 80 because they are the grandparents of the criminal. Did they really deserve it? The architectural eighteenth-century grandparents of the Germany of Goethe did not deserve to pay the price for Hitler's régime.

Victor Klemperer, the Jewish professor who, as if by a miracle, survived the holocaust, the bombing and the five years of hunger, persecution mania and harassment, described in his diaries what an inferno the night of the great bombardment was. This mild-mannered native of Dresden, an erudite Romanist and linguist who identified with the Germany of Goethe, Heine and Thomas Mann, who felt himself a European German through and through, kept, with dismay and disbelief, but also meticulously and with superhuman perseverance, a diary of the twelve years of the Beast. On 5 July 1944, he noted: 'We're all convinced that Dresden will be spared and we find the journey to the air raid shelter an annoying and unnecessary interruption. A time-consuming game.' His refusal to believe that Dresden could ever be bombed flat is finally proved wrong after all and, as the bombers come sweeping down low over the city night after night, he knows that the end is approaching. With a mixture of relief – Hitler's fall is at hand! – and horrible pain at the destruction of his wonderful Baroque city, he wanders through the burning heaps of rubble, and after this infernal night sits again in the first chill light of morning for the first time on the *Brühlsche Terrasse*, once called 'the balcony of Europe', a spot where for five years no Jews had been able to set foot. A battered, aimlessly milling throng rushes from nowhere to nowhere along the banks of the Elbe. There are still flames everywhere, the sound of buildings collapsing, the smell of destruction, a wind that is fanned by the heat and seems to come from hell. He sees a soldier lying there with a death rattle in his throat. It has no effect on him. His wife tries to light a cigarette she has got somewhere from a spark on the ground and realizes that it is a burning body. And yet the destruction of the city is described as an abstract dream, all around him the brutal Baroque of the apocalypse is present, but what matters is a little warmth, a mouthful of coffee, a sweater or a cellar to hide in. He flees as far as Munich under a false name and does not return until June 1945. He is to experience the reconstruction of the city in the GDR as a reinstated prominent citizen.

Somewhere it must be possible to find a connection between the Baroque that the Venetian Canaletto saw and painted, and the one that the Saxon Canaletto tried to immortalize. But, by the eighteenth century, the Venetian Baroque was already decidedly one of decline – to an even greater extent than we can now imagine in this restored city; in close observation of the first Canaletto, there is already a way of looking which heralds the vampiristic love of the sketching Ruskin, the redeeming and moral vision that delights in the passing of time because it gives him the opportunity of being its keeper, the magic evoker of the indifferent effect that the light has on faces, façades and years. And yet the light of Canaletto shines over things and faces as if on the first day. The Baroque of Canaletto, like that of Vivaldi, has to rely on a strange experience – the ordering of a sense of life, an experience of space where the centre of the city has known for ever that it has been reflected by something treacherous and unreliable, that constantly causes passions to flare up – the light of the sea that radiates over the façades from the Lido. The Baroque of the first Canaletto is that of history and its everyday enchantment.

Seen in this context, how different is the perspective of the younger, Saxon Canaletto: the Baroque that he paints is that of self-assured spatial perspective of architecturally conceived streets and squares, it is the rhetoric of a history that stands still at the peak of its dignity, or at least tries to. Where the first Canaletto painted a Mediterranean existentialism, the second told us about a place, an effect and the light was only a device for reassuring the inhabitants within that historical scene of an heroic present. While the first Canaletto lived on a Baroque sense of life like a rhythm of time caused by the algae and the colours, something that emerged in the brackish streets between old façades from the Adriatic and its flickering reflection, the second lived on the smug dignity of a city on a calm river, a Baroque that had to invent itself as a style. The first Canaletto painted the effects of an existence, the second painted the existence of the effects.

The art historian Corrado Ricci said of the Venetian Canaletto that if Venice were to be destroyed, it would still be incomparably with us thanks to Canaletto's paintings. A few years after Ricci's book, this pronouncement became gruesomely true of the paintings of Dresden by the other Canaletto.

But the irony of history goes even further. The Dresden

Canaletto actually experienced the destruction of Dresden. In the summer of 1756, Frederick II, King of Prussia, invaded Saxony without a preceding declaration of war. The Saxon forces capitulated on 14 October, but the war dragged on for years and, in 1760, the city was pounded into rubble by the Prussian armies. A Prussian officer noted: 'The fire blazed fearsomely in and around the city, many distinguished streets were burning along their whole length. Splendid palaces, which would have graced any city in Italy, fell victim to the flames. At every moment houses many storeys high collapsed . . .' Goethe too, who visited Dresden afterwards, lamented: 'Now the royal chateaux are destroyed, the splendid Brühl buildings have been laid waste . . .' In so doing, he was virtually singing the first couplet of the dirge that Gerhard Hauptmann completed.

In 1765, Detto Canaletto painted the heaps of rubble of the Kreuzkirche. Even at that time, people talked of the final destruction of the Baroque pearl in Europe's crown. The city was rebuilt. The Saxon Canaletto also painted the Frauenkirche. In Bellotto's time, it was virtually brand new: it was finished only in 1743 from a design by the architect, George Bähr. So that when, in the second destruction, Dresden was reduced to a few scorched stones by the Allies, it was almost exactly 200 years old. After his return in 1945, Victor Klemperer lived with this image of the destroyed jewel in the Protestant crown as if with a daily reality. He did not have much talent for rhetoric and no predisposition at all to religious emotion. This quiet scholar, who had been hounded like a cur, who in his youth had fought in the First World War as a volunteer in the German Army in Flanders, and who for the sake of his wife had in a fairly business-like way 'converted' to Protestantism, felt himself through and through a German in the great humanist tradition. He only became a Jew through the paranoia, the plunder, the isolation, the starvation and the fear of the Nazi period. In the GDR period, however, he became a member of the Communist Party and was awarded an honorary doctorate by his beloved Technische Hochschule, from which he had been dismissed like a dog in 1935 with virtually no pension. He may have walked past these ruins many times, grinning, with his typical reservations and daily grumbles, happy that he could wear socks again, could drink coffee and some 'alcohol' as he called it eagerly during the period of abstinence, could again drive a car clumsily and could keep lots of cats for the love of his wife. He is buried in Dölzschen, a municipality above the town centre, with lots of greenery, where, in the difficult 1930s, despite persecution by a National Socialist mayor, he built a small house that was then confiscated by the Gestapo and to which, after the bombings, starving and exhausted, he finally returned one hot June day ten years later. Klemperer still knew the Zwinger as a whole, and he saw it destroyed. He did not live to see it in its form as rebuilt by the GDR (he died in 1960). For the greater part of his life, he saw the Frauenkirche as something self-evident and he saw it destroyed. I do not know if he could have imagined the reconstruction. In his diaries from those years, which run to over 1,000 pages, he says little about the enchantment of the river in the city. It wasn't really the time for it; life under constantly threatening pogroms and the harassment of the Gestapo made him sick with fear, although he kept hoping doggedly that it would change one day. In one of the three Jewish houses where he was forced to live during the war, on some winter mornings, when he wasn't hounded to go to the factory before six in the morning, he was astonished to see a piece of the city on the Elbe – but everything is seen fleetingly, as if it were incidental. A person can come to live so steeped in the obviousness of the ordinary, thinking it will always be there. When someone walks through Dresden in 2005, the 'model' for the *vedute* of Detto Canaletto will again be there to be admired as if it had always stood there. In this way, the Dresden of Canaletto is rising from its own ashes and the Dresden of Klemperer with which the GDR lived is disappearing.

The anti-monuments of the war. Monuments that with every scorched stone must say: 'Never again'. Should one really restore this Frauenkirche? This blackened, sad navel of Dresden, should it gleam again? What is a monument, I wonder, as I watch the builders busily ascending and descending scaffolding. If a monument is a keeper of memory and history, then the destroyed Frauenkirche is perhaps the ultimate monument. So, hands off? In 1997, behind the church, on the Neumarkt, there is the most moving archaeological museum that one can imagine. It can only be seen through the mesh of a fence and it looks like a builder's yard – which it is. It consists of endless rows of neatly arranged numbered stones. To work this out must have taken years of dogged puzzling that must have depressed people anew everyday. The architraves, fragments of saints' images, cornerstones, bits of window frames and countless anonymous-looking stones torn apart by the bombardment are ready. Everything has been catalogued. Even the twisted iron on which the clock hung is neatly stacked with the other twisted iron, numbered. The stubborn energy that can emanate from *Trauerarbeit*. It is not our usual image of the work done in the GDR. And I don't know how I'm supposed to interpret it, I can't find any familiar perspective. I have not taken any travel photos for a long time, there's little point. The real image in any case is always deeper, photos only diminish memory. But now I am suddenly overcome by the need to record something, perhaps it is because of this uniquely sad display of carefully catalogued stones, I don't know. I go into a camera shop and buy a roll of film in one of those cardboard boxes with a lens in it. It takes wonderful photographs, the woman in the shop assures me. It has a kind of wide-angle lens inside. A Canaletto box? I feel sheepish with the thing in my hand and after a few shots, stuff it deeply inside a coat pocket.

As if by a miracle, when the bombing stopped on 14 February, the Frauenkirche was still standing. The gigantic dome, known in Dresden as the 'stone bell', had obviously protected it. But in the morning of the following day, the survivors of hell heard an ear-splitting roar, the completely gutted church finally collapsed under the weight of the dome that had protected it. A church that dies like an animal. They must have been apocalyptic moments. Sodom and Gomorrah. And anyone who looks back turns into a pillar of salt. At least the latter seems to be the historical motto of the capitalist *Wessies*, who are investing gigantic sums in this region. But their optimism, aimed at forgetting a piece of history, makes one feel as uncomfortable as the unbearably black ruins.

There is a huge shortfall in funding for the restoring of the Frauenkirche, and yet the aim is to have the restoration completed by 2008, when Dresden will be one of the European cities of culture. In principle, the famous dome should be on the church again by 2005. Less than ten years to build what in the past took 50 years and more. The destruction took a moment. Bombs away, and that was that. *Archie the undaunted stormer,* as Mulisch called the pilot. Mission accomplished. Canaletto Bellotto made a splendid painting of this colossus, almost 100 metres high, seen from the Neumarkt. There is a reproduction in the tourist guide, next to the famous photo of the black Angel on the town hall, looking down on the smouldering ruins.

Am I trying to gloss over something? I think there is a different point. I am standing in front of a moribund monument that exudes history like a nightmare. Contradictions pile up. Why am I feeling pity for a Baroque religious monument? Because it suddenly stands for the preservation of culture and memory, also the culture of violence, which always had a close pact with the culture of *joie de vivre*? Ecological sentiment of those who live after Auschwitz? In a narrow street right opposite the church, one can see a great mural, a kind of nineteenth-century strip cartoon, about 50 metres long, depicting the history of the Saxon princes. The changing costumes constitute the only differences between historical figures; the facial expressions, from the mediaeval to the latest, clearly modern figures, are the same.

On one side, the church has been completely wrapped up. There is scaffolding around it, on which great strips of plastic sheeting hang. When the sun breaks through at about noon, workmen pull away the sheeting. In the restaurants opposite, solid Saxon food with slightly sparkling beer is served. The most delicious thing that Dresden has to offer, as it says on the advertising hoardings. Near the church you can now buy Swatches. A quarter of the proceeds of sales goes towards the reconstruction of the Frauenkirche (what happens to the other three-quarters, you wonder immediately, and instead of idealism looms capitalism – without which, of course, this church would remain a black hole in the city).

Above the Elbe, a bird rises into the wind, glides high above the walkers strolling across the Blue Wonder, disappears above the cars racing along the river in the direction of the wine-growing slopes outside the city. The light is as vague as in a Canaletto.

I hang the framed reproduction carefully back on the thick wall of the ancient, cool Mediterranean room where I am writing this. Outside it is gradually getting hot. The noon hangs above the hills like a silence measuring kilometres across.

Forgetting is a strange power, because it makes memory possible. That is why all architecture from the past is something like the music of space, which surrounds us and sends us images that we constantly have to interpret. Perhaps for every view that we want to absorb, whether it is a landscape or a townscape, we have to take up three or four positions before we can make a composite image. And even then, looking is impossible because layer upon layer is hidden by the light of the day.

In cities, visibility is the ultimate fiction of history.

Intercity

A city becomes a world when you love one of its inhabitants . . .
LAWRENCE DURRELL

Lawrence Durrell, a now almost forgotten writer who in the 1960s was all the rage with his four-part novel, *The Alexandria Quartet,* in his description of the mysterious and impenetrable Justine constantly combed the streets and alleyways of Alexandria, searching for what he could not grasp, for something that seemed to be hidden like a promise in the body of the woman he desired and that nevertheless constantly eluded or at least exceeded his comprehension.

What his phlegmatic character, Darley, is slowly able to unveil of the secrets of this city, seems to exist concretely and tangibly in Justine's body, but at the same time the maze of the city shows him how much more there is – how the streets say in code that there is something more complicated in that woman, something that extends in time and space and can only be deciphered in the body of his beloved Justine as an allegory; so that the city in fact becomes the allegory of her body and its secrets and her body the key to the secrets of the city.

City and body of the beloved merge, assume each other's characteristics and disguises. The mirage of a street after rain and the sweating skin of a lover whom we have just left – although we have only just met her – both appear with greatest intensity when we are without them. The lover is constantly in your mind when you walk alone through the city, which you have come to know through her; and you constantly see the streets of the city, which you are beginning to love, in unsuspected dream perspectives when you fall asleep to the rhythm of her breathing.

You only get to know cities when you love someone there – only then is the scrap of newspaper blowing across the pavement meaningful, does every face have something to speak to you, is there something around every corner that can bring the dream to a stop or make it continue. Walking through streets that are burgeoning because of a new love: it is something like a constantly threatening danger, you are on the alert because a neglected detail can throw you back on yourself, back to the beginning, hitch-hiking on the motorway, or standing on a platform holding a paper with a date on it that you would most like to forget as soon as possible.

I got to know Amsterdam almost twenty years ago now on a small Greek island, because a young woman from Amsterdam spoke to me in the late afternoon sun. I had just waved goodbye to someone leaving on a sloop across the shallow bay. The small, rather grubby terrace of the otherwise uninhabited section of the island where about 50 of us were sleeping on the beach at night, was behind me. I waved goodbye to the friend, shook my head at the misunderstandings that had arisen between us, stood for a little looking out over the water glistening in the sun and turned around. I saw her sitting there and it was as if I had been struck in the face. Her long red hair was tied back, she had put her feet on a chair that she had drawn up. She sat calmly rolling a cigarette, looked at me with wonderful green eyes and said, 'Hey, your nose is burned.' She grinned broadly and pointed to the chair next to her. I walked over to her, felt my nose with the tip of my finger, realized that this was idiotic, burst out laughing, took the newly rolled cigarette out of her hands, bent over to her and was given a light. She rolled a second one. We both grinned. The tobacco pricked our throats. Gradually the adrenaline level rose as we said nothing. In the dry hills behind us, a few goats were grazing. Everyone was staring at the sea and waiting for that one flat-bottomed boat that would bring vegetables, fruit and meat for another day, so that the taciturn old man in the concrete hut could make food for us all. Hours later, we swam in the shallow salty bay, got sea urchin spines in our feet. The wind rose from the mountains and we were swimming back but we could scarcely make any headway; after a while we reached the beach exhausted and remained in each other's arms gasping for breath. The sudden feeling that everything in the world is possible at a moment like that. The first stars appeared over the uninhabited, empty land. We smoked and looked. We stayed together for a week, then went our separate ways. I spent a few confused days in Athens, but had the feeling that there was only one road open: the one that led to Amsterdam. A month and a half later, I saw her again in a street in Amsterdam and caught my breath. I was subsequently to spend four years of my life with her. But long after those four years, something has remained that will last all my life, when we meet up for a coffee and when we still go walking together now and again, sit in the pub like brother and sister, worried or happy because the other is: all that has become inextricably linked with Amsterdam, it has the smell of canal water or the atmosphere of the Leidseplein at two-thirty in the morning, it sounds like the click of the step when you get off the tram – a sound that, in the first few months after we said goodbye, pursued me into my dreams as the symbol of what I had lost because I could never choose. Amsterdam had really become a home. Whenever I drove into the city, saw the building on the Frederiksplein in the distance, parked in one of the streets named after seventeenth-century landscape painters, and later walked with her through the Albert Cuyp market, shopped and took the aroma of cinnamon, curry and olives with us up to her small loft, I knew that more than anywhere else in the world I had come home, and yet it was a home that I could only experience if that other home, far away in Belgium, was there too. I got to know the city from the inside, like people know it who have lived there for ages. I adopted habits, things you do there at set times, things you preferably do on Sunday (having a coffee in the Stedelijk Museum or a bike trip out of town along the Amstel, for example), but also the ordinary things that you can only do during the week, and all the things that you do or experience anyway simply because you are there living your own life: Indonesian cooking, getting into conversation with an arguing couple in the Marnixstraat, making a date in Frascati, getting drunk in the 'The Years' café, but that wasn't there at the time, though the imagery comes in handy. I got to know the strange paradoxes of a city where I bought books without suspecting that I would one day publish there myself, learned its narrow and wide-open sides, visited all kinds of friends and acquaintances with my girlfriend, went on pub crawls with her, sometimes had the feeling that anything was possible in that city, and then again that everything was terribly well-regulated. Anyone who realizes the nature of that alternation, I lectured, is beginning to understand something about Amsterdam; but the code is never expressly stated, you have to fathom it for yourself, and every signal has a specific meaning – meanings that were totally different in my traditional Flemish home town. I started, as it were, translating gestures, a look, a sentence broken off in a significant way, a waving hand, into another language, in a city that, like most big cities, was self-consciously reflected in its inhabitants, who combine a great feeling of solidarity with an always possible shrugging of the shoulders at other people and the place where they live. The labyrinth gradually revealed itself and only when everything started to become a little clearer, did I see how naked I myself had been for my friends and acquaintances in the city. Not only did the body of the city become the body of the woman I loved, but I also learned that the city was increasingly becoming the mirror of my sense of being different, of the fact that I had grown up in an entirely different framework. And although I tried to learn as quickly as possible all the elusive things that had to be learned (terms to be used at the baker's, for example, none of which were the same as in my native dialect), I simply realized that, in that growing intimacy with the city, I was beginning to feel ever more keenly the tiniest aspects of my existence as an outsider. After a while, I knew the nuances of the seasons in an Amsterdam street, the noise of fireworks in the night at New Year and the feeling of emptiness after the bang in the street with cars parked bumper to bumper, the regularly recurring three rising tones of the ambulance at night. How different a rainy Wednesday afternoon there was compared with a Wednesday in the city I came from and constantly returned to. I learned the sore points for the average city-dweller and how best to cope with them, how to make things clear that you initially thought were inexplicable. I learned a little to empathize with how immigrants in my own city and perhaps in this town too often felt – I also learned how untypical and, at the same time, completely representative Amsterdam is of the rest of the Netherlands. All clichés, of course. But clichés come to life when you live somewhere and what you thought you'd left behind you taps you on the shoulder again. It is a matter of lots of tiny nuances, the way you say something, a look, that whole language that I learned at close quarters because someone loved me and I loved her. It is that intangible surplus that I now recognize when I read a book by an Amsterdam writer, things that I can't explain but in which I know most people in Belgium see only words where I, like everyone who has spent a while in Amsterdam, am aware of a specific smell or a room with a view of back gardens, or sense an implied, typically Amsterdam quirk. In a chance sentence, I sometimes hear how words sound on a narrow staircase where bikes hang on a hook, how the ringing of the doorbell becomes inextricably bound up with the rope on the landing of a flat with which you open the lock; the kind of things people say while they're standing waiting for a table they have reserved to become vacant, or I remember that it can be useful for a drunken newcomer to remember the sentence '*Piet Koopt Hoge Schoenen*' (a mnemonic for remembering the order of the canals, Prinsengracht, Keizersgracht, Herengracht, Singel).

Perhaps you should have the courage to write precisely about clichés especially, if you want to know who you have become. They are the things that pursue you when you go to a place less often: the taste of coffee with milk (milk heated in the saucepan, very cumbersome thinks the Belgian – disgusting if the milk is cold, thinks the Dutchman); the atmosphere at the newsagent's; the Bijenkorf department store compared with L'Innovation. Voices, things and faces connected with an attitude to life. Only years later have you plotted something essential, less by thinking of clichés than by forgetting about them, but at that moment you are no longer able to put your finger on it as cheerfully as your compatriots who visit the city now and then. Forming opinions about a city is something for tourists, I thought, but in those days that was exactly what I did. I sometimes long almost pathetically for the bread, already half-stale by Monday morning that I bought on Saturday afternoon on the Ceintuurbaan (an inconvenience that is non-existent in Belgium with its extra well-stocked bakers on Sunday) or I miss the mixture of exotic and disgusting smells in the Albert Cuyp market. Then I know that it's time to ring my girlfriend there.

The only members of your family who really count, you make for yourself, by loving and doing stupid things, by for-giving and seeing each other again. In that sense, Amsterdam is a city where I come home to but that I also have to get away from again, because I obviously couldn't live there permanently: for writing, I need a different kind of space, where people are less hectic and opinionated, where there is a lull without opinions, where absence reveals its elusive poetry, where I can take distance from what I long for. So something of the home-less person gets into you, although you always return to a fixed spot. You take the tram aimlessly, you just walk through the city at night and everything and nothing at once is what you want to see: this strange and new combination between too much and too little, too few people and too little space – this atmosphere of an international village, on which modesty is wasted, although there is nowhere else that one wants to create such a strong impression of critical awareness; but where on the other hand self-consciousness is quite rightly rooted in words, not in the look of the streets. Because of this linguistic awareness, I've always found something Jewish about Amsterdam, more Jewish than anywhere else, something with which I feel myself at home without myself partaking of, but for which I longed, it seemed to promise something that in our Belgian, linguistically chaotic upbringing had all too often been absent – I mean the experience of constant linguistic criticism as an identity, but I also mean the associated process in which the urban ambitions of the city, which in other cities is a primary concern, becomes incidental – a kind of nonchalance about material things. At the same time there was something of a Jewish Biblical scholar about many Amsterdam intellectuals – perhaps something of what was lost in Dresden, Warsaw, Paris or Berlin, but something less interrupted here than elsewhere: a sense of continuity. The way in which people discuss things has grown up in a tradition of self-conscious language. This abundance of critical self-consciousness, on the one hand, and a complacent belonging-here-and-nowhere-else, on the other, is what sometimes gets too much for me, so that I want to quickly return to the Flemish provincial calm of a smaller city and relish there an indefinable sense of the proximity of the French cultural sphere; though, after a few weeks, months at most, I am nevertheless filled with homesickness and have the feeling that I urgently want to feel it all around me again and know where I really stand in regard to myself and the other people with whom I live. Amsterdam is a place where I adjust my compass, on a terrace in the sun, in a crowded cage full of urbanely twittering budgerigars.

In those years, something of my stay there crept into the accent of my Dutch, an eloquent witness to what apart from that is just my own business and my own history. In the meantime, I have long since lost that accent but, whenever I get to Amsterdam, it is back immediately, whether I like it or not. The accent, of which I was often not even aware, invariably annoyed people in Belgium: there it counts as a form of posing, speaking Dutch that smacks even a little of language usage north of the great rivers. In fact you are some kind of traitor if you get rid of your typical Flemish accent, even though you don't do it deliberately. This is supposed to be giving in to Dutch linguistic imperialism. All too often even the most progressive Flemings come to Amsterdam with that covert national feeling: it's a form of self-affirmation for them to see how Amsterdamers frown at certain expressions that are generally used in Belgium. They enjoy laying it on a bit thick and start talking in even broader dialect to lure the average Dutchman into adopting his most easily-caricatured position of schoolmaster. The average Fleming reckons that it does not take very much to do that. Speaking dialect constitutes the last provincial attitude of resistance, it is a bloody-minded reaction to the ever-ready fussing, the friendly or arrogant correction of every sentence or expression that doesn't immediately belong to Northern language usage, and it's understandable that all this should now and then get right up the nose of Flemings: when six million people use a certain expression, then of course it is a natural part of that language and, even from a sociological point of view, it has a right to exist. It's the same attitude with which an inhabitant of Marseilles comes to Paris, the inhabitant of Trieste to Milan, the inhabitant of Vienna to Frankfurt or Berlin. Yet that kind of tug-of-war is lost on me now because the defensive self-consciousness of many Flemings annoys me just as much. In this way, you soon find yourself belonging nowhere and that's perhaps just as well. In Belgium I am constantly incensed by Flemish self-conscious linguistic laziness, in Amsterdam I am often fed up with Dutch self-conscious linguistic zealotry. But I am already talking about those endlessly chewed-over contrasts that do not interest me. The essential thing about Amsterdam is what I hear when I dial the number of a male or female friend and hear a familiar voice with a questioning tone or when I arrive and hear the click-back step on its spring when I get off the tram, when I climb up to the flat, past hanging bicycles and am welcomed: coming home to the city to which, long before I had a girlfriend there, I had fled with a sweetheart, some time in the mid-1970s. At that time, we fairly abruptly got to know the seamy side of the city. Much in my life has begun and equally often ended there.

Almost fifteen years later, I walked through a city with the same feeling of being homeless and new in a city that I have known since my childhood, but which only now, because of a new love, began to speak at every street corner of that fearful, mutual merger of body and city, which makes the smallest things become threatening and promising: Brussels. Although I had known the city since my childhood, it only now began to speak of the images that lay hidden deep inside me, the vague, dusky delicatessen store of a Brussels uncle, whom I hadn't seen for twenty years – the street where the shop was located was no longer there; my memories of the time when as a student I worked in the great customs complex in the harbour, in the huge building of Thurn & Taxis, the African smells in the afternoon around the North Station. I walked with her through streets that I only remembered after long hesitation, which I must have passed through as child, as if I had to decipher a cryptic map. In this way, I learned how different is the fall of the light in a Brussels flat on a big avenue compared with a room in an Amsterdam street, though in fact objectively there is nothing happening to the light, only to your consciousness; I went into houses in suburbs, where there was something of a Parisian atmosphere, walked through the desolate empty spaces of this badly wounded city and paradoxically enough became happy precisely because of it.

There is no handier cliché conceivable to represent all the misunderstandings that exist between Belgians and Dutchmen than to think of Amsterdam while walking in Brussels, and of Brussels in Amsterdam. And most clichés are actually immediately confirmed in the look of the streets: just in the same way as some leading citizens of Amsterdam take their bikes to the poshest reception, the poorest devil in Brussels comes tearing along in his third-hand Mercedes to pop round the corner for a packet of cigarettes. For Dutch people, it must feel a little like a southern city, whereas it does not even strike the average Belgian as anything specific. Identity is the blind spot in your consciousness. Identity is the incomprehensibility of the cliché. Really being in Brussels means being prepared to relativize, forget your place in the world, your identity, your language to a large extent, to be absorbed in the vital and really cosmopolitan character of this unimaginably chaotic society: its bastardized culture, its lack of self-respect, its blurred sense of standards, its cynical lack of urbanization. If you want to assert yourself there as a self-conscious Fleming, you must limit yourself to one of the ten pubs where it is known that all the Flemings living in Brussels meet – that means in concrete terms that you can decide to move in a kind of Flemish Brabant village within the city, an imaginary and oppressive kind of homeland that has to be marked out with invisible lines within a metropolis. So that means that you can decide to exist in a rather cosy and small-town Flemish way in a city which is quite simply 80 per cent Gallicized. But if you do not cling to your provincial identity of 'threatened minority', you can move in the best atmosphere that Belgium, this 'corridor of Europe', has to offer; a feeling that is completely opposed to what you find in Amsterdam – a loss of solidarity, of identity, of morality in the neat, bourgeois sense, of effective action, of talent for organization and critical awareness – virtually none of the ordered manageability in which opinions can be weighed to the nearest gram, but instead a kind of expanding of the personality that can only happen to you in metropolises. As far as mentality is concerned, Brussels, you sometimes hear said, may have more in common with Buenos Aires than with Amsterdam (another cliché that is precious to Dutch-speaking Bruxellois; they look down on Amsterdam and call it a village in the 'polder', and thus show that they simply fail to notice the completely different focus of the cosmopolitanism of that city).

Brussels makes at least one thing immediately clear: that there are two kinds of Dutch-speakers: about sixteen million who belong to the Germanic sphere, and six million who belong to the Latin sphere. To a large extent, the deeper cultural conflicts can be traced back to this rift. Fashion in Amsterdam shows a clear influence of Berlin, London and New York, fashion in Brussels favours Paris and Milan. Architecture in Amsterdam has stylistic characteristics that you find as far north as Oslo and beyond; architecture in Brussels displays aspects that you find as far south as Rome and beyond. The Amsterdam weekly, *Vrij Nederland*, has something about it of the *Times Literary Supplement*; the Flemish daily, *De Morgen*, seems rather to have taken its inspiration from *Libération*. Dutch people interested in literary programmes abroad can hear Marcel Reich-Ranicki talking about books on German TV, but for years a foreign model for Flemings was *Bouillon de culture* with Bernard Pivot. Among intellectuals in Flanders, Laure Adler with her intellectual Parisian interviews is a minor celebrity; in the Netherlands, people read French philosophers in English or German translation. In Flanders, the artistic channel Arte is broadcast in the French version; in the Netherlands, that would undoubtedly be the German version, if it ever gets that far. My generation of Flemings learned French as its second language (from the first year at school); Dutch people of my age had English as their second language, which for me was a third language. All this has persistent effects: literary examples, painting, philosophy, development of taste. Before we know it, we are astonished at completely different assessments of literary work, films, theatrical performances and other cultural questions, 'even though we speak the same language after all'. Because people tend to think egocentrically, the two Dutch-speaking communities regularly call each other 'stupid'. Usually people on both sides are content to blame the differences on the opposition Calvinist–Catholic, but as an explanation that is inadequate. Flemish Protestants are still much more like Flemish Catholics than Dutch Protestants, and Dutch Catholics have little in common with Flemish ones. In turn, certain kinds of old-fashioned Flemish Catholics have more in common with the atmospheric Walloon bigotry of small villages than they themselves care to admit. The historic choices for those two religions, even in the sixteenth century, were inspired by the Germanic and Latin influence respectively. The historical roots of those clichés constantly resurface. Flemings find Dutch people 'annoyingly American', and Dutch people find that Flemings do everything 'in a nonchalant French style'. Most Dutch expressions which include the word 'French' are not really meant very positively. This distinction, based on ineradicable and often idiotic clichés, cannot be bridged by language because it is deeply embedded in culture and from there it finds its way to psychology, communication, even public morality, however charged that subject has become in Belgium in recent years.

And yet. The 'lightness of being' in Brussels only strikes you if you are prepared to abandon yourself to the messy border areas of language and society in which by now millions of people all over the world live: expressing themselves in languages that are not their own, getting by with a handful of expressions that they have learned on the street; pidgin English, bastardized French, the dying Brussels dialect with its inextricable combination of French and broad Brabant dialect, a dreadfully tortured kind of 'parcellation Flemish', as Geert van Istendael has called it – all this in a city with a plan that bears testimony to a far from innocent colonial past, a city without rights and with an incredibly flashy Palace of Justice, a city with improbably high rents and a huge number of unoccupied buildings, bragging and aberrations, endless disputes between municipalities, no official language, no clear representation, a bureaucracy swollen to monstrous proportions that is completely cut off from the impoverished demographic mix – in short, a chaos in which people no longer feel that we are talking about their city – this is precisely what makes me love Brussels, and why, in the eyes of my Amsterdam friends, I will probably always remain an odd Belgian and in the eyes of nationalist Flemings, a traitor.

For Brussels belongs to no one and everyone. Both the nationalist Flemings and the nostalgic Walloon movements have turned their backs on the city. Of all the administrators, bureaucrats and politicians who take decisions about this city, almost none personally live in the city. What does the urban decline matter to them? From their ugly office buildings and royal suites, the Flemings commute hastily back to their rural estates – those awful stone camping sites that have swallowed up all the public spaces in Flanders.They daily abandon their capital with frivolous indifference. There is now also a deep rift between the urban Francophones and the Walloons from the more rural districts and small towns. Liège and Brussels appear to be in the same country purely by chance; even here, there is no longer any question of collaboration or solidarity. Brussels is a shop full of spoiled goods, where people come holding their noses to steal what hasn't quite perished, and then to disappear back to their own little plot. It is a capital without a country, and hence a city without responsibility or morality. In the division of Belgium, Brussels should become an independent fourth element, alongside the other three language communities, Dutch, French and German. No one has a consistent plan for the city; no one frets about its symbolic function. The European party states saw that very clearly; all those things that aren't allowed anywhere else, can be done in Brussels. Nobody cares. Provided the money rolls under the table, everything is possible. That's why the real city dwellers are powerless to confront the chaos: decisions are taken about their city in the narrow-minded sphere of the provinces and in the seclusion of international lobbies, an atmosphere that each day penetrates effortlessly as far as Parliament. In the much-flaunted new Flemish 'Glass House' where the Flemish government resides in its village-like pseudo-transparency, there is a buzz of East Flemish, West Flemish, Antwerp and Limburg rhetorical tricks. Local politicians are 'dispatched' from their provincial nests to Brussels, to defend local interests there. No one is concerned about the city where they are sitting squabbling.

Neither Flemings nor Walloons regard Brussels as their capital. Only the languishing Brussels population does, and here and there some people with cultural awareness, who are usually written off as old-fashioned Belgian nationalists. In this social vacuum, the speculators have set up their stall eagerly, and this can be seen from the city. In Amsterdam, Amsterdamers have some say in things. But in Brussels, there are no natives of Brussels in power. The people of Brussels do their deals in the twilight zone. *On se débrouille*, they get by. And the town council, which is made up of native Bruxelloix, suffers far too often from the small-minded municipal belly-aching that pre-empts any fundamental discussion in advance. Brussels' mayors look more often like retired croupiers than civil servants with an eye for political morality. That can all be seen from the graft – Brussels is a city without vision, and hence an urban jungle with unexpected perspectives. It resembles a gigantic messy kitchen used by countless tenants, but where no one feels it is their fault if people don't clear up. Brussels is therefore a city that lives in its undefinability – something that paradoxically enough sometimes gives rise to sublime moments in a view of the city, an empty plot or an old district. It is the effect of historical indifference, such as could be seen on the bare, fallow Potzdamer Platz. The appearance, in a flash, of an almost film-like exaltation in a sordid detail, this sense of being charged with an elusive history, jerks the walker in Brussels out of his familiar identity in the narrow sense. You certainly can't say that of Amsterdam: there you will feel only too quickly where your place is, where you belong or do not belong.

In that borderline area of careless use of language and space lies the whole meaning of the whorish charm of Brussels – as though language adapts itself to the chaotic town planning; or was that there first and did people learn to speak as crookedly as they built? The core of the Brussels experience lies in the fact that language is peripheral, that both at official occasions and in the smallest and seediest all-night bar you can suddenly have the feeling that you're everywhere and nowhere at the same time, because you can't tell from what you hear spoken around you – nor can you see it, except perhaps by seeing that there are no standards for your attitude and behaviour, that there is in any case no secret code (such as exists in Amsterdam) that decides whether or not you belong to the 'in-crowd'. You can perhaps only discover this Brussels by loving one of its inhabitants and thus finding a way back into that secret surplus in the odours, gestures and the fall of the light, which otherwise you can only observe as an outsider. But how are you ever supposed to be at home in this culture if you love a city without a spiritual centre? Only by not being 'home' anywhere, perhaps, can you exist radically with an idea of a city, with a utopian plan (to achieve this, you must perhaps make a careful drawing of your lover's body). The moment you start dreaming of non-existent maps, your cities start overlapping in your memory, even if they are extremes like Brussels and Amsterdam. And although it is inconceivable that one would confuse the smell of a rainy street in Saint-Josse or Ixelles with one in Oud-Zuid or near the Kleine Gartman Park, there is still something that you can only carry in yourself: the fact that, if you want to be at home in Brussels, Amsterdam or in any city, you don't belong anywhere except with the people to whom you matter.

The delusions of grandeur of the Baroque architecture, combined with the cynical neglect of valuable old properties in Brussels, make the walker homeless, simply from critical self-defence; the flats piled on top of each other in a kind of Bruges that has outgrown itself (that Amsterdam sometimes resembles) make people there long for a statement, some clarity, an indefinable longing for clarity, which I sometimes passionately completely share, and then again abhor. Brussels resembles the description of the world by the French philosopher of doom, Jean Baudrillard: semblance constantly takes the place of what you thought you detected – you live with the simulacrum of a culture. No wonder that many people in Belgium find Baudrillard's theories very plausible, while many in Amsterdam consider his ideas total nonsense: there is no relevant situation that provides that experience. Because every-thing in Holland is 'genuine', just as in Belgium everything seems real, but 'is not real'. Perhaps that is the reason for the constantly recurring philosophical misunderstandings between people who have Brussels as a capital, and people who experi-ence Amsterdam as the guideline of their thoughts and actions: misunderstandings that we can perhaps solve better by walk-ing through each other's streets and listening to the city at night, than by having conferences with gentlemen in made-to-measure suits, stiff civil servants and administrators who are never absorbed into the nameless city and into that sea of details about which almost no one speaks, an elusive whole that says everything about cultures and their limitations.

Bratislava: The Age of Anachronism

I didn't want advice, I wanted to hear a story.
CHRISTOPH RANSMAYR

A man stands on the platform. He looks intently at a woman opposite him. While she is saying something, in mid-sentence, he carefully puts two fingers on her upper lip and with a quick tug pulls out a hair, a sort of stray moustache hair. The woman starts, gives a little cry, slaps the man and immediately afterwards kisses him.

On the Stefánikova, the long street that leads to the old town centre, it is empty and silent. There is only the rustling of the elder blossoms in the front gardens and the rising scent of heating asphalt. In a park completely abandoned by human beings and animals, in deathly forgotten silence, there is a statue of Johann Nepomuk Hummel, the famous composer from Pressburg, among wildly blooming irises and waving chestnut blossoms. At the foot of the column on which his bust stands, there are a few of those dreadful, typical 'little Hummels', fat-bellied Baroque boys who invariably look like piglets, with their rolls of fat, their rounded cheeks, their sentimental curls and their little penises. Strange that such ultra-'bourgeois' things should have outlived anti-bourgeois communism, amusing to think that they stood there quite simply and stayed there in the period of Husak. Then too no one gave them a second glance, but now tourism is beginning to penetrate even here, people are beginning to take some trouble over the local Hummel museum, which I will discover later in the day in the old town centre. The opening times are rather awkward, the museum is completely closed during the

93

opening hours indicated, you have to ring, you are shown in, must wait for a guide. I rush outside again because of a sudden attack of claustrophobia. But I haven't got that far yet.

At the end of the boulevard I see the first cars; and suddenly you enter the old city through an arch. The first sight is dismaying: almost every street is being dug up, people go on working on Saturday afternoon, the sparse shops are closed, the old, cracked asphalt is being dug up, here and there the beginnings of a new pavement are visible: Bratislava is working on its new pedestrianized shopping centre. A little further on you find yourself in a few completely empty streets, all the houses are unoccupied and windowless, ruin after ruin. Silence, a smell of mildew and old wood, not a soul to be seen. It looks like a district after a civil war.

In the small town centre, a few streets are already finished. The Baroque façades have been given a new coat of paint, some are already a little paler, perhaps painted just before the *Wende*. But the new, scarcely laid paving stones seem to be hoping for many walkers who, for the time being, haven't materialized; people of a different kind, people who stroll instead of hurrying to their work. Why should they stroll if there is nothing to buy; in Bratislava I was warned, there's nothing to see. It's true. I'm fascinated. Between some dilapidated houses there stands an artificially neat Baroque façade: the Berlitz School. A priest in a brown habit, straight out of an old cartoon, walks past it with his robes flapping.

Pressburg, as Bratislava was called for centuries, was once an important town, the capital of the Hungarian kingdom. With the liberation of the areas occupied by the Turks in southern Europe in the second half of the eighteenth century, this centre considerably extended its power southwards into Europe. The Archbishop had an ancient Gothic house in the city. The earliest parts of the so-called Primatial Palace were already three centuries old. The wealthy and famous Esterhazys further extended the central palace. Here worked the notorious face-puller and virtuoso Baroque sculptor Franz

Xaver Messerschmidt, all of whose statues have at present been loaned out for the great summer exhibition that Harald Szeemann is now putting together in Lyons – I will see them, three months later, there in Lyons in the great 'Hall Tony Garnier', and will topple back into that day, that instant in the Primatial Palace, when I stood looking around rather hesitantly and was disappointed not to be able to see the smooth capricious heads. Just as with the Canalettos, things suddenly came together there in an unexpected place. Travelling is often finding something in retrospect that you hadn't been looking for.

But here in Bratislava, the peace of Pressburg was signed in 1806. A painful affair for Emperor Franz I who, because of the conquests of Napoleon, lost his hold on important areas: Venice, Istria, Dalmatia and Tyrol. Franz I asked Lichtenstein to sign in his name, Napoleon sent Talleyrand. This marked the beginning of a drastic contraction of the German Roman Empire. But even today many Viennese still stubbornly call Bratislava 'Pressburg'. When you drive from Vienna in the direction of Bratislava, the city is still signposted as Pressburg in Viennese territory; after a few kilometres, that is, outside Viennese territory, it is designated as Bratislava. A detail perhaps, but significant. Nevertheless, the city retains almost nothing of its Habsburg flair; it will probably re-evoke it now, for the benefit of tourism, from the countless Baroque buildings that fell into decay during communism. But the necessary know-how has to be imported. The moment you board the waiting train to Bratislava in the rather grubby-looking Ostbahnhof in Vienna, another world begins – a world of dust, smells of fat and engine oil, of vague heat and body odours. Gone are the clean young Viennese with their big-city cool, gone is the chilly, reserved behaviour and the averted glances that carefully avoid any contact, gone are the tarts of the *Graben* parading past in clouds of perfume. The train is suddenly chock-full of young boys and girls with torn jeans and headphones. A girl right opposite me is sitting kissing her friend, but she is angled so that she can keep looking me straight in the eye. She has wonderful black eyes. Intently chewing and smoking, adolescent boys listen to American music on their Walkmans, so loud that everyone can hear it. Unlike their parents, they can't understand a word of German but speak a kind of broken four-letter-word English mixed with their Slovak, which they rattle off in rapid tempo. They look a little cynical and when they laugh, they make a sound like a German shepherd-dog with a bad cold. At the same time they're naïve. You feel that they think it's wonderful to be able – and most of all to be allowed – to behave in this way. Every ten seconds, in the intervals between eager drags on a cigarette, a young boy propels a tiny wad of spit out of the window and looks defiantly at the ticket collector. 'Fuck!' he shouts triumphantly and puts his legs on the seat in front of him, so that the shy girl opposite him starts. He's reading an English-language rock magazine. It is the older people, whom I will later see in the city, who still know a bit of German but because the borders have been closed for 50 years, it is vague and old-fashioned German, still dating from their almost-forgotten youth, larded with expressions that now strike us as literary. They do not show much enthusiasm to revive that memory. I myself, less than ten minutes' journey from Vienna, have no urge at all to speak another word of German.

The gorgeous girl at the reception desk of my hotel also speaks fluent Berlitz English. At every English *th* the tip of her tongue slips out through her perfect teeth. The hotel is clean and post-modern but it is situated on an old street and hides behind an old-fashioned façade. The city has a completely dead and abandoned look, except for the few strolling tourists. Not one shop is open. The Slovaks have not yet discovered late shopping days, and the greatest pastime in the West – throwing a fixed weekly budget down the drain on Saturday afternoon as you trudge lazily past window displays – is obviously not yet in vogue here. So you really can't do anything at all in a weekend in Bratislava, and that fires the imagination. I walk down the empty grey streets, see building after desolate building, sooty black and decayed blocks of flats with dark stairwells covered in peeling Baroque motifs, and again am amazed at what my generation has seen, at the unbelievably disastrous experiment of which we have been the historic witnesses: a system that was unaffordable, in which gas, water and electricity, indeed even the houses were virtually free, but where apart from that, there was no freedom left and finally less and less could be obtained, so that everything simply went on decaying for half a century. The bankruptcy of communism can still be read from the vast majority of the façades. We are witnesses to the ruins of a system, of an economically non-viable ideology. For a little while, we can still see in countless details how this system allowed half of Europe, and architecturally indisputably the most beautiful half, to go to rack and ruin, flake away, become mildewed and crumble to dust – in the name of a humanist utopia that went wrong. This is an historically striking fact which, in countries like Poland with its countless propped-up old mammoth buildings and abandoned factory sites, has something apocalyptic about it, something quite as exceptional as the sights people who went round Europe after the plague epidemics must have seen. Not so pathetic and awful, but on just as huge a scale. Thousands of kilometres of decay, rusty gates, broken windowsills, almost faded pale paint, hundreds of thousands of kilometres of cracked asphalt of dubious quality. But there are also wonderful old gateways everywhere with an almost mediaeval darkness, which have only survived because of the same neglect: in the West they've been long replaced by properties without a history. Communism lasted just as long as it takes to wear out a nineteenth-century building completely without maintaining or repairing anything. It lived as it were on what there was and finally let go of it again, just before it collapsed. In that sense, communism was also bound to collapse: all monuments, nineteenth-century blocks of houses, palaces, facilities, street paving, flats from the period of Art Nouveau or the Habsburg period, had simply worn out, were simply finished.

During the weekend that I am here a referendum is being held: should the Slovaks join NATO or not? President Kovak is in favour. Kovak is not worried about the Russian growling of the great White Bear Yeltsin. But his fairly dictatorial Premier, Meciár, is against this manoeuvre, which he sees as far too much geared to the West. On the forms, on which initially only a yes or no had to be filled in, the cunning question has been added: do you also agree that in that case American nuclear weapons should be stored on Slovak soil and if necessary also be fired from here? Elsewhere the addition of this question would be condemned as an inadmissible manipulation of the referendum. But things don't weigh that heavily here yet: Meciár proudly signs a big contract for a gigantic nuclear reactor which will for the first time combine Western and Russian technology – something that is repeated at every turn in newspaper articles. Symbols in technology.

But apart from that, there is no sign at all of the referendum on which even many Western television stations will report that evening. Bratislava waits motionless and, it seems, indifferently for the result. Certainly, there is a small faded poster here and there, although usually with the slogan 'Go West' stuck over it. Though both examples – the referendum on NATO and the cigarette advert – are fundamentally about an obsession with America, this is why the Slovaks do not maintain cordial relations with their Austrian neighbours: they are fixated on something else, something that has been withheld from them for so long that they have immediately made a caricature of it in the midst of an economy in decline. A strange paradox also originates here: Austria, which is so capitalist, so convinced of its own rightness, suddenly looks old-fashioned when you see these post-communist young people wandering around in Bratislava, so run-down, so excitingly chaotic. Vienna continues to suck on its deepest and oldest roots, however far advanced its economy may be, however fashion-ably the women parade there, however large the advertising hoardings may be; Bratislava scarcely has a past any longer, hardly anything to suppress, and America marches in – a second Marshall Plan is being introduced into Europe, this time the eastern part. Here something has come into being that Peter Handke may also have felt when he attended his Serbian football matches, a highly explosive mix of unhistoric living and longing for a future without a label, but with an image – freedom, with all the trimmings, a ragout of chilli pepper, cola and cheeseburger against a decaying and, here and there, apocalyptic backdrop. These post-communist young people would survive more easily in the Bronx and Soho than those from the old Josefstadt: a combination of rampant capitalism and decay is familiar to them. In the background, there are episodes of vague longing for a past – a provincial funda-mentalism, images from before communism, broken toys that have to be patched up. In the local McDonald's the progressive rabble assembles. In contrast to the unbearably banal atmosphere of these kinds of establishments in the West, the McDonald's here is the place to be: hip-hoppers, caps, heads shaking to thumping rhythms of music listened to on Walkmans and gyrating bottoms, Nikes that have been scrimped and saved for and sometimes even the odd roller-blader. Next door there is still a decrepit rusty old administrative thing with broken windows. Pepped up, hip capitalism against old, memory-less rust.

In-between: nothingness.

In-between: the lost nuance.

In-between: memory.

In-between, a chasm.

In-between, the Now, excitement.

A chasm from which a complicated truth rises – that of anachronism. In his excellent essay on Heiner Müller, the famous German scholar, Hans Mayer, described this life in anachronism:

The situation of life in an anachronism is well known. Social order is dissolving, because none of the events happening at that moment are regarded as valid or remarkable . . .

Among the Frenchmen who wrote about a *Weltschmerz* that originated from a deep dislike, hence not so much from a longing for the downfall of the Ancien Régime and the restoration of the Bourbons as from the sight of bourgeois consumer culture, a culture described at the time by Ludwig Börne in Paris as 'a poisonous money economy' – was the aristocrat and great poet, Alfred de Musset. He was also the person who found the appropriate way of expressing the constantly recurring constellations of a life amid social anachronism. In his biographical work, *Confessions d'un enfant du siècle*, a diagnosis was formulated: 'Everything that was there, is no longer there, everything which will one day be is not yet there. Here is the origin of our suffering.' That was the correct diagnosis. The so-called *Weltschmerz* arose from suffering from a reality that one despised. It was about a deep social dislike. It was therefore also pure cynicism to interpret such a thing as romantic or even provincial Biedermeier fashion.

Two hundred years after the storming of the Bastille on 14 July 1789, a new form of life in anachronism had come into being in the so-called European West. The decline of the past bourgeois community and hence of the bourgeois Enlightenment but without any prospect of a longed-for or conceived Not Yet.

Mayer is of course alluding here to the situation in which the young GDR found itself, no longer wanting to base its social contracts on outmoded individualist humanism, but also with too little experience of the individual in the new economy based on the Stalinist model. At such moments, there is no longer any valid model for regulating interpersonal action; for this reason, strict, empty rituals are created which fill up the whole vision with an immediate presence in which the external becomes of great importance. This is why the workers in Müller's early plays constantly have moral conflicts that are supposed to regulate human interaction in new complex situations for which there is not yet any solution. What you can see in cities like Bratislava shows a great similarity with the process described; and just as it was unjust to speak of romantic

Weltschmerz while the romantics were questioning the whole order politically and ideologically, so it is naïve to think that the flashy, aimless posing of the young people hanging around here eating cheeseburgers is without content: they are cutting a high profile in an empty world, and the first thing human beings look for in such a situation is an attitude. This has severe repercussions for the way in which one thinks about the rights of the individual. What is important is not the content of their provocative, rather provincial reflexes, but what is behind their behaviour that they themselves do not yet know, what is being put at stake. The No More and the Not Yet.

In such a no-man's-land there emerges something not understood, but with a great vital force that throws itself recklessly into the future. According to Mayer, these are periods in which the most important texts for a future view of the world are created. In that sense, I am also reminded of the provocative text by Peter Handke on former Yugoslavia and I am again inclined to give his texts the benefit of the doubt, however dubious his lyrical report on the Serbs may be; not because of what he says, but because of what he set in motion in a new Europe that was shaping itself unpredictably. Hans Mayer presents us with two periods of anachronism – the French Revolution and the young GDR. But now, at the end of the twentieth century and the beginning of the third millennium, more people than ever live in a world of indecision. Here in Bratislava too. They live with strip cartoons and chips, drum and bass, pirated versions of video games, mannerisms and attitudes learned in discotheques, magazines that present self-images of the momentary, pep talk, tasteless beer (XTC is still too expensive here), quick sex behind a desolate concrete building, but still make do materially as well as one can in dilapidated old houses, with worn-out furniture, second-hand equipment, clapped-out mopeds, a few of which slalom slowly between the stinking public transport, desolate streets with nothing but flaking and ruined façades, horribly unattractive shops, the mess of the confused beginning that means the beginning of a free market; they have young and impatient bodies and they want to move forward to something that is unknown and precisely for this reason, so attractive. Nowhere else can the coarsest clichés of glitter, eroticism of the purely external and unrealistic success rage so freely as in these free zones where history no longer has a face. It is not humanism, not totalitarianism, not ideology, not freedom in the traditional sense, not individualism like that of May 1968, not collectivism – it is all that mixed up together, and the sum is nevertheless something different which will be given a name later – an Eastern European form of post-modernism perhaps. Bratislava: an empty quay on the Danube, five guys and music by Tina Turner by a stall with faded sex magazines, beer and cigarettes; a couple of floating restaurants on flat boats without imagination, obviously from before the *Wende* but now patched up somewhat.

A shabby drunken man attacks a flashily made-up woman, with peroxide hair, in McDonald's because she takes a photograph. He shouts and threatens to smash her camera, tries to wrench it out of her hands. With his free hand he hits her arm. The woman starts to cry. A hamburger Rambo in a striped shirt rushes from behind the till and intervenes at lightning speed, throwing the violently struggling man out of the door. Gives him a firm push in the back. He slips off the pavement with one foot. Turns round insulted and shouts, with fists clenched, at the front of the building. The glass door is locked for a moment. The dirty old tram passing by creaks on the bend on a bed of cracked concrete like a groaning dinosaur. A girl wearing a McDonald's cap and an apron comes to spray the table where the man was sitting with disinfectant. She cleans the tabletop. The glass door is open again. The scene continues.

There is new money in this worn-out city. There is sauna with massage in the newer hotels (but conversely the simplest things like lighting do not work that well after seven years of free market economy). It gets dark here considerably earlier and, towards dusk, strikingly beautiful young women emerge all over the place, and without exception look you straight in the eye. No, in its former satellite town of Pressburg, Vienna seems a planet away; London seems actually more of a vague dream for the new youth, but behind it looms a shadow that is not understood – of Stalingrad, perhaps. That too is the explosive cocktail of a still undecided history. And at the only busy restaurant, Spaghetti and Co, New York-Italian in the new style with a copious salad bar and smooth à la carte, the cakes with the espresso come from Lembeke, near Eeklo in East Flanders, of all fucking places – the ploughed fields of my youth that have since declined into cosy suburbia. Even the Belgians are marching into Eastern Europe via the kitchen. I drink too much Lambrusco, smoke and watch.

Have men and women ever been so banally beautiful and anonymous, so almost meaninglessly interchangeable as now at the end of the second millennium? All 'personality' and as superfluous and identical as fishes in a school of herrings? Perhaps the view that you get as an outsider in one new city after another, is playing me false. Life appears anonymous, overwhelming and attractive because you don't see anything of the relationships and the complicated situations that link people together. You see the outside, the gestures and the bodies, the eyes and the now and you actually live in a dream of history and space. You are inclined to think in general terms, so you must look at the small things, the individual, or you will begin to think that you understand the world – the surest way not to understand it. But individual glitter is also massively present, it comes and disappears again, you are constantly fascinated for a few seconds and then distracted by something else.

Darkness. A small round gateway with a bare lamp fronting a barrel vault. A smell of mildew and piss. At the end of the old, massive corridor, a gate. Behind that gate, a courtyard. All around four floors of dark windows, only three of them sparsely and poorly lit. I count fifteen broken windows in varying states of decay. At the end of the courtyard, a strange, wooden staircase with again a bare lamp. Another gate, smaller this time. It is half open. The staircase sounds hollow and is rickety. At the top of the stairs, a round gateway, behind it a landing above a second courtyard. When you've reached the other side, another old wooden staircase awaits you, which gives onto a kind of higher-level courtyard, behind which there are again steps leading further. I must now be virtually on the third floor and have penetrated about half a street into the complex of buildings. They're actually private hallways, but I don't meet anyone. Now and again, there is a faint glow, a vague sound of a radio or a trio of voices. I've found myself in a labyrinth in the middle of the city, simply by stepping through one of the many open gateways. I don't know where it will end, but it reminds me of the houses that Gustav Meyrinck described in *The Golem*. Under the communist regime, countless people simply went on living here in the oppressive, early twentieth-century world of Franz Kafka, while the Stones, prosperity and flower power raged through the West. Somewhere meat is being cooked, it smells disgustingly greasy, elsewhere I smell roast paprika and hear a man growling at a woman. Always new staircases, more doors, it goes on and on. I no longer have the slightest notion where I am and if I were to bump into anyone, I could not explain why I am in this completely closed-off, for me completely chaotic world – actually a private space and yet at the same time public. At first sight, everything looks desolate and later, inhabited after all. It is a variant of the halls in apartment blocks but follows the organic pattern of mediaeval cities that sets your imagination racing. It is perhaps typically Slav but it reminds me of the vanished Jews. These ghetto-like inner worlds were fatal to them – they seemed as if made for the pogroms. You close the great gate and there is no escape for an unknown number of people. Like rats in a trap – their own labyrinthine houses. And in the night, having lost my way here, I sit down on a higher wooden staircase further on, and I think I'm sitting in a mausoleum, in another time in any case, in a Europe that I thought had died out. Until I nearly have a heart attack when a cat jumps onto my shoulder from a darkness higher up. Like a small black ghost it disappears under the staircase. Odradek.

I wander on a little further, then return, take the wrong turning a couple of times, finally find my way out of the innocent-looking gate behind which a whole city seemed to be hiding, and I am standing behind an old church, in a little square that already exudes the banal atmosphere of restoration. I have recognized a kaleidoscope of smells that were stored deep in my memory, smells from my youth in the 1950s. Within a few years the restoration will perhaps have swept away this whole hidden, silent labyrinth.

In contrast to Vienna where, in the evening, I either sit on the terraces of the old Josefstadt drinking or reading or go to the theatre or the opera, here I dive into the night life with a Cuban guy. Bubbling, crowded cafes, many willing girls and aggressive boys, a multicoloured mixture of the best rock music of the 1960s to the 1990s, then after three or so pubs, after a long walk along a bare avenue, at the end of a dark street a closed garage door – a private club where we have to ring three times. Striptease, immediately a girl next to you. In my case a Thai girl; she is 28, she has something aristocratic about her and she knows how to tease. We drink the obligatory champagne and talk. The acts are pretty naff, my concern is with the girls. I tell her that it doesn't excite me, but makes me curious about what those girls are thinking. We talk about this. She thinks that, as a man, I'm completely crazy to talk like that. I regularly ask how old a girl is, where she comes from, why she does this. 'Darling', she says with her dark lipstick-covered mouth against mine, 'you are sweet but you make me so nervous!' We order another bottle and drink it together. She smokes my packet of Marlboro at high speed and gives me a few kisses, routine and clumsy at the same time. Her hands try all kinds of things, but after a while she also thinks that it's better to talk, that we've already said too much to play 'the usual game'. Her story is the universal clichéd one, so clichéd that I think she's dishing it up to entertain me: she sends her money home and somewhere in a village in Thailand supports thirteen brothers and sisters. In any case, I have to pay her a gruesomely high amount for the bottles and the company and I say that I want to go. She pulls a shrewd, ugly face, asks whether I don't think she's beautiful. Yes, she's dazzling. Good, well, will I take her out to dinner the next day then? For that, I have to buy her freedom from the bar for a day, a small fortune. I say I don't think so. She shrugs her shoulders and strokes me again. Baby. My Cuban friend is nowhere to be seen.

I walk on for hours, almost till morning, down empty suburban streets, districts with front gardens and then down more empty, deserted asphalt roads, in the greenery of night-time parks, hidden old churches alongside appalling concrete blocks of flats. The night seems to grow warmer towards morning; a sensation that I have never felt before.

Back in my hotel room I find hypocritical pornography on two of the four channels, with nothing but bad actors dressed up as Nazis fucking women they have taken prisoner, mechanically, with terrible lighting, camera work that's obviously determined by the censorship laws, the whole list of obligatory acts is worked through, but the camera just avoids showing any genitalia – something that leads to the most unimaginable, sometimes ridiculous, but actually mostly disgustingly ugly acrobatics, with wobbling bottoms at the edge of the shot, mouths and bellies seemingly devoid of every normal human anatomical feature. It is always about 'Nazis and prisoners' who have to behave like 'sluts', who perform the game of power and submission with leering mouths, pointed tongues and rolling eyes in a mutual contract. There is something unbelievably repulsive about it. It is obviously the intention that the bad taste should be exciting – the seedy, unimaginative lighting, the pale colours, the camera sometimes clumsily zooming in, the wobbly hand-held camera, shadows of the film crew falling across the characters. The man performing sex in post-communist Slovakia is obviously still the Other, the Beast. And in a post-communist world what archetype can evoke the exciting psychological cocktail of perversion, alienation, self-disgust and identification for the viewer of pornography better than the good old Nazi, preferably played by an ugly, bad actor with a pale poker face? The soulless characters allow themselves to be sucked off with a bored expression while they wave a whip above their heads. For minutes on end you see a woman's head pumping up and down, they push a kneeling woman away from them with their pelvis, they stick out their bottom lip or they take a woman from behind as if they were standing together in the urinal of their youth (you see only a neck and a back sliding backwards and forwards, in an attitude that exudes humiliation, and then for two minutes that ugly head with the vicious mouth). It is so disgustingly caricatured that for a while I can't take my eyes off it; I realize that I'm looking into the private dreams of a proportion of this population, and it's fantastic to see how the censorship standards operate in something as concrete as the movements of a cameraman devoid of talent, who thoughtlessly and soullessly masters this craft of not quite showing. He himself belongs to the nomenclatura of the porno business, who can see everything; but with an exhaustible pleasure he withholds from his eagerly frustrated public precisely what they want: to see the Hidden Thing. Ideologically, there's no better caricature of the past system that could be devised, and yet it presents itself as one of the excrescences of the new age, imported from the West. Apart from that, of course, Evil emerges here in exactly the same way as the Devil used to in the Christian world; there Satan was the excuse for doing what people can't help doing; getting involved with sex and pretending that it's dirty because it's fun and much nicer precisely because of this sphere of taboo: 'good old Hitler' as the phantasma of the forbidden game. It is, I realize again, with a gradually clearing head, the period of an historical anachronism. The bad champagne has given me a headache. Markiza Television suddenly disappears from the screen, filling the morning silence with snow. Outside the first black-bird is singing.

But the following morning, when the ghosts of the night have dissolved in a shining southern sun, the Slovaks troop into church *en masse* to attend the Sunday service. An hour later they stream out again – the older ones with a blissful peace about them, because all this has again become possible during their lifetime: rediscovering the things of their youth in all their childlike innocence. There is probably nothing more to the ritual than that, but it must not be underestimated in its uncon-scious enchantment. The old Church Fathers knew perfectly well that, in order to partake of the sacred it is enough to do the exercises. For the most bigoted among them, there is probably no more than a dark rift of 50 years gaping in their history. Those 50 years, however much they marked them, disappear in their memories like the last grey cloud dissolving in the pierc-ing sunlight above the square.

    I decide to fill up the emptiness of the Sunday with a visit to the Narodna Galeria, the local National Gallery. There is a retrospective exhibition of the British artist, Tony Cragg, and I'm curious to see how that will be tackled here. At the counter there is some .consternation that a visitor has suddenly appeared; when I ask how much it is to get in, there is embar-rassed giggling – it is free. The catalogue is grey and small and ugly, only in Slovak, but I am kindly accompanied by a woman who takes me by the arm through the parquet-covered rooms full of *Flamsky* and *Hollandsky maliars* – the dominant presence of Flemish and Dutch painters is most striking here, perhaps explainable from the earlier wealth of surrounding castles, which in the Habsburg period collected art but with the advent of communism saw their possessions confiscated or had to sell them for lack of money. Whatever the case, at the back of the last room a modern staircase has been fitted. With a slightly pitying look and with her hand stuck out like a captain on a ship spying land, the woman indicates that I must climb that staircase, go through the great glass doors and there, for God's sake, must gape at the rubbish of that strange Brit who is not even a *maliar*. I suddenly find myself in a new wing obviously built under communism, with the desolate suicidal lighting of which they had the patent at the time.

For a whole hour, perhaps longer, I am the only visitor in the large retrospective exhibition. Not a soul, not one person, not one attendant takes the trouble to check what I'm getting up to, alone with the stones, the plastic, the objects of Cragg. In the West this is already old hat, but here it has such a 'displaced' effect that it fascinates me. One of the infamous and famous works with the hundreds of broken plastic objects, in a great right-angle, arranged by colour and laid out on the floor as the booty of a child-like beachcomber – perhaps this is the work which makes one laugh most here – seems to be a collection of melancholy remnants of a submerged civilization, collected by a post-modernist, British Walter Benjamin. Here in this city that is doing its utmost not to miss its connection with modern-day life, this must be incomprehensible: a beach spade, a broken lighter, a strainer, a frog, a plastic duck, a spout of a watering can split down the middle, everything a little worn or eaten away by having lain too long in the water or the sand. Here, without the chattering art snobs around me, the world begins to speak of history, of lost life – now I am completely alone with it as if the exhibition had been left there solely for me. Who did that strange little ring there belong to, this yellow lighter, this thermos flask case? Where did they wash up, what did these discarded, spurned plastic objects experience – that fire engine without wheels: has the child who played with it by now become a man? And did that broken red lighter lie on a bedside table, while someone lay smoking in bed, or did two people have an argument, then make up and, after making love, reach for it for the 'cigarette after'? I can stand looking at these touching things for hours, the loneliness of the abandoned museum makes them flower with a poetry that I've never felt so strongly. A goldmine for anyone who wants to invent stories: start with the first blue button and end with that red screw, that broken sieve there, that goblin's boot standing touchingly upright over there, the plastic duck with a burn mark in it, the cake mould, the tray bobbled by the heat, the green top of a bottle of detergent, that rose of pale purple plastic, that dull-red bracelet. Archaeology of a recent time, which now already seems as sunken as the booty of the *Titanic*. But then suddenly, an attendant comes and looks rather grumpily at what I've been doing for so long with those things – it does not seem probable to him that I want to take them with me, but I must have a screw loose to spend so long there looking at rubbish on the ground. The poetry of what has been lost says nothing to a community that for 40 years has lived with those rotten objects of a system without any form of consumption. The later work of Tony Cragg, better constructed, more aesthetic and more carefully structured with ready-made objects of metal, glass and stone, pale in their self-consciousness beside the elusive poetry of the first work. Later, Cragg becomes too conscious of the process, you can see that he starts having opinions instead of depicting experiences. It becomes a concept and the blood of imagined life gradually flows out of it. Gone is the call to 'linger' with things, art criticism marches through the shapes and the sculptures, however elegant the piles of bromide glasses may be. It all seems like mannerism in the light of those pale, shoddy plastic things from 1979, with their simplicity of a twentieth-century Pompeii tending towards the sublime. A strange clash, the poetry of what has been lost, which throughout the city is being wiped away very industriously (even on Sunday the hectic street paving in the town centre goes on), is here displayed in abandoned silence with an ironic melancholy that no one understands any longer and that, at the same time, is not yet understood, despised and pityingly supervised by bored attendants. There's nothing here to throw away except the past. Again then, this living in anachronism, the rift between the No More and the Not Yet. Tony Cragg's things lie in that rift of what has been forgotten and is undecided on a Sunday morning, in an empty museum by the equally empty bank of the Danube in a provincial town, which is the capital of a new state. And only then do I realize that he collected them along the banks of the Rhine, where months before I saw the glitter of an elusive past from the train. It could scarcely be any more symbolic.

Later I stroll around the collection of older works: the Flemings and the Dutchmen are in the majority, mostly second-rate work, anecdotal or rather clumsily painted, but sometimes also surprising. And there hangs, in all its glory, an image at which I have to blink in order to believe it: a St Sebastian by an 'artist from Naples, painted between 1620 and 1630' – the captions here are always so vague that you invariably become suspicious – who with one hand squeezes his left nipple and with the other closed hand clutches two arrows, just in front of his crotch and diagonally upwards. There is no way of not seeing it: a Sebastian who is quite openly and shamelessly jerking off, between the stately portraits, the landscapes and the distinguished heads in frames. I look at first disbelievingly, and then with an ironically curious gaze at the old woman who watches this room grumpily knitting, but her eyes are empty and hostile when she looks at me. I ask if there is a reproduction of the painting, it takes minutes for the monolingual Slovakian woman to understand me. No, there is no reproduction. No, I'm not allowed to take a photograph, no, no and no again, and that Sebastian goes on grinning, pinching his nipple and quietly jerking off. As if there is some devil involved, I pass a side staircase downwards and see a second Sebastian, and it seems to be a sequel picture: the Saint has collapsed backwards between two cloths, he still has one arrow in his hand, he has clearly fallen, but there is no question of pain or grief, rather of being caught doing all kinds of things that we have to find out for ourselves. I burst out laughing, a female attendant comes immediately to see what's happening, but the fact that it's hanging and happening there doesn't occur to her. Here too there is no indication, no identification, it's a little Caravaggio-like in its dramatic contrast, but apart from that nothing.

I go outside, the light is suddenly overwhelming – with a smell of distant meadows by the water.

The referendum on joining NATO is over – it produces nothing concrete. As was to be expected, the Slovaks are divided, but the world remains empty and there are dust clouds around the small diggers in the street because there life goes on in these small material perspectives, in this tearing up of neglect. A land waking up from a sleep that it no longer understands.

Bratislava is as sunny and lively this Sunday as it seemed grey and desolate to me the day before. On the only flourishing terrace they serve excellent Italian coffee from Segafredo cups, again people are eating lasagne and spaghetti for all they're worth, the local *G'sprizter* – white wine diluted with sparkling mineral water – is flowing abundantly. There on the old square the old trams are moving across the cracked asphalt like prehistoric fossils, a dark reminder of something that is rapidly vanishing, while here on the brand new terrace the assertive girls are displaying their make-up in the sun and are twisting their bottoms coquettishly at the machos, who strike an attitude by putting a toothpick between their lips and letting a lighter dangle on a chain, which is swung round with obsessive repetition. Now people are suddenly walking along the Danube, even though there are only a score of them. A little further on there are young boys dancing to a Slovak mixture of heavy metal and grunge. A fat Frenchman is sitting showing off appallingly in front of a shy Slovak man. All the weather forecasts for this weekend were gloomy but towards noon the sun burns as in the Mediterranean. The already restored Baroque façades shine in the light, doze in the talk, in the strolling, in the sound of birds and children, in a haze of dazzling present around them.

In the middle of one of the dug-up streets, a bride in white stumbles through the gravel grinning awkwardly on her mother's arm. A little further on, at a restored and pink-painted round gateway into a courtyard with a rusty futuristic fountain,

The library at Melk.

a number of men are waiting. One of them has a camera with him. It is the bridegroom.

On leaving the city, I drop in to an old run-down church. It still slumbers fully in the magic of what has been forgotten, seething with damp and old dust, silent and dark. This is how, I think as I look at the worn frescoes, Umberto Eco must have seen the monastery of Melk in the Wachau, before the restoration which began in about 1983. The Austrian *Stift* on the Danube was then still faded and ancient. In the library in the church he must have seen the traces of history, the magic of what had gone. I myself arrived in Melk far too late: I saw only the dazzlingly clean and restored monastery, odourless, taste-less, tourist toys, a décor of stupid latex and plaster, a pizza stall with Coca-Cola at the entrance and photos of the restora-tion, an exercise in the erasing of memory. Eco's post-modernism had already worked its magic on the monastery: it shone and gleamed like a huge plaster meringue, a theme park of the past without depth or experience.

But here in this old church of St Maria of Loreto in Bratislava, I can smell the enchantment. And where Eco must have seen mainly the dust of ages of monastic silence in Melk, I see the stone rot of communist decline. I do not want to be nostalgic, what matter to me are the traces, but I'm appalled by the hectically digging machines in the sun on the square, which I can see from this lonely damp darkness. No, not because I am nostalgic, but perhaps because I read Michel Foucault long ago, I, like many people, have become fascinated with the archaeological layers of the present in which I live and forget.

Some days before, I spoke to someone who teaches Dutch in Bratislava about the epiphanies that come over those of us born in the 1950s in the former Eastern bloc countries. That all our waffle about the happiness of brown coal and old wallpaper must seem crazy to people here: stories of spoiled little boys who are nostalgic for their worn-out bikes in the bike shed, but who wouldn't survive for a year in the circumstances in which people live here: poetry as an excuse for a lack of understanding.

I leave the old city through the gate and find myself in the empty, long streets of the suburbs, leave the city through the leafy Stefánikova Ulica, with a smell of roast fat hanging in the doorways.

When I reach the station, a dark man tries to trip me up and when I quickly avoid him and so don't stumble he says viciously, close to my ear: 'Omoseksuál'.

I have the urge to turn round and say: 'So what?'

But suddenly something else occurs to me. I turn towards the man, point to his moustache and gesture to say that he should pull it out hair by hair.

Then I have to beat a hasty retreat. Luckily the train to Vienna Ostbahnhof is full-up again.

I sink down next to a man with a mobile phone and three gold rings who, immediately after pressing the last key, starts talking at me and, as an internationally-minded Turkish citizen, explains how he is 'pissed off' with all our whining about the

Kurds, those villains, that bunch of terrorists and how we over there in Brussels are to blame for everything. Well, that one hit home.

Vienna

Cities, like people, can be recognised by their walk.
ROBERT MUSIL

An insignificant opening sentence from a book, I forget which book, that occurred to me as I drove along the great Ringstrasse: 'And so I wound up in this city.'

People walk up and down the hallway of this seedy apartment block, the worn-out Italian restaurant manageress screeches at a shut door: *'Momi! Momi! Bistu da?'* And behind it you can hear, as if from far away, the croaking answer of an elderly person. The front doors all have a large window of reinforced glass behind which you can see ghosts moving about, the flicker of a television set, a child running through the room. The only free room is gloomy, north-facing and looks out over the tall house fronts on the other side like a child cowers before an adult who has behaved in a grown-up and threatening way. Not even a chink of the sky; everything made of stone, rows of balconies and windows, closed curtains. Garage doors; small shops, grumpy girls at tills in little suburban supermarkets and the red and yellow trams, cutting through the tailbacks on the main street around the corner – the old Josefstadt, where Elfriede Jelinek grew up. Being alone is a strange activity, with which the traveller can fill his long empty days. He nods off to sleep after the umpteenth walk, exhausted and alienated from everyone because he seldom speaks. Before he realizes the girls at the tills look at him more grumpily than at the others and he begins to suspect that he has really started looking different from other people, he starts awake from a cat-nap because he remembers a sentence in his dream – a sentence he cannot

116

recover; where does its dreaming effect come from, the nagging in his head? 'So, so this is where people come to live, I'd be more inclined to think they came here to die' – a pathetic and astonished sentence, somehow taken out of context, a sentence that woke him up. And things and people have become so inconceivably remote from him, driven away by sleep, that everything seems abstract to him, a joke that has been played on him: not only do his own face and history seem suddenly incomprehensible, but so does the aeroplane above the cities and the mountains, arriving in the midday traffic queues, the first glimpse of the strange, exciting atmosphere, the city where he is going to live for a month. As if catching a glimpse of a person with whom he was to share his bed for an indefinite period, he notices how that person passes him and doesn't yet greet him, because he – the traveller, that is – has for the time being remained equally invisible to that other person, who is already desired and does not yet know it. But the obligatory bride comes rushing past on her rollerblades with chewing gum in her mouth. And each detail acquires something of a first enchantment, the prelude to falling in love and throwing away the street plan. It only lasts for a moment; very soon the familiar will move in, the stimuli of the former will give way to the humdrum life in which he is trapped, the history of an imagination and a body, that's the sum of it all, that's all there is. And although in his youth it had seemed endless, it's now a kind of prison, the oh-so-familiar prison of recognition that overtakes people once they have reached a halfway point in their lives.

So, this is where people come to live or die, it doesn't matter which. And standing in the bathroom, with his hands under the stream of lukewarm water, that sentence comes into his head again, and he has the urge to hold onto it. He saves it for a moment and again makes plans: perhaps there's still something to be done that might be worthwhile? Something that doesn't give you the feeling that everything has already been done? Something that would make him look in astonishment at

117

all the life around him that has previously been observed to death? But a person gets suspicious as he gets older. He is ready to pounce critically on himself at the slightest impulse and there is always another, older, unjust self that puffs contemptuously and says: oh, off you go again, you know what this will lead to. And he dries his hands on the still spotless white towel, he looks in a mirror that he does not yet know and whose frame particularly catches his attention, gold with serrated bits and pieces. And he turns to the empty room and he says aloud, I want music. And in the hall again, he hears the overwrought woman going to and fro, and her fist pounding on the door so that the plate glass rattles: '*Momi, Momi, hörsdu mich?*' And the rattling of the window reminds him of a window blown shut this afternoon by some gust of wind in the wide street; the people who had been sitting below it drinking coffee, perhaps for an hour, were just getting up talking, a boy was holding out his hands to a smiling woman and, because he was at least twenty centimetres taller, he bent over as he did so. And just at that moment, on the third floor, a window slammed shut with a huge crash because of the spring wind, slammed thought- lessly and with the great violence of a child running fast through a room that is too small and bangs its head on the edge of a cupboard; and the slivers rained down in great pieces, a bright guillotine that flickered in the sun and, because the boy was just bending his head to the smiling woman, the great pieces of the broken window grazed his neck and smashed into a hundred pieces behind him. And, scarcely startled, they turned their heads, laughed in astonishment at the slivers and walked off, so light-heartedly that it was obvious that they didn't realize what might have happened. The young boy put his arm in the woman's and they disappeared around the corner. And the man with whom I was sitting eating saw in it a symbol of what he was saying, that one must let everything happen as it happens and not chase after anything – 'letting go' is what he called it and his eyes shone with a strange glow: let everything go, there's no point at all in chasing after anything or trying to avoid anything. And he talked about Oedipus who, by trying to flee his fate, in fact ran straight into its arms. 'Letting go' – I looked in alarm at the slivers on the terrace a little way away – and I heard the woman pounding on the window of the door a little way along the corridor, and I looked at the edges of the old mirror eaten away by soap in the slightly seedy bathroom, and I lost all sense of connection, of meaning, and the emptiness yawned in my eyes that were staring back at themselves; I didn't know the man who was standing staring at me there, groggily, a face with a history, a man in a strange city on the first day. And that was enough to evoke the familiar feeling that succeeded it: that of erotic desire, the urge to put my jacket on and go strolling through the twilight, looking straight at people strolling past in the full awareness that it made some women see me as a creep, and the men perhaps as a simpleton. And it streamed into my consciousness like a wave, the familiar feverish tune: that life was nothing, that I understood nothing about it, that it was all for nothing – life is nothing, as I had heard a poet repeat in a drunken voice to a half-full auditorium: life is nothing, it is nothing, it's all for nothing.

And he conceived a plan, that very evening, back in the desolate room, to write down a merciless story that had been running through his mind for some days; that he would follow it with another and a third – bleak, violent and pornographic, without any ray of light, without a single edifying thought – only the constantly recurring encounters described in the minutest detail which always led to the same thing, to bleakly repeated and furious acts, bleakly spread and exhausted limbs, in the most banal style, and that at the end he would constantly repeat the refrain more obsessively: life is nothing, you've got worked up over nothing, it's dust in the street, it's the dead mouse under the stairs, it's the gurgling in the drainpipe, a gurgling that can make you feel sick if you've thought too hard about it; it's the scum in the washing-up basin; the bubbles look like the still disgusting, slightly moving brains that once long ago you felt in the palm of your hand when a lamb was slaughtered;

it is the suffocating effect of association, that's all; at the same time, it's nothing, it's for nothing, it's nothing, it's a mish-mash of sticky semen and blood, a burst vein in an eye, a deformed swelling on a lip or the weals on a hand with a disgustingly thick gold ring; it's the thought through which the human being, standing in wonderful spring sunshine, a prey to the chaos in his head, sobs with a bitter expression and curses other people, throws himself in front of the tram with the stubbornness which is suddenly filled with the stupidly lost purity he had always sought and had never regained, except now, in this last moment; because life is nothing, it's all for nothing, and there's nothing to be understood.

And he did not put his jacket on, and he did not go walking through the streets, the summer night was lost on him while his thoughts spun, his hands under the lukewarm stream of water remained behind like a constantly rewound fragment of film, constantly back again and then again that action, and when his hands were completely washed away like a piece of soap, he grabbed his own face while the slivers crashed just missing his back on the bathroom floor. He wasn't conscious of anything, and the angels sang and the rats stuck their noses out behind the rotting edge of the shower compartment, their pointed snouts snuffled like the tenderest and most sensitive mechanism that the devil could have devised; there was something exalted about all this, and life was nothing, stripped of all importance, and he suddenly recognized in this conscious peering at the unconscious, the feeling that he was terrified of: the emptiness of a man who is past the mid-point of his life and has woken from the hallucination that up till then had passed for reality – the dream of a conscious, enlightened world without all those pointlessly pullulating lives. It was the enlightened child's dream of the naïve, arrogant linguist, with whom he once had an argument, a man who prided himself on the most infantile form of rationality and who, as he did so, stubbornly continued to deny any form of repression. But finally he'd picked an argument about nothing because what a person doesn't feel can't be explained to him, there's nothing about experience that is useful to anyone else. People must manage to get to the bottom of everything for themselves, although there's nothing, nothing at all. Across the street, the lights went on, one by one, like stars looming up in the dusk and two taxi drivers sat smoking and waiting in their cabs, and it was all completely incomprehensible to him: he'd arrived in a new city, he was to live there for a while, as best he could.

He sat down, and began his story: 'I'd seen this woman several times before, and each time it had struck me that . . .' And when after just a few pages he described the murder in detail while he had the man climax, hissing between his teeth like a filthy dog, he sighed, hunted for a cigarette and muttered that it was all for nothing, that life was nothing, that his imagination had been infected by everything that had happened in the last year in Belgium, the insignificant, hectic country from which he'd been delivered for a short while, and that he was tired, and that a woman came up to one of the taxi drivers on the other side of the street, the street where that afternoon he'd moved into a shabby apartment, and spoke a few words that he could not hear, only intuit. She got in (he saw the skirt riding up above her narrow thighs as they disappeared into the car) and he peered like a simple-minded voyeur through a chink in the curtains, but there was nothing, the city seemed like nothing, and in a line, in a strange silence, with engines turned off the taxis in the taxi rank slid further down the sloping street, now the first one had disappeared from view; there was really nothing, nothing at all, and strangely enough that reassured him. Perhaps he would now be able to sleep after all.

Someone sat in the gigantic, stately reading room of the library for German literature, reading a book aloud and laughing, and the man who was sitting listening listened, but did not laugh. The further the first man read, the more exuberant his mood became, he kept reading new passages, which he accompanied with a neighing laugh, pointed with his finger to the passages

121

in question, went back to the book, leafed through it a little further, then exclaimed 'And here', and began to quote again, stopped hiccuping with laughter halfway through a sentence, and the other sat, listened and did not laugh: as if for him the things that made the first man laugh had a completely different meaning, at any rate one which was not anything to laugh about; he seemed to be sinking more and more into himself the more the other emerged from himself – as it were, emerged from his own head, exalting like a courageous adventurer planting a flag on the roof of his own head. The reading room in the German library retreated into the silence of its countless dark racks and volumes, into its staircases, galleries and alcoves. The day passed on clocks and in windows, cars roared around the quiet building where they were sitting, somewhere a cyclist was run over by a car, the leaves of the book waved in the hands of the man who was reading aloud, gold shone for a moment on the table, somewhere in a toilet the sound of running water erupted. The man who had been listening got up, went out of the large room without speaking, walked down the monumental stairs. Outside it was raining. The city became a backdrop for anonymous running. He was amazed at the lack of coherence in what he saw. Everything I've ever said, he thought, consisted of repression, of pushing aside things I was frightened to think about; and if I were to say aloud what was the point of it all, then the value of it would immediately evaporate. He looked at the evening, the ending of a day in the emptiness of being alone, a day of not speaking, because there was no one, among all the countless anonymous running people. He had the feeling of having to go to a workplace instead of to a room to live: a workplace where heavy things would have to be moved in his head, pushed aside, others pulled up. 'Momi!' He heard from the steps the dreadful voice that bored through everything, 'Momi, schläfst du denn?'

And because there was nothing to do, because he had nothing to say, he realized that a new challenge awaited him; to accept the following hour, the following day, the following week, the following month without any plan – to live without the hallucination of a plan. He tried to confront that without fear – perhaps something like the first step towards an acceptance of finally dying, so that everything was suddenly significant, but significant in a way that was of no use to him – and therefore as if for the first time, terrifyingly and totally significant. That was also, he suddenly realized, the only reason why people in strange cities can be so terribly lonely and abandoned; because this challenge to *let go* terrifies them – just as it did him.

> If you notice the sorrow of the thresholds, you are not a tourist; there is a chance of a transition. (Peter Handke)

I walk through the squares in the underground with Keith Jarrett's *Vienna Concert* in the Discman; the world appears as a film, the passers-by float past like fish: the wind that blows through the tunnels of the metro seems to herald a mild last judgement and above ground, I heard an old woman say, 'It's started raining again.' In the Burgtheater, a new text by an author whom I often reject totally and yet read again and again with great involvement: the amateur prophet, the grown-up little boy, the precious defender of what has been lost – Peter Handke. There is an intangible but obvious relationship between Peter Handke and Keith Jarrett: their longing in the midst of hectic society to hold on to something of distance, the aura of longing for a timeless image in which things and sounds of every day have a coherence once more – very typically end-of-the-century, but without the usual cynicism – it requires courage to run such a great risk of misunderstandings.

The red-haired woman with whom I had dinner near the Stephansdom yesterday evening, loved me and shared my bed for four years – and I was equally in love with her – I only heard at the last moment that she was here, the enchantment of long ago had just the right fraction of time to take effect. First in the square, sudden gusts of wind with a low red sun through which pieces of paper scuttled and skirts pressed against thighs, as if something were approaching from which it was best to flee indoors – then in the restaurant, as if twenty years had not passed since the first time, the slightly drunk laugh, as if the years had lasted only a few hours; her sweet, familiar hand with the rather thick fingers on my knee and the light in her eyes great and green. And because towards midnight we were somewhere–nowhere, and of course there was no history and just a kind of astonishing now, we kissed each other in the underground, like long ago, where the air stood still and a boy by a ticket machine sat hunched, trembling and rocking. Later I took an empty train to the beginnings of suburbia where I live. Under the awning of the restaurant past which I can reach the courtyard, it stank of congealed fat and rotting vegetables. A Serbian girl, who must have a room somewhere on the same corridor, stood gazing at me. I heard the hissing cymbals of the drums grating in her Walkman as she chewed gum with her mouth open, leered at me stupidly and provocatively and just stood there and put all her energy into being in the world.

In this city, over ten years ago in the hotel opposite Café Hawelka, I pushed my anti-asthma spray into the teeth of Bert S. and said, 'Breathe in, Bert, breathe in deeply, and it'll pass.' He sat on the ground gasping and blue in the face, in the early morning, and obediently did as I said. After just ten seconds or so the phenoterol gave his heart a boost that made him start. Gradually he came round, all the wrinkles in his mouth were suddenly in the right creases, he grinned and said, 'Just pour me another whisky.' And laughed as only an angel expelled from heaven can laugh.

'Instead of grace', says Handke, 'we could just as well speak of an adrenaline rush,' but that doesn't fit as well into a poem. I myself think that the adrenaline rush fits better than grace – because that's the cause, the other is an interpretation. 'Technique in writing means: being aware of as many possibilities as possible' – the same Handke.

124

A day in the life of the Central European metropolis. While the successful young progressive politician throws himself under the subway train early in the morning because of a failed marriage, a spokesman of the FPÖ, the extreme right-wing party of Jörg Haider, is infuriated by the Mouflon sheep in the Lainzer Tiergarten – according to this brilliant strategist, foreign sheep no longer have any place in the typical Viennese zoo. Meanwhile in the town council it is decided that the 'Bosnian bonus', a scheme whereby Bosnian refugees can receive an unemployment benefit, is to be withdrawn. Future immigration policy will have to take more account of 'a broad definition of key occupations' – that means that 'for example, ice hockey players and managers are welcome': they can also rely on Austrian hospitality if they wish to 'import' (*mitherein-nehmen*) a secretary.

The Cabinet is today considering the lot of the asylum seekers: a new 'integration package' is coming – that means mainly a reduced one, which destroys the morale of the human rights organizations, and which still doesn't go far enough for Jörg Haider. What does go far enough for his egoistic politics? The extermination of everything that we would prefer not to see in the mirror? That can only happen if one destroys the mirror itself – the past century has taught us that, but obviously to no effect.

In the city of Graz, it's been decided that an exhibition on the war crimes of the German army between 1941 and 1944 will not receive a subsidy and in fact is not desirable, because as the Chief Minister of Stiermarken, Waltraud Klasnic explains patiently, she 'only wants exhibitions people enjoy'.

Live in Austria for a few weeks, and you immediately understand that the despair of Georg Trakl, the rage and hatred of Karl Kraus, of Thomas Bernhardt, Elfriede Jelinek and Werner Schwab are the most normal thing in the world: how else are you supposed to react?

While Handke's newest 'royal drama' (*Preparations for Immortality*) is being performed in the Burgtheater the polemics around his 'Travels' to Serbia, which are full of misdirected and political frivolity, go on: an angry, slightly hyperventilating Croat, Branimir Souček, long resident in Austria, has written a pamphlet in which he lists all the misapprehensions of Handke; but his rhetorical sweeps larded with exclamation marks, ridiculous digressions and irrelevant rhetorical asides are here and there just as absurd as Handke's political inanities. So it is impossible to take sides. And yet I read the better writer, the same Handke again, in his irritating, and then again unequalled reflections, from which he himself could have learned something: 'For things I almost always have a focus in my eyes, for people only exceptionally (and I don't blame myself for that) . . .'

'Fantasies of repetition', he called these reflections somewhat clairvoyantly, over ten years ago.

One day I take my girlfriend, who has just arrived here, to the old university on the Lueger-Ring, walk with her through the enormous stairwell, lead her up the wide marble steps, show her the marvellous library of *Germanistik* – a high room, books on the walls in wonderful old cases, and everywhere people in the circle of lamplight, green opaline lamps that can be turned on above each reading desk. The silence envelops us, we've just come from the bustle of the metro; the light falls through the high windows onto books and silently bent heads, my girl-friend squeezes my arm, she suddenly seems deeply moved. I realize that she's thinking back with melancholy to the period of her studies. She looks around slowly and while she opens wide her moistening eyes, she whispers: 'we're living the wrong way.'

Six months later I will have the same kind of shock in Madrid – running hectically through the city, searching for medicine for my son who has fallen ill, I suddenly see the Ateneo, the old public library. The high stairs in the elegant hall are beckoning in pale lamplight; I walk up the stately wooden stairs, enter the room where there is a rustle of people reading, of pages being turned, of faintly creaking wooden floors. The daylight glows vaguely in the glass doors of the high book-cases. Here and there a hinge squeaks; apart from that, silence. There is nothing so blissful as collective silence, it's something that many of you people build up together to evoke unanimity, although you can remain completely yourself. The magic ritual of scores of people sitting together reading, a disappearing world. Later I meet someone who has also seen the library and who says quite bluntly, 'Can you imagine something like that in the age of the Internet?' Well, it is undoubtedly a vanished way of life, sitting in libraries during the day and becoming absorbed in a movement of people reading around you. Just as it's different seeing a film in the cinema rather than watching it alone on your video, reading in libraries was a great collective ritual that said something about a culture. Perhaps the disappearing public libraries are a kind of last memorial to a gradually vanishing sense of life. Perhaps we're living the wrong way.

SALZBURG

At the top of the Kapuzinerberg, wonderful fresh Sunday morning, all the bells in the Altstadt suddenly start ringing at once; in the distance, through the young greenery of the beeches, the snow-capped mountain peaks. This view must have been very familiar to Georg Trakl. An aeroplane takes off, thunders over the blue land dominated by the sound of birds. The world, which in my imagination has for decades been polluted, noisy and banal, lies here pristine and Arcadian, dozing in the sun like a dream from a distant past. This is the end of the second millennium. The second thousand-year empire has gone, the empire of Christianity, the great ideologies and art. What follows is disintegration and at the same time, a universal uniformity: empty and extremely vital, chaotic exoticism in a swirl of impulses, which is what the first view of the following millennium offers. The third millennium will begin with confusion, excitement and disorientation – just like the last.

Perhaps that is how it must be: in a small, banal hotel room, the peeping and rustling of gypsy-like music that comes over the Alps from Sarajevo to Salzburg – when, more than can be explained in words, you realize what an incomprehensible and impossible thing Europe is. And the macho Salzburg Home Guard, and the noisy American tourist with his unbearable wife, and the fifteen begging punks in the Linzer Strasse, the Mozart kitsch, the Trakl kitsch and the cry of the gypsy on the radio, who suddenly, out of the blue, yells 'Africa!' – followed by a jingle in which one can again and again hear 'Bosnia Radio' – perhaps you need all that to understand for an odd moment what cannot be understood. That you're living in a history impossible to disentangle and precisely because of that, you want to live, although life slides past faster than a dream.

The contemporary knows nothing. (Victor Klemperer)

And there, alone in that badly-lit room with plywood furniture in Salzburg, through an endlessly repeated and thrusting Bosnia-Herzegovina mostly followed by a long sentence in which the word *problemi* cropped up in a language that apart from that was incomprehensible to me, alternating with music that made me melancholy – music which made a distance open up, a destroyed land, useless passions – I suddenly felt great excitement, which through my loneliness and the longing for my distant lover was given space to grow into an obsession: I would go to Sarajevo after all, alone, with the uncertainty and longing like an intoxication in me, even if it was only to avenge myself of my overweening critical statements of a few years before. Because you do not understand anything that hasn't become an experience; you judge and you are as blind as the chess computer that can beat Kasparov but has no idea of what playing chess actually means to human beings. And I didn't sleep that night, I stayed awake and worried feverishly – I, who had come to the city of Trakl as a learned child to realize that I had to go to Sarajevo, lured by a melody and a number of

128

constantly recurring sentences in an incomprehensible language, larded with *problemi*. I, with my indignation at Handke's public taking of sides in Serbia, with my sceptical remarks about Bernard-Henri Lévy, I had to and was going to. I lay awake and a little later thought of my son, not yet a year old, who with his tiny warm hands pinched my lover's face and as he did so enjoyed the terrible face that a human being pulls if you grab them and pull hard on their lower lip, but who finally gave her a snotty dribbly kiss and laughed – and I was frightened of losing something, whatever I did. Then on the radio there was the sound of something familiar, fairly surprising to tell the truth, in the middle of all that hundred-fold repeated Radio Bosnia-Herzegovina, namely 'Let it be' by the Beatles, exactly, letting go; let it happen, let it all hang out, and I thought that I would wait and see.

And in the end I didn't go, of course not, I didn't have time; there were unforeseen circumstances and apart from that, who was I to join the queue of disaster tourists? So a few days later I was just walking around in Vienna again, saw the Serbian girl in the corridor, invited her out, drunk two or three glasses with her and then, sated with the absurd nonsense pouring from her broadly grinning mouth (she talked exclusively about *tolle Diskotheken* and *wilde Typen*) and went back to my room and rang my lover, to ask if she was OK, if the baby was asleep, if she'd locked the front door. And drinking a last glass in my oxygen-starved room, with the rain lashing the windows, I saw something like a glimpse of history, very briefly, because a lot is required for us to see something for a moment before it's immediately gone again – a glimpse of a whole in which we belong without being able to get a view of the whole.

While the new play by Peter Handke in the Burgtheater is about how two kings' sons are unable to prevent a 'noble people isolated from the world' from becoming caught up in the confusion of the modern world, the chess computer Deep Blue defeats Kasparov, who is close to tears: the rooks, knights and a king tumble, the papers talk of the last human illusions being destroyed. In *Der Standard*, Galileo, Darwin and Freud are invoked as the previous great destroyers of illusions and in the street where I live, an unsightly old man sells second-hand newspapers – that is, he never sells anything but he is there, in the street, in the swing of things and that seems fun enough for him. I don't know what he lives on but, however dirty and out-of-date he is, he looks happy and when I come past with my rolls from the Anker baker he grins because the day before yesterday I bought an old *Die Presse* from him; ridiculous of course, buying old newspapers out of sentiment, but it creates a bond. And in that issue of *Die Presse*, there is a report that ends with the by now famous words uttered by Kasparov after his historic duel: 'I am ashamed.' Kasparov is ashamed on our behalf, he is ashamed on behalf of all human beings, just as the first man on the moon took a step on our behalf, he is ashamed heroically and historically. I think it is unnecessary; he did not lose to something metaphysical, but to something made by another human being. 'I'm ashamed.' I am too, when the old man tries to sell me a paper again that I bought the day before. But there is shame and shame.

Typical Viennese anecdote. In front of the bench on the platform of Wien Mitte, where I sit waiting with my lover for the train that after a few days' stay is to take her back to the airport, there is a little spot covered with vomit-like mess. A bright and chirpy elderly woman comes to the bench, is about to sit down next to us, notices the mess and starts telling us about the *Fremden* who are destroying Vienna, making everything *schmutzig*, while the Austrians are *sauber*, 'so wie die Deutschen, verstehen Sie'. Is it the same where you come from? We sigh in boredom. She asks where we live and if it's as bad there too, and when my girlfriend finally answers with a sigh that she comes from Brussels, the fireworks really start: Yes, *Brüssel*, the EU makes everything *kaputt*, the Belgians are bastards, child molesters and so on, all for money, Belgium is making everything go down the drain, everything is becoming too expensive to buy in Vienna, the fault of Brussels, everything completely smashed. Once there was *Dis-zi-plin*, do you know what that is? No, we admit. There go our last five minutes together. I go on protesting that we're not Eurocrats, that Vienna is more expensive than Brussels, and much more so, and that the EU is the business of her wonderful Germans, but it does no good. A Jörg Haider woman, pure theatre, you simply have to put this woman in Brussels or Amsterdam in a chair on the stage and bingo!: you have pure Werner Schwab, the whole theatrical world will be rolling in the aisles for weeks, crying with unstoppable laughter. Like this, with our nose on top of it, we think it's a little less amusing. We endure it, until my girlfriend, straightening herself a little, says gently to the woman: that there, it isn't sick, it's melted ice, just there a sweet Austrian girl of ten years old, with blue eyes and blonde hair, dropped her ice cream. The old woman gasps for breath for a moment, gets up, announces that she's going to the beautiful free nature in the Wachau for a day out, and leaves the platform. And look, there comes the train that is going to separate us again for weeks. I get in too, we'll see. Only hours later do I pass the bench on the platform again. A man is sitting reading a letter and with one foot he stirs the now almost completely dried up mess. In the evening, I see an interview with Roman Herzog, the German Chief Rabbi. He tells the Austrians in a friendly but forceful way that they must join the EU. So the Germans again? But meanwhile I notice from the complete military paranoia around and in the wonderfully appointed Imperial Hotel that the German President is hoping for a quiet Austrian night.

A year ago in a small town in southern France I had felt the same hatred of an abstract bureaucratic Brussels that everyone always blames, and for which now obviously every Belgian must pay the price: a man in a big car, dashing like crazy through the traffic and forced to brake because I stop at a traffic light which turns to red, drives up alongside me, opens his window and screams that I should go back to my fucking Brussels, that Europe can get on without us fucking Belgians (*ces connards des belges*) and then, virtually foaming at the mouth, shoots the red traffic lights, almost collides with two cars and disappears. By the traffic lights, I see only then, a pair of birds are mating in an old plane tree.

There are other things in Vienna to set against that old Werner Schwab-battle-axe, the dusty, sultry inner parks in the old Josef-stadt, where the Balkan languages intermingle, the Croatian Serbian bookshop in my street, the proximity one senses every-where of Eastern Europe, the old-fashioned easy-going life in the working-class districts where no tourists venture any more, the charm of things that with us have long since vanished, and that make life more poetic, give more room to thought, and standing still and observing things.

Now and again I get faxes from people from Holland and Flanders expressing their sympathy: what a torture, a month in such a terrible city. But meanwhile, I've got to know a city that is almost unknown to us – far beyond the centre, in a timeless grey openness, where the excitement of Eastern Europe begins.

One evening I go to a performance of Heiner Müller's *Germania 3*, somewhat overdone to my feeling – an old-fashioned production, with caricatured Soviet soldiers and an hysterical Hitler caricature, consequently nice, safe non-committal theatre: no actor takes off his professional mask for a moment to give the public in the auditorium a hint that the plays of Müller are not about a distant past, but about the beast in the present. Older Viennese are shocked by the play, the others leave the theatre full of enthusiasm, but I think they do it in large part to tease the older ones.

As soon as you get into the opinionated society in the city centre, the rift is radical: rabid conservatives against radical, almost anarchistic left-wingers. The infamous Hermann Nitzsch who, as long ago as the 1970s, haunted Vienna with his *Wiener Aktion,* his rituals full of blood, intestines and disembowelled animals, is in this month of May holding a party for his friends. The blood and filth are already coming off the poster. That means that the conservatives are maintaining their position here: all left-wingers are beasts, and the left-wingers are keeping to their point of view: all conservatives are idiots. In this atmosphere, in this impossibility of finding a reasonable compromise, the work of Thomas Bernhardt has originated, but also that of Elfriede Jelinek and certainly that of Werner Schwab (who is openly called the greatest theatrical writer of the century). But the work of Georg Trakl was also marked by it: in peaceful, bourgeois Salzburg, this biscuit barrel made of meringue, in which a poet walked around as early as 1910 and managed to get his own supply of cocaine in the cellars of the wonderful Engel Pharmacy (where I bought an anti-hayfever medicine and afterwards read the poem on the plaque outside, everything dark and gloomy in the poet's head, while outside the *Grüssgotts* and the *Schöner Tags heute* twinkle and twitter). Nowhere else has a European culture grown up in an atmosphere which so clearly and obviously lacks a reasonable democratic centre; one is either right-wing, conservative according to the clichés of the record, or one belongs to the hard, radical alternative *scene*. On both sides, this attitude remains surprisingly rigid and unchanging: a lack of relativism, absolutism, purity of principles. Equally refreshing, there is no blasé feeling of non-committal vagueness as in our culture, but a volcano of energy, even if no one knows what's going to happen. As yet, Vienna has lost none of its absurd theatrical power since the time when Kraus and Musil sat here writing furiously, but it has lost its meaning for the outside world and this frustration makes the people in the streets grumpy and overly self-conscious about the external view of their culture.

The enemy is our own question in the shape of a human being. (Heiner Müller)

I write poems, the young poetess says to me frankly, which are avant garde. When she notices my eyes open wide with astonishment, she clarifies her statement: like Jandl against the *Kleinbürger*. She goes on talking, but my eyes wander to a poster a little further on: 'Anarchistische Buchhandlung'. And above it 'Formerly Monte Verità.' I burst out laughing at what I see, but when I try to explain, the girl looks surprised, in turn.

Elfriede Jelinek spent her youth in this old Josefstadt. Somewhere near here, around the corner, was the old cow from her book, *The Pianist*. Here Jelinek became embittered as she walked around these streets as a schoolgirl. Soon the Burgtheater is putting on one of her new plays; she has meanwhile given up the embargo on Austrian performances, which leads to scoffing remarks in the press and to indignation on her part. Her unstable, furious relationship with this country, seems to me more and more Viennese: love me because I hate you. I assume that this thought makes her even more furious. This is the way that Austrians are extremely – and fatefully – linked together. It is a strange society, old-fashioned and unfathomable, with an historical mortgage that is much too large, too broad, too heavy, and yet at the same time, it sustains an impulsive anarchistic theatricality. One evening, though, I notice from a memorial close by that the well-behaved, untimely Stefan Zweig wrote silently and diligently here for twelve years – before he went to kill himself in South America because the old international Habsburg Empire had sunk into a German caricature.

'Hating one's own people', says the old Gregor von Rezzori, 'is mostly a sign that one belongs to the real élite of that people.'

In conversation, a student says that she specializes in women's studies in gender ideology, that Austria should forget Jelinek and should attach itself again to the humiliations and the nuanced struggle of Ingeborg Bachmann in her novel *Malina*, which is much more radical. I can't fathom whether her remark is supposed to make me see her as rather conservative or, on the contrary, very broad-minded.

134

Christoph Ransmayr, who comes from Nieder-Österreich (but lives in Ireland), also talks about this in his most recent book, *The Way to Surabaya*:

> The German part of the Habsburg world is to blame for the disappearance of internationalism in central Europe. It was the only great supra-national state [the second, I think, as I read, is very small but historically just as valuable as the Habsburgs once were: Belgium]. The Germans wanted the *Anschluss* and the Austrians are still linked with them, but they are tormented by Germany, with what Germany thinks about them; they dismiss the contempt of the Germans, but call themselves proudly 'Germans' as opposed to the Czechs, the Slovaks, the Hungarians, the Slovenians, the Croatians and the Serbs. With this German obsession, they have the downfall of Central European internationalism on their conscience.

Ransmayr tells anecdotes from the Austria that is slowly disappearing – the pathetic visits of the last Empress Zita who, just before her death, returned to the country; stories about a grave-digger around Braunau (the village where Hitler was born); apocalyptic scenes depicting the building of a dam somewhere high in the mountains, using the forced labour of political prisoners; a strange eccentric who has collected 8,600 *Lichtbilder* on the lost Austria of the past.

These are refreshingly intelligent analyses of Austria, which Ransmayr produces with these narrative reports, but they always have something unspeakably oppressive about them.

At the same time, I begin to like this city - its confusion, its strange young people, its ancient wrinkles, riding the subway aimlessly and at length, the sultry continental and windless warmth, the countless, breathtaking Slav types walking in the dusk, the 'melting pot'.

For the moment, it has absolutely no significance that I was sitting in the early evening in my shirtsleeves on a Viennese terrace, still puffing about the heat, eating and laughing with a friend, and that a few hours later, as night fell, I was walking back to the old city after a theatre performance, shivering in the rain. But one day it will be (my) history, and then there will be perhaps one person who has the feeling that something has been lost – something that was obvious for me: a smell, a view of a building which still exists, imagining what the wet asphalt must have looked like in the 'last century'. Things which are present for me, but which are unobtainable for the future generation. Things for poems. Very many things only acquire value when they are no longer there. Just like a nameless evening in the city, somewhere in your life. Perhaps it's a special day for someone, a moment that is important, if only because of an image. For we don't have many more memories to fall back on in our heads. A modest reporter like Victor Klemperer understood that perfectly. So I shall record it now, the waving plants next to our table, the wide arches of the gallery in which the twenty tables or so stand, the people strolling through a park around a fountain on the other side of the wide avenue, the boy getting off his heavy motorbike and taking a tiny little dog out of his leather jacket, the cheeky street sparrow which comes almost up to my plate to peck at my food, and when he nips onto the plate of an older woman behind me, I hear her say with affection, 'So, my little street urchin.'

Till 2.30 in the morning, I look at a German-dubbed version of Robert Altman's *Short Cuts* on Austrian television. Terrible, but I can't get enough of it: Tom Waits grins and mumbles in a Jörg Haider voice: '*Komm hier, mein Schatz.*' He truly takes on the appearance of Boris Karloff as Dracula.

The way in which, in this city, I am constantly being thrown back into my own imaginative world, despite my longing for other people, is the only thing that is tangible, has a meaning. An unforgiving school in which to learn to understand something of myself.

I eat in Ristorante al Caminetto, because it is a regular haunt of the Italians living in Vienna, and because I find it a relief to listen to Italian for an hour. Oh, the longing for Italy, what a jaded and yet constantly recurring feeling. Being an Italian: what a clichéd longing of Flemings, Dutchmen, English, Germans, Parisians, New Yorkers. What a frustration since Shelley and Keats, for us Northerners not to be able to reel off Italian as fluently as the girl next to us on the bench, not to be part of a culture which has in the meantime been reduced by the RAI, Gianni Nannini and Eros Ramazotti to a colour picture, to be able to order saltimbocca mozzarella, carciofini, mortadella, Lambrusco and sambuca, not only because we really love those things – which we of course do, but because they're twice as delicious in comparison with our own jaded world. So by coming and sitting here and ordering in Italian like a perfect student, I can forget *Belgio*, because you come from there, don't you, *signore*? *'Oh, Belgio, Belgio molto bene, my grosspapa da gearbeitet. Liège e bello! Ecco! Schön, ja.'*

And I think of someone who was on the point of becoming my friend and who, the day before, one morning in the south, simply collapsed incomprehensibly in the street and fell down dead; it pains me to have to learn to understand this, and it strikes me that life is nothing, it is all nothing, we've got worked up about nothing, but it's all we have. I want to get just a little more drunk before I go back into town, take the metro, see people. So I reopen my register of spaghetti Italian.

'Signor, si prego, encora un caffè e un sambuca. Si, grande. Sono molto triste stassera.'

One morning, my Slovakian cleaner comes in with a spray can: next door, *Herr Professor*, there are Indians, and she was in there to clean, and oh dear, oh dear, everything was *schmutzig*, terrible, and because she is frightened of creepy crawlies you understand *verstehen Sie bitte*, and before I can say anything she starts spraying the whole floor with a spray can which stinks terribly. In great haste, I remove bread, butter and coffee but she is already coming after me and gives the small dark kitchen a spray too, and then the bathroom. As if she wants to kill all little devils, little Indians no doubt – this woman who herself is exploited as an immigrant for five thousand schillings per month – until my whole apartment is one big poison cupboard. She indulges her fear of infection by my Indian neighbours so voluptuously that she starts panting and giggling as she works. Don't open the windows! She cries and rushes off again. I immediately open everything wide and let the draught blow through it. Two days later she is back, she's a little calmer, she's worked here for six months but has decided to return to Brno in Moravia, she's fed up with exploitation, my boss is *schlimm schlimm*, I'm going to study economics she says with a hand that is red and swollen because of the cleaning products on her expansive bosom, and then I'll also know how things work, *Herr Professor!*

In Gugging, in the large Leo Navratil asylum for the insane in one of the suburbs of Vienna, I finally walk along the paths of the mentally unbalanced poet, Ernst Herbeck, I see the images that were etched unforgettably into me by the mentally unbalanced draughtsman, Oswald Tschirtner, whose portrait has been in my memory for years: walking along the corridor, he is just passing a Coca-Cola machine where the text under the photo reads: 'This is how I am, always the same.' The images which I had in mind when I wrote the last pages of my text *Suture* on this unbalanced, brilliant melancholic, loom up in front of me: 'The heat is in the head \ The heat is in the hair \ The heat is in a little corner \ The patient is allowed to walk \ The patient is allowed to play table tennis: the patient is allowed to relax \ To dally with fifteen leaves \ Of the mulberry tree \ We go shoulder to shoulder through the night . . .'

And, strolling among the silent, awkward figures who sometimes stare at me and sometimes rush off into a brightly coloured corridor, I suddenly see into a small room, and someone points out to me a man with a nodding head, who is sitting wiping his eyes with a handkerchief. And he says to me: 'That is Oswald Tschirtner.' I have a shock, because I thought this

138

'This is how I am, always the same' – Oswald Tschirtner.

man had died years ago, like Ernst Herbeck, but no: here he sits, an old angel, not of this world, the draughtsman of endless series of extended, pale human figures, *Immer gleich*. And I go up to him, put out my hand, say that I am moved to meet him (thinking the whole time: God, how he's aged since the photo), he takes my hand, looks up as if he needs to think for a long time, says that he is pleased, pleased, yes how pleasant something like that is, that he is pleased that he is pleased and goodbye goodbye and yes see you again yes I hope to see you again and he rocks my hand for a long time, suddenly releases it and looks straight ahead of him. I stand there clumsily and with a lump in my throat, nod at him again and go back into the corridor. There are photos on the walls of the most famous inmate, the poet Alexander, actually Ernst Herbeck, the man who was the inspiration for the famous anti-psychiatric novel *März* by Heinar Kipphardt. This is in the depths of Austria, a slope full of green silence above an idyllic village, with a collection of drawing, painting and writing mentally disturbed melancholics. Along one of the paths, where W. G. Sebald may also have walked with Herbeck, there is an abandoned building, and sprayed on it, in red trembling letters: 'Help we want to get out!' And in my imagination, Sebald is walking behind Herbeck and Herbeck is walking behind Robert Walser and Walser behind Trakl and Trakl behind Lenz and Lenz behind Hölderlin and Hölderlin behind Kaspar Hauser and I walk and talk with someone, a woman who I only got to know this afternoon, and who has all the light of the day in her eyes, pointing to the desperate graffiti: they seem to have been sprayed there for a film, this is too real too typical, what we have to imagine. And the day is open and full of summer smells, a couple of lunatics shuffle past us and mumble all kinds of things that we can't understand, while we walk down a steep path, a path under the mulberry tree.

> Anyone who has never heard the rattle of projectors in the back of his head, does not know what memories are, nor does he know the visions of the present, those morose images that seep through the screen and cast their arbitrary forms on unintended back-drops. (from Louis Ferron, *Turkish Vespers*, a novel about Vienna)

I had arranged to meet her in front of the house where Kafka died; earlier that day I had driven to Baden with the friend who was practising 'letting go', had stood looking among the vineyards behind his house and heard the first cuckoo of the year. It was May, everything was abundantly fertile, moist and warm, with what was already almost a stifling Hungarian heat – it was reminiscent of the southern French hills, with the same smell of vines and old cellars. The friend had brought me to the suburbs of Vienna and there we saw a woman who I had imagined differently – not so radiant, not so naturally there in the bright afternoon: I had tried to ring her a few times on the advice of a woman friend, I had heard her voice on the answering machine a few times, the light erotic lisp of the 's' in her name and somehow I had formed a picture of someone who was dark-haired. Now the moment of farewell had come from my friend, we both became unsure of ourselves in the presence of an unknown third person. So he came up the stairs with me for a moment – the woman had had the house where Kafka died specially opened for us on this Saturday afternoon – and the three of us stood on the balcony on the second floor, at the back, and looked at the peaceful gardens and the wooded slopes behind. This had been *his* balcony, the view that Kafka saw every day in his last few months. Not much can have changed about it; trees and slopes and magpies and tits. Below, against the back wall of what was then a private institution for severe TB patients a few dark figures were sitting in the conservatory in the afternoon sun, a little pale. He must have sometimes sat among them, though without much enthusiasm – he would now have finally found in Dora Dymant a woman with whom cohabitation might have been possible, a possible homecoming to a love that he had always felt to be impossible. We stood on the balcony not really knowing what to say. The woman still unknown to us stood next to us. There was the occasional sentence that was unanswered. Looking filled the whole event, time and space. A return seemed possible for a moment, we would see him, the black thin figure with the piercing look, we would have shaken hands with him and

141

when we were startled by these kinds of naïve reflections, we knew that the time for farewell had come. Somehow that was accompanied by a strange kind of emotion not expected by any of us; the girl went and stood in the hall, and when she rejoined me on the narrow wooden balcony, the two of us were alone - on a balcony that then, in the month of May, was still intact, still completely the same as when he had sat there silently dying; but in the month of December, that same year, the papers reported that the balcony had been dismantled and sold, plank by plank. A small museum that, in order to survive financially, sells the reason for its existence. Thus even the return to my memory is already becoming historic. I have never written or wanted to write about Kafka; he fills too much symbolic space, and too naturally, in the life of people who write and as a result do not do countless things that other people do, they prefer to sit at their desks while everyone is outside enjoying life. All too soon, writing about Kafka either becomes filled with the inexhaustible extended riddle of his stories, or with the pathos of his fate; and everyone who writes has to go easy on this. The fact that I can't and could not write a single word about him is all due to his dominating presence. But then with someone whom I met there, in a glowing afternoon, on the very terrace where he more or less sat dying, a small opening was created, a tear, a rip in the wallpaper under which I preserve him for myself, and as I write this, I feel now this enchantment returning in the unexpected fact that I'm writing about it – realizing that I began this spontaneously and it's precisely a month ago to the day that I experienced it – as if this crazy calendar with its chance games could give an explanation for what a person does or doesn't do.

But I turn to the woman, she asks me a question – after all, we had to do something to get to know each other, now we'd followed up each other's telephonic summonses – and I replied to her, I don't remember to what, and she looked astonished, even laughed, looking almost ironic: why? – and leant over the balustrade again, as if trying to find something in the view.

From the house where Kafka died, we walked to the paths of Herbeck in Gugging, and from Gugging we took the bus back to the centre. She showed me things by the Danube and landmarks in grey streets. We went to the Jewish cemetery near the Berggasse – a courtyard surrounded by a tall, unimaginative newly built old people's home on which were the old, lopsided round stones with the Hebrew texts; lost, pushed into a corner, but even then, the town council obviously had too many scruples to simply demolish them. Lost stones with Jewish inscriptions, a few of them with large branches of hanging crowns above them, grass which had shot up, a spot like an old mouth with a few teeth left in it, an irritating spot for the elderly Austrians, who would have preferred to put their deckchairs down there in the sun and hold their intolerable coffee gatherings. But the city has to take heed of protests by humanist souls who still crop up here and there, people with scruples; the old Jewish stones remain in the centre of the city like a remnant from a mythical time, the time of the Diaspora, and they bear witness to its unimaginably dreadful ending. As I stand there looking at them, rather undecided, I think back to Kafka, and it is as if these Jewish graves, almost hidden from the outsider among the glass and aluminium of an asylum for the moribund, are silently screaming about a life that has become incomprehensible, a life with a text to which the key is finally missing, as if we were to encounter hieroglyphics in a corridor in the underground; and this place, this spot which is saturated with decayed Jewish bones, symbolizes the grave of Kafka; not his personally, nor the sentimental grave of the philosemite, but the grave of an unknown and extinct people, a people that has very little to do with the hawks of present-day Israel – the Kafka people with its TB and its stories, a people without land which here has a piece of ground around which the vultures hunt for carrion.

The expulsion of the Jews from Vienna in 1938 meant the immediate murder of the great cosmopolitan Vienna. The young people who are now filling up this empty shell no longer have any link at all with my generation. (Gregor von Rezzori)

In my memory it will open: 'the cemetery of the nameless', the remote little cemetery of the drowned on the Danube, about ten kilometres outside Vienna.

Hidden behind an earth wall, at the end of an industrial site, snowed under by the fluff of blooming poplars, with a couple of threateningly large silos in the background, is an idyllic piece of ground with horse chestnuts around it. In the middle the graves are crowded close together; time after time they have no other inscription except 'nameless, unknown'. When there are names, they are Polak, Novak, Gutmann – perhaps not coincidentally the names of a Pole, a Czech and a Jew. People who came from elsewhere, who did not feel accepted and then had themselves accepted by something greater: the swaying motion of the river that, behind the earthen wall for a couple of kilometres in the direction of Vienna, divides into two so that by the head of the strip of land in the middle, a current is created that brings their bodies back to the surface. Cross after cross after old-fashioned iron cross: nameless, nameless, unknown. And among them one cross with: 'Unforgettable'. That more or less strikes one dumb. Unforgettable, but nameless: what does that mean, or at least what did someone once mean by it? Was the sight of this washed up dead person unforgettable? Was it about someone who was recognized? Or a child, or a person who had drowned before someone's eyes, come up to the surface, submerge again and rise again? Was it the sight of the nameless person that was unforgettable or the event of death? Had a dead face been damaged by a dredging hook, or had something else happened which beggars the imagination?

The landlord of the small tavern that lies hidden a little further on among the waving crowns, has seen the processions, year after year, day after day. The drowned ones of the Danube. This is a place at the end of the world. With the charming woman, whom I already seem to have known much longer (though it is still just that same long enchanting day), I have cycled about ten kilometres along the banks of the Danube, leaving from the well-known building, Urania, with its strange dome, in the centre of the city. Gradually the streets open out, we leave the city walkers, the roller-bladers and the leaping dogs behind us on the banks, catch sight of the four old gas reservoirs at the edge of the city, then the oil refinery, and beyond it the vague, great spaces of industry. She points things out to me laughing, with her arm outstretched, cycles alongside me talking and opens the day further and further till it glows. To the right of us roars the highway to Bratislava and that too bends in a different direction after a few kilometres. We are completely alone on an endless, straight asphalt road between bushes and broken-down advertising hoardings. Swallows shoot above our heads, through the bushes we catch a glimpse of the strong current of the river to our left. We cycle on hard, the woman laughs and tells me stories and shakes her thick bush of curly hair and gives me the feeling that the day is perfect because she has thought it up for me. After cycling for three-quarters of an hour, we pass an old stationary row of train carriages with the ineradicable sadness of war transports. They're simply standing alongside the road, they've probably stood there as long as the great grain silos built and left behind by the Nazis, along which we now let our cycles free-wheel, getting our breath back and looking around. An old sausage stall has been shut for years. The cranes which I remember from my childhood, the old cranes near the harbour, here they stand like rusty birds from mythical stories alongside a few more recent metal silos by the bank, which themselves lie hidden behind the old storage depots. And, suddenly emerging green past a trio of parked lorries, that nameplate: *Friedhof der Namenlosen*. There's a round chapel, but you only see that when you've crossed over an earth wall, so deep is it sunk in the ground. Since last year there has been a commemorative plate, a tribute to Josef Fuchs, the man who for more than 60 years tended the cemetery and the graves day by day, planted

145

flowers on them, raked the paths and, from nameless one to nameless one, with always the same care, lit the candles in the old-fashioned iron lamps, repainted the flaking silver of the letters and the black of the plates. He began this work in 1935, even before the cemetery was officially closed, and died less than a year before I am standing here. Two gigantic old Robinia trees, which he must have seen all his life, have just been up-rooted. No more dead added here, but he remained faithful to this resting company of those who had been washed up together.

Washed up together, like a poem on a black plate in the middle of the cemetery says, just as we are washed up together for the day of judgement, on which they, the poem goes on to say, will not be forgotten: an unusually tolerant attitude for suicides, who according to official doctrine must generally be deprived of happiness after death.

> When peace and quiet you have sought,
> You sorely troubled hearts,
> Far from the world, which sought you,
> Here there are no more sorrows.
>
> Although the modern muck is missing,
> No single cross gives your names,
> Here you rest in god's hand,
> In his peace amen.

On the stump of one of the sawn-off trees that is still sticking out of the earth, waiting and thinking, sits my guide with her blonde bush of hair that is set in motion by the slightest breeze. I see her, through the nameless crosses, as a glowing spot. She smokes, meditates and gives me time to get used to this place as she has done herself. And I sit down next to her on the tree stump and look at the cemetery from there – it is a little like Jan Fabre's host of blue crosses with the names of insects, and only an artist could dream up something like this: a cemetery filled time after time with 'nameless'. Austria, she says pensively, has the highest percentage of suicides in the whole of Europe; and Vienna in turn the most in the whole of Austria. They washed

146

up here, the people who did not see the second Great War, who simply stepped out of history after they had come here, on their way to the great collapsed empire of the Habsburgs. Were there already people who had had the fear of death put into them by the early brutalities and intimidations of the SA? For a long time, Austria remained idyllic, idyllic in its typical, unbearable way. Undoubtedly, as the cemetery opened in 1901, there were also victims from the first Great War, or people who had just heard that a fatal shot had been fired in Sarajevo and that the great central European kingdom was coming to an end, or simply someone who was absent-minded or incautious, a walker who suddenly had enough of it, a child that stumbles by the bank, one day in June, let's say 16 June 1904, the day on which Nora Barnacle kissed Jim Joyce for the first time.

Here the water churned their bodies up, swollen and bruised by the stones on the shore, blue like all bodies which surface, with their hidden history, their battered bodies, their swollen abdomens and their eyes strange and lightly sunk, human fishes from a bad dream. I tell her about the film on the drowned people of the Seine, how Peter Greenaway had virtuoso copies of the bodies made and how the row of the drowned lives always has something of a *mise-en scène* of the whole of life, of missed chances, beauty, violence, lost intimacy, discouragement, final phase. She looks at me with her large open look, thinks and smokes and points out to me after a long silence a commemorative stone hidden by a fir. It is the grave of the former caretaker of the cemetery, the man who saw the lost, drowned and rejected lives put into the ground here: finally he had himself buried here, the only dead person one could easily identify, because he lies where he lived – a caretaker of the drowned, and he has a name.

Through the crowns of two brotherly trees, the three large silos glow yellow.

We get up, walk to the tavern a little way along under the trees. A few people are sitting drinking something. A girl walks along the grass-grown banks with a dog. A lorry driver steers his puffing juggernaut to just by the tables of the terrace, as if

147

he wanted to slowly smash them. The top of his truck scrapes past a few low-hanging branches. We hear for a moment the pounding of the hi-fi, he jumps out of his high cab and goes inside for something to eat. He has forgotten to put on the hand brake. The heavy lorry gradually rolls a metre backwards in the direction of the banks and then remains swaying in a hollow spot in the sand. We drink, smoke and watch. A large barge is sailing on the Danube, in the direction of Vienna. The motor pounds slowly behind the low bank, and with its blades it churns up the water, and water then churns things up, that's how it happens, it's inevitable, and I think of the idyllic Danube banks behind the high monastery of Melk, 80 kilometres upstream, the place where Umberto Eco has *The Name of the Rose* written by an aged local monk – I think of the abandoned Danube quay near Bratislava and from there of the Margareta Island in Budapest where people lie sunbathing in the summer, and from there it goes southwards in the direction of Pecs, the Banat, former Yugoslavia (where perhaps other bodies have lain in recent history) and from there to Ruschuk, the city of Canetti's youth, and then through Romania, the whole stretch that Claudio Magris has described in his book *Danube*.

We cycle the ten kilometres back to Vienna, into the wind, arrive back in the city in the dusk with faces flushed, eat in an Egyptian restaurant, get drunk as we laugh, and life is no more than this, this weightless getting to know someone who makes you happy, makes you glow within. We become a little exuberant, her cheeks blush, but now from the drink and warmth that we are ourselves exuding. It's raining in Vienna, a nocturnal soft rain, and the city is in my imagination again a port to another still not understood Europe, where everything must begin again. The time of the anachronism. Through the street walk a few North Africans, washed up in this city.

And there suddenly on a quiet Sunday evening that I'm fighting with my loneliness, in the last sun, there is a didgeridoo player in the Kärtnerstrasse in Vienna. I hear the sound and am, as it were, catapulted back to Circular Quay in Sidney, and stay as if rooted to the ground. And, after listening for some time, I'm unable to leave, the rhythmic pumping of the deep note paralyses me and has me totally in its spell. How long did I stand there? Half an hour? An hour? I don't know. Around me and the player, the city flared on like a dream from a distant future. Now and then, approximately every two minutes, the man quickly opened a bloodshot eye and as he did so, looked at me with more and more attention. His body moved with the pulsating bass tones that were pumped in my direction. Then he closed his eyes again and suddenly extracted from the pipe of the basses a high sounding note, almost like the cry of an animal and then let the rhythmically repeated tone sink down until it vanished into the lowest notes. His body swayed softly to the pumping primeval sound. I began to share his ecstasy, and he knew it. He was white, about 30, but he had the broad features of an Aboriginal. His eyes were deep-set and his eyebrows were thick and almost white. His lips were red and obscene from hours of blowing, defenceless and swollen like the cunt of a woman after long love making. He mastered the whole complex and complicated technique of the various embouchures perfectly, and with his free left hand beat a small drum that he had wedged under one leg. He went through all the turns, twists, growling notes and high notes, the depths and heights of this one strange, timeless instrument, it growled and roared like an unearthly being, a god from the depths of time. I had the feeling I was gradually becoming completely stoned. He, I knew that for sure, was in his mind going back through a section of the outback, he was walking through a hot empty landscape that he could see before his closed eyes. *The song lines*. And I walked a part of the way with him. When he stopped it was as if we came to a stop with a jolt and found ourselves in Vienna together in astonishment. But I had been around the planet for a while and he, completely high with blowing, slowly opened his eyes. He looked at me penetratingly, blinked his eyes emphatically a couple of times, laughed for a moment and then slowly nodded his head towards me. But he was still far away. The cold of the banal shopping street and the parading Viennese filled him with disgust. He took the second, shorter pipe, surveyed it for a moment. Further along the street a boy was twittering 'La donna è mobile.' There must have been 200 people watching him. He and I were alone here. As if he wanted to banish the noise of the twittering singer as far as possible from his hearing, he put his mouth to the very simply painted smaller didgeridoo, gave me a wink and again set out on a journey through the bush, to a thousand years ago, in the heat in the emptiness. I suddenly longed terribly for Australia. For the dry smell, for the endlessly undulating hills, the gurgling cry of brightly coloured birds that were unknown to me, the screeching of the troupes of white corellas flapping to and fro, the hares and the dry creeks, the lizards under the eucalyptus trees, the sleepy koalas high in the branches, the deserted beaches with the playing sea lions, yes even the unbearable emptiness in a desolate street in Adelaide where for the first time I had had to confront my own fear of dying.

Oh, you can't keep it up for two minutes without starting to find yourself amusing. Boring postcards from all the places in the world immediately slide past your longing gaze and you realize that you are just one of the hundreds of thousands who long to really believe that escape is possible, has any point or whatever. Paradise is camp. And I walk through the stupid Kärtnerstrasse full of Viennese kitsch, the terraces were crowded, people were twittering and chattering, the opera was just coming out, waiters dashed between the customers with fully laden trays. I walked away from the noise, it died out painfully slowly but painfully softly behind me. The opera singer started up again, this time with 'Signorina mille tre'. And I thought of my frank friend Michel, laughing rather breathlessly from all the smoking, who, striding along Circular Quay like a drunken pope, looked round at me and said with a pedantic expression that he thought bridges were more beautiful than koalas.

That night I hear in my sleep nothing but the deep monotonous rhythm, swelling and then dying away, coming and then disappearing in an empty heat, addictive. But it is not there, there is nothing but the night and the emptiness of the boring Josefstadt that Jelinek disdains so much, there is nothing at all, because life is nothing and I think of the poets who have sung this refrain – Christine D'Haen and Leonard Nolens – and I am in Vienna, Jesus Christ, in a narrow bed in a stuffy room, alone. I am longing for my girlfriend and my child, but I can't telephone because it's four o'clock in the stupid godforsaken Viennese morning and that's so incomprehensible that I have to think about it, fret, wrack my brains until I fall asleep again to the rustling of the first tram in the Alserstrasse.

> Perhaps a city is not made of views, and the city is not the correlate of a series of objective points of view. Perhaps the city is invisible. (Bart Verschaffel)

Marseilles: Urban Legends and Sardines

In the early summer of 1940, a boy cycles from Boom near Antwerp to Marseilles. He is eighteen and has fled the summons by the German occupiers to go and fight or work in Germany, he is not sure which. At that moment nothing is certain any longer. So, preferring to be safe rather than sorry, he says good-bye to his parents and jumps on his bike. Rides and rides, all day and all night. Rides through the Ardennes, through the broad rolling hills of north-east France and through the valley of the Marne, sleeps here and there in farms on a haystack or under a shelter, from a distance sees the movement of troops – has the Vichy government already been set up? – sometimes hides, on occasion meets with understanding and on occasion suspicion when he says that he comes from Belgium. Exhausted by the long climb, he passes the walled town of Langres, where it is cold, and descends in the direction of Dijon and the Gothic Flemish-like Beaune, after first riding through the vineyards of Nuit St Georges, Gevrey-Chambertin, Romanée-Conti, Aloxe Corton – the names mean nothing to him at that moment. Everything lies there as if peace has never come to an end, although it is sometimes busy on the roads: green lorries, columns and then again endless expanses of land, light and the movement in his legs. Rides and rides, through the night, through the day. Encounters control posts, is some-times taken for a deserting German. From Lyons onwards it is blisteringly hot. He passes Valence, Montélimar, Orange, Avignon. Doesn't stop, goes on riding. Sleeps in the vineyards of a vague area somewhere behind an ancient wall. Rides on the following day, turns eastwards, to Aix, around which he rides in an arc, and then on through the heat in the plain of the almost dry Durance. And so weeks later he arrives in Marseilles, *Massilia*, at the harbour that was already mentioned by Herodotus, Thucydides and Aristotle, and was praised by Plutarch, Caesar, Livy and Tacitus. 'Ten thousand stages and another ten thousand stages', he has biked in order to escape the summons of the Nazis and he sees the sea – 'thalassa, thalassa!' He stands by the Venetian-looking Vieux Port, dazzled by the light and the reflections in the water, walks unsteadily and, with his legs trembling, pushing his bike along the Quai des Belges; and then turns, looking around in amazement, onto the Canebière, sees the statue of the first round-the-world traveller, Pytheas of Massilia, on the front of the Stock Exchange and then strolls along the shady Cours Belsunce, and towards evening finds a room in a small hotel in the Rue de Rome. It has two entrances, one for the down-at-heel guests and another for the whores at night.

What he did, fleeing the German call-up, is only the umpteenth repetition of an odyssey to this city, a twentieth-century version of what countless people have done before him, whether they came from the south, the east or the north: seeing Marseilles and standing in amazement on the quay, walking in astonishment through the streets, hearing dozens of languages, seeing the self-confident women, the cries of the fishermen by the quay, the dazzling African types in the streets behind the Porte d'Aix, the Boulevard des Dames and Jules Guesde Square and further on the infamous old Panier. Casanova did it, Chateaubriand did it, Stendhal did it, indeed even Schopenhauer and Walter Benjamin did it: looked in amazement at the sense of liberation in a city where they had really not expected anything.

The boy is to stay there for more than two months and will be put to work by the French. He becomes a repair mechanic in a technical team where French tanks are assembled. He hears about the Resistance, he is young and absent-minded and good-looking, in the evening he stands on the quay watching the weighing of the catch, tuna of more than two hundred kilos – and as he stands smoking a cigarette with jet black tobacco in it, he occasionally picks a piece of black grease from under his fingernails. His wavy hair is stirred by the wind and along the quay a number of laughing girls have their eye on him, but he doesn't see that, he is thinking of his Flemish sweetheart at home and feels homesick while the city has him in tow.

He is my future father and it will be more than half a century before I ring him, almost naked in front of a window on an upstairs floor of a hotel looking out over the Vieux Port sweltering in the afternoon heat, and tell him where I am, whereupon he, sitting quietly in his garden having his afternoon coffee, will start, and will say and go on repeating, 'But my boy'. And then I have to tell him exactly where I'm standing, and he says that he knows the spot and again he can't believe it and I can hear the emotion in his voice, a whole world is opening up for him. Have I been in the Rue de Rome yet? Are there still hotels there? The one where he stayed will probably have disappeared? Is that district still there where the streets are so narrow that on the top floors on one side of the street you can shake hands with somebody on the other and where they simply throw their household rubbish out of the window into the streets? No, father, there's a book shop-cum-huge shopping centre there now, air-conditioned.

As I put down the telephone I have the feeling of having closed a circle. His grandson is standing on the fourth-floor terrace with his hands round the iron railings screaming euphorically and wordlessly at the roaring cars below, the teeming of people by the water, the seagulls swooping over his head and the flickering of the sea. I take him in my arms, with a laugh show him to his mother who is getting changed, and she says, 'Come and get dressed, we're going into town.'

Marseilles is less the city of a particular topography than a city that hangs together with stories. Apart from the Panier, the Cours Belsunce, the Rue de Canebière and the Vieux Port, all writers who wanted to say something about Marseilles talk about stories, not about places. The presence of North Africans, which has been powerful for centuries, has produced a reservoir of myths, stories in which crime, darkness, menace and erotic tension are constants. Add to that the continually recurring mythical stories about the Greek origin of the city – according to one legend a king's daughter is supposed to have given her hand in marriage to a Greek navigator from Phocea in Ionia and in this way the city of Massilia is supposed to have been founded – and it is clear that Marseilles is a place *par excellence* of urban legends where it is not so much topography as historiography that colours in the city plan. The only positioning that the inhabitants of Marseilles grant themselves is, from a nationalistic point of view, a negative one: in fact they are descended from the Greeks, have nothing to do with the hinterland – Provence – and live with their faces turned towards the glistening sea. They also live *from* the sea, and Marseilles simply passes its lavish gifts on to the interior, but requires nothing in return – except cash. The feeling of living in a kind of enclave which, at the same time, guarantees a greater freedom than the peasant country described for centuries as backward in the hot hills of the Lubéron, the Vaucluse and the Drôme, colours daily life with a greater intensity – which as, in many big cities, is secretly fired by disdain for what surrounds city-dwellers. For centuries, Marseilles has cherished the highest ambitions. In the past, it has been called a Provençal Athens, it was the only non-Greek city to be given a temple in Delphi and, strangely enough, it was not laid waste by Caesar when it rebelled against him. For centuries, it enjoyed the esteem of Rome and through its clever policies succeeded in having its greatest adversary in the Mediterranean, Carthage, wiped out.

On virtually any morning, anyone living in Marseilles can take a boat from the quay to the North African coast – Oran, Tangiers, Algiers – just as Dutchmen and Belgians can go to London. Sitting here on a terrace near the Vieux Port, with a cool glass in the shadow of the La Samaritaine, you feel that somehow the world of Paul Bowles and of Camus' outsider is actually already beginning in a way. An exotic mixture of passivity and boastfulness causes the inhabitants of Marseilles to make rather complacent and affectionate fun of Paris – 'If the Canebière were in Paris, it would be a little Marseilles' – and the contemptuous intellectualism of the Parisians only confirms them in their sense of difference. At the same time, the presence of the immigrants, currently the target of the Front National, constitutes the core of the identity of the people of Marseilles; for that reason, racism here is more than elsewhere a matter of complete cultural schizophrenia. But those who live or walk around the city see a different reality from that of politics: a sophisticated and, at the same time, rather vulgar culture of great naturalness and obviousness. Politicians, on the other hand, are so outspoken in their ideas that they overlook the complexity of reality.

The North African element, a part of the Mediterranean face of the city, has spread over the whole urban population: that is, even the most entrenched racist cannot really imagine life here without these districts, without these exotically stinking alley-ways behind the Porte d'Aix, Jules Guesde Square or the small streets behind the Rue de Rome – because the disappearance of the immigrants would rob Marseilles of its identity. What would Marseilles be without the North Africans? A provincial hole, every bit as backward as the despised hinterland. The North-African character has spread like an age-old rumour, an atmosphere that intensifies everything without there necessarily being any tangible factual basis, without anything actually happening. The immigrant population forms the living core of a constant crisis of identity that, in its turn, produces the great vitality of the city. It is 'almost' always present and it is feared as much as it is desired – the dark shadow of the city, what makes it attractive and sexy, something that people are proud of yet at the same time torments and irritates.

People also manipulate it. From the small ghettos, the smell of the dream rises but no one can point out the territory where it is now really 'happening'. In order to remain even tougher

156

than this self-created image, the Marseillais must therefore constantly appear a little overblown, be a little rougher than the imagined toughness of the criminal immigrant from the stories (who has often lived for generations in Marseilles, who feels 100 per cent Marseillais and in most cases is no more criminal than the average poor city-dweller in other big cities – unless like Chirac you see the smoking of a joint as a crime). This is the origin of the obsession of the 'French' Marseillais to 'go further', to long for something extreme without knowing precisely what, to bawl out his neighbour, drive the car at crazy speeds, to have pounding music on the whole time and making windows and doors rattle. Because blood will out, people have developed something else here, a language which bristles with superlatives and power words, a loud cackling, hilarious spluttering and swearing that disappears over the sea like the sound of the flapping of ten thousand newly-released birds. The only calm, serene types are found among the Africans – particularly the darkest ones who, like noble savages, look at the fat-bellied and loudly talking Marseillais walking past and keep their thoughts to themselves. But just when you're beginning to fathom this, or are at least cocky enough to think that you understand something of it, suddenly you are somewhere deep in the city standing in front of a small dark hairdressing salon from which a rancid aroma rises in the heat of the siesta; Eastern-sounding music comes out of the dark doorway, above it hangs a hand painted sign: 'Coiffeur Africa moderne'. And beneath this it says 'Speciality, hair straightening'.

All these contradictory stories make Marseilles a place *par excellence* of the Logos, of narration and the Word and equally of the inflation of the word, the never-arriving Last Word of the unknowable Truth, which every day hangs anew above the districts like a sword of Damocles, in the view of a courtyard, a messy alleyway, in the gloomy shops with live chickens in stinking cages, on the dreary concrete balconies in the suburbs. The Word that whispers along the courtyards and only comes to a halt in the great spaces of the contemporary metropolis –

157

such as the gigantic Virgin Megastore shopping centre, where young people dissolve into the colourless codes of an internationally imposed attitude.

It is therefore only superficially true that Marseilles and Paris are antipodes. Firstly, cities like Lille, Lyons and Paris, for example, probably have more foreigners than Marseilles by now and so its inhabitants no longer need to pride themselves so loudly on the presence of the immigrants. The only difference in this respect is culture: the immigrants of Marseilles have been there for so many generations that they form an essential part of the city. Secondly, the much-discussed rivalry with Paris is simply an invention of the last two centuries (previously Marseilles was only ever compared with other Mediterranean cities), invented by the comparative commentaries of Madame de Sévigné, Georges Sand, Emile Zola or Victor Hugo, indeed even Antonin Artaud. Incidentally, the last of these was a native Marseillais, which perhaps explains a good deal of his later literary development in Paris where quite typically he became obsessed by the tendency always to 'go a little further' than others.

The central paradox of Marseilles, of course, resides in this separatist attitude to the rest of France, and then particularly, since the beginning of this century, by contrasting itself without any clarity and only playfully with Paris (as I heard in a conversation on a terrace: '*Oui, ça c'est très typique pour les Français ça! Mais où donc est-ce que cela est arrivé? Ah, à Paris, mais ça ce n'est pas la France, dis-donc.*')

Is it France, or on the contrary not France at all, or the only real France? Marseilles serves it up to you à la carte.

Oh, perhaps Marseilles is the anti-city par excellence, and before you know you walk right into the trap, and it is the trap of the word, the urban legend, the story of the 'French Chicago on the Mediterranean', Babel in miniature.

No other city has a stronger anti-tourist record than Marseilles. The slightly cowardly rich, who have in the meantime poisoned the whole of Provence with their precious search for 'truth' and 'authenticity', avoid this city like the plague. Marseilles? *Dis-donc*, don't go there! You can't park; 'they' will steal the wheels off your car in broad daylight; 'they' will pinch your car radio while you are paying at the petrol station; avoid the northern districts like the plague; all hotels there are dangerous or stink; 'they' carry knives under their shirts; never walk beyond the Porte d'Aix; never look 'them' in the eyes if you simply have to go there, for God's sake, and let's hope we see you alive again. On the terraces near the Vieux Port they sit smiling at their bouillabaisse, the Marseillais, and they let them cackle there in the hinterland, these red-boiled tourist crabs with their Michelins, their dog-eared books by Peter Mayle (*A Year in Provence*) and their *poteries* bought at outrageous prices. A little further on, someone cries above all the other voices: '*Et qu'est-ce que ça peut me foutre alors!*'

A crackle of laughter breaks out, infects the adjoining tables and passes through the whole restaurant like a wave, someone raises his glass to someone else whom he doesn't know who has also burst out laughing and finally everyone raises their glass, they're shouting and toasting and the commotion spreads to the tables on the pavement where even the passers-by stop to see what's going on. Nothing turns into something, and there is no getting away from it, because it is pure energy.

Places without a name – those are the real places in Marseilles. The toilets on the island of the Château d'If, for example, are so filthy and stink so appallingly – gusts of some hot sea wind come wafting in through a rattling and rusty old window – that you cannot help thinking of the prison which Alexandre Dumas turned it into for his hero, who is still commemorated here: the Count of Monte Cristo.

This sturdily built room, because of its anonymous rankness, reminds one of dilapidated Oriental bathhouses, and in the old Roman arches of the cool, urine-drenched stairwell I see for the first time something that might be in accord with the much-vaunted Roman past. A past that apart from this lies violated

159

by the most unimaginative blocks of flats and forgotten along the hot rocky coasts past the Corniche John F. Kennedy, with unbelievable stretches of pseudo-California, beaches with grotesque buildings, quays with nothing but kitsch, and past the point where the city fades like an idea and the last angular forms are dissolved by the rocks and the light, while in the hinterland the storm clouds pile up like glistening towers in the late afternoon beyond the bay.

The Château d'If, says Paul Theroux in an enchanting book on the countries round the Mediterranean, is a combination of Alcatraz and the Enchanted Kingdom, a Disney prison. That stone mass amidst blowing sand, waste paper casually thrown away by tourists, fragments of concrete and sharp stones on which you sprain your ankles, reminds him of stale cake. And he feels happy because sailing here, on this sea, gives one the feeling that nations are unimportant.

This grubby idea of the deep south is cherished in a sophisticated way, in this particular contrast between the sordid and the dazzling – and all this while in northern Paris the paper of progressive intellectuals, *Libération,* has for weeks been praising the exoticism of Faulkner's work, meditating and commenting on precisely the same heat, precisely the same tensions. In the evening, when I look at a map of the world, I see that Marseilles is after all a lot further north than Faulkner's world. *Mais qu'est-ce que ça peut me foutre alors?*

Places without a name – in the past it has been pointed out so often that Marseilles has no historical monuments, not even any architectural proofs of its illustrious Roman past. No arenas like Arles and Orange, no gate like Saint-Rémy. Nothing but sand, light, the smell of fish, salt water dripping off tables, hot tarmac on dreary looking avenues and the unexpected charm of the side streets. A sober park near the Prado, that's true, and a fairly obligatory stock exchange building and, of course, a fairly pompous jewel box up on the hill – the church of Notre Dame de la Garde (*'Elle nous protège tous'*, says an old man earnestly to us with his finger raised, swaying near the railing on a boat). But apart from that, Marseilles is mainly a place of nameless, direct presence, of immersing yourself in the crowds in the street, the excitement of the day, the waiting for a boat or a bus or a connection in a metro station.

The archaeological excavations that were carried out with brute force when the foundations of the great shopping centre, La Bourse, were being dug, revealed an old Roman ship and, halfway through the twentieth century, anyone who put a spade in the ground could find a few Roman utensils. They lie carelessly exhibited in display cabinets in the Historical Museum, which you have to look for on the ground floor of the corny shopping centre, down an escalator past the tacky shops, through a clumsy glass door in the basement. There you also find the *vestiges*, a fragment of the defensive walls of the ancient city. In a large case you see a model of Massilia (as the Romans called the city; in the time of the Greeks actually Massalia). The planning of this hypothetical construction shows a transparent architecture achieved through the effects of the columns and galleries on the large buildings. The temples of Artemis and Apollo dominate the skyline. The Vieux Port is a creek, a natural whim of the water where Pytheas moored when he came home from one of his world voyages. Not much more than the bay that two thousand years later the English convicts were to call Botany Bay.

The historical library that is also housed in the basement of the department store has mainly exotic-looking readers who are being surveyed in silence by two pale, sour-faced ladies. It comes as a shock: finding in a place where underground car parks are usually found, a studious silence, a place where something like reflection can emerge – so untypical of this city.

For Marseilles does not have a university. Young people with intellectual ambitions flee the city to study in Aix or Paris. Half of them never come back from Paris, unless it is much later, when homesickness begins to bite, but then never for good. Marseilles has this brain drain partly to thank for its provincial epicureanism. In fact, only Lyons is a real counterpart to Parisian cultural hegemony. Marseilles does not qualify for this in any way; and if there is a 'little Paris' in the south of France, it is Aix, with its leafy lanes where the chic students with their vituperative style and expensive sunglasses dominate the ambience.

So Marseilles is not after all the 'other France', at least not in a topographic or cultural sense. Otherwise, Nice and Cannes would have that 'otherness' too, and that is, as we know, definitely not the case. No, Marseilles stands for another piece of French *history*: the link with the Arab world, the experiences of the Algerian war which are still traumatic for many Marseillais, and the resulting difficult relationship with almost all North Africans – a problem that did not present itself in this form in the eighteenth and nineteenth centuries, when the immigrants were already there and when Géricault could draw with no embarrassment his scenes of a lion hunt in Morocco, or Flaubert could brag about Egyptian whores. Here in this historical legacy, in this paradoxical French link with North Africa, in this point of *La France profonde*, almost invisible for the foreigner, there is a deep and usually hidden meaning for something that sometimes astonishes northerners: that sometimes the conservative Jacques Chirac plays the Arab card politically against the Zionist Bill Clinton. And something that is not only concerned with France's economic interests – it is partly connected with a hidden erotic cultural element that takes shape when you walk through the streets of Marseilles, and that you can also find in the books of Camus (his depiction of Oran), Yann Queffélec or Didier van Cauwelaert. A number of the leading intellectuals in present-day Paris, such as Bernard-Henri Lévy and Jacques Derrida, were born in North Africa and return there regularly.

And in this way, yes of course, Marseilles is France's only exotic alternative to the centralist *Île de France*.

The oldest celebrated inhabitant of Marseilles is called Pytheas of Massilia. He was the first world traveller known to us, the

Pytheas of Massilia; photo by the author.

predecessor of Ibn Battuta, Marco Polo and company. He went
in search of the furthest point north that was still habitable –
the Ancients were convinced that life in the cold must stop
somewhere, up there a few thousand kilometres above their

heads. Pytheas travelled widely. On his own testimony he reached the northernmost point, Thule. He wrote at least two extensive works on his voyages, but these have been lost. There are a great many polemics on the question of whether Pytheas went to Norway, Iceland or Greenland. What did he mean by Thule? The question still greatly preoccupies a number of scholars. Pytheas was the first explorer who, approximately the same time as Pythagoras, maintained that the earth is round; he had established this for himself as a navigator. What was at stake here was not insignificant, and the historians of his time greatly underestimated or ridiculed the implications of his assertions. In fact, he was the first Greek to discover Western Europe. Strabo, a Greek geographer from the time of Christ, openly calls him a liar and a fantasist. The founder of the later urban legends of a port city, perhaps?

If we are to believe Pytheas, somewhere north of Brittany very savage people must still live who lead a dreadful life because of the cold. But Pytheas, who on so many other occasions was able to pull the wool over people's eyes, undoubtedly lied about this matter too. So says Strabo. But the Romans are already honouring him, and the bust in Rome is itself a homage to this first planetary wanderer.

Eighteen centuries later, Alexandre Dumas goes completely off his head when he talks about Marseilles and he calls it this 'Ionian city, contemporary of Tire and Sidon, perfumed by the feasts devoted to Diana, completely under the spell of the stories of Pytheas'. You can find his statue on the front of the Stock Market building. He might just as well be an immortalized speculator. He stands staring straight ahead rather boastfully with a stick in one hand and the snout of a seal under one foot. He seems scarcely interested in the hectic colourful life below him on the Canebière.

A young classical scholar assured me that not one of the texts about Pytheas has been translated into Dutch. She has resolved to do something about it. Together we search through the drawers of index cards; half the references refer to worthless re-tellings of the well-known legends. Pytheas escapes between the rows and racks, and hides among the figures of a quizzical mulatto girl who sits staring straight ahead, chewing her pencil into splinters.

Apart from this, Marseilles has done no more than name a street after him. A short street behind the Quai des Belges, where there is also a slightly seedy Pizzeria Pythéas. The heavy shadows in the Rue de Pythéas, at about two in the afternoon, blur things and make you uncertain whether you are seeing what you're seeing. What do you see? Someone is sitting scribbling in a notebook as if his life depends on it. The classics scholar takes a photo of a street sign. Just behind her heels, a car screeches towards the far too close end of the street, someone starts swearing, the sound is lost in the dazzling tumbling of light.

Jean Giono, a Provençal writer, implicitly evokes the image of Chekhov's three sisters when he says that the people of Manosque – the small town in Haute Provence from which he himself comes – have been able to say all their lives: We're going to Marseilles. Without actually ever getting round to it. There the city becomes a focus for the longing for excitement, the antithesis of the rural reflectiveness from Virgil's first Eclogue, where Tityrus sits dozing under the canopy of his cooling oak. Just as Chekhov's three sisters stay in their peaceful dacha, and experience a perverse pleasure from what we could call with Jacques Lacan the *objet petit a* 'Moscow', so the elderly person drinking pastis under his plane tree in front of the Bar Tabac can say all his life that he will go to Marseilles and thereby satisfy his longing by saying it and not doing it.

So people who never go to Marseilles and stay in their little village somewhere in the mountains, are still not cut off from it. The stories in the newspapers take Marseilles every day to the furthest plane tree and oak. By preference, the stories are striking and they confirm the ambiguity of fear and longing. A man of 35 was murdered in the street yesterday by a quartet of boys from fifteen to seventeen; he got fed up with his mentally handicapped brother being jeered at, teased, stoned and assaulted by the adolescent vandals. The boy had become so traumatized that he scarcely dared go out any more. The brother took his part, was kicked down on the pavement and then had a small sabre (sic, this is the city of the three musketeers), thrust in his back. The day after the murder there is a procession through the streets of Marseilles, which stops in front of the town hall. There, members of the Front National of Le Pen try to take over the demonstration by loudly shouting racist slogans. The demonstrators resist and immediately distance themselves from this 'politicization of a human drama'. Only now does the newspaper reader realize that the murderous adolescents may have been foreigners. But the report leaves that uncertain: another way of not abandoning Marseilles to Le Pen? But it is very doubtful whether cosy multicultural optimism, as the Dutch writer Anil Ramdas calls it, can neutralize such tensions.

And yet the real centre of Marseilles has that solid historical basis. So that the FN – like the Vlaams Blok in Belgium – remains a party of the inflating of arguments between neighbours into the sordid politics of hatred. The real cultural desert where racism can flourish structurally and institutionally is in the suburbs. Vitrolles already has an FN mayor and the clique that has come to power there under the leadership of the ranting Catherine Mégret has deprived all cultural associations of their funds, purged management ranks of all foreign names, eliminated people, in brief pursued a policy identical to that of the Nazis in the 1930s. This means that the kind of people now in power are those from whom my father fled on his bike in 1940. L'Estaque, the once delightful little bay where Cézanne came to paint, is now a dilapidated place where the beach is dominated by macho and racist tensions, a place without any space beyond the industrial port and hemmed in by the slip roads of the great motorways. All the suburbs whose name begins with *Saint* have problems, as a bitter-faced elderly resident says to me. It is a fact that all the places where architecture, urban planning (or the lack of it) and demography no longer give one a feeling that the residents live in a meaningful community are descending into contemporary barbarism: ugly streets, subjective insecurity escalating into indifference and later into hostility, prejudices about and subsequently dislike of others, primarily competing survival behaviour and finally human catastrophes. Just as Musil once said that Vienna at the beginning of the century was a laboratory for the downfall of the world, it is perhaps possible to argue that throughout Europe the present-day suburbs are the laboratory for the final downfall of the nineteenth-century humanistic principles of civilized society and, in that sense, are a preliminary stage of life in a permanent civil war in the twenty-first century, as it is depicted in not always very tasteful strip cartoons, a hi-tech equipped desert with tribal disputes in gutted subways. Compared with life in the cultural desert of most suburbs, life in the historical centre of the large European cities which, at the end of the 1970s was almost impossible and extremely uncomfortable, can now, because of the ecological turn, again be called almost an idyllic village life: restoration, small-scale, traffic-calmed streets, room for culture, terraces and bistros, pruned trees and courtyards with lamp-posts and picturesque paraphernalia. Post-modern imitation of the charm, elegance and reflection of the lost tradition of the bourgeois. Restoration of the 'authentic' for the benefit of the tourist industry. Compare that with the average suburb: appallingly ugly super-markets, building suppliers and storage depots, sloppy planning, contempt for the quality of the environment, traffic flows that take no prisoners, bored faces, tensions, masses of shiny jogging suits on useless parking lots, rubbish tips on the last remaining piece of countryside, vague and dilapidated areas and second-hand cars covered with plastic spoilers racing through the streets.

For example, anyone driving into Avignon – where the beautiful lie of the historical town centre disguises the demographic problems – first passes through a vast commercial estate that is a travesty of everything that the cultural brochures maintain.

The difference in quality of life, culture and political vision between the city centre and the suburbs can therefore only increase in the coming decades, and in all larger urban centres of Western Europe.

But it is of course equally true that these suburban deserts appeal to the imagination because they show the emptiness of life unashamedly and in the raw, and so form the basis of a new kind of city life in a great, future-orientated indifference, which is neither urban, nor rural, simply undefined. A kind of gold-mine for a writer's imagination that produces worlds like that of Thomas Pynchon.

In his book, *The Limitless City*, the Dutch philosopher Willem Koerse argues that urbanization has in fact long since swallowed up the countryside; certainly at least as regards utilities, facilities and lifestyle in public places, the 'urban' has of course established itself as far as the smallest suburb, even in the villages. The farmer in his house hemmed in by driveways also sees the demonstration in Paris on television in the evening. For Koerse, however, there seems to be no distinction between cultural cities and the urban agglomerations of the Netherlands. But perhaps the difference lies in the fact that typical urban phenomena have no basis in the non-urban areas, no basis from which they have logically sprung. This historical emptiness of urban phenomena in the countryside gives one the inescapable feeling that the modern there is fake and therefore wilder, the basis for everything that is conceivable, hence also mindless excess.

It is remarkable, once you start paying attention, how many important artists of this age grew up in suburbs deprived of culture or in areas that are hard to define. The life of the great, peaceful bourgeoisie that can remain in the old patrician houses in, for example, the Bois de Boulogne, Kensington Gardens, the old canals of Amsterdam or the great avenues in Ukkel, obviously does not provide the kinds of frustration and chaotic longings that make someone into an original artist. In the centre of the cities – just as in the villa areas surrounded by woods – the doctors breed doctors, the lawyers lawyers and the culture vultures culture vultures, and life is pleasant in its insignificant security. But everything that takes place, looms up and teems in the intermediate areas, in all its violent emptiness, is the basis for the new that we fear and long for. Just as the old resident of Manosque who perhaps, must go to Marseilles tomorrow, if only once, when it's not raining and isn't too hot, when it's not too busy on the road, the *garrigue* is not on fire and when . . .

In the last two centuries, writers about Marseilles have regularly complained that it has never become an intellectual city, that it has opted for the carefree commercial existence of a southern port, proud of a distant and vague past, but without present-day ambitions. Unlike Trieste, which has succeeded in using the fruits of port commerce to extend an upper middle class with a knowledge of culture and literature, Marseilles has become a city where trade, tied to the industry of the lower middle classes has produced nothing except its own activity. The famous Provençal writer, Mistral, once proclaimed in rhapsodic tones that Marseilles must become 'the capital of the Latin' but, half a century later, Blaise Cendrars and Jean Ballard can only say that this party never took place. Marseilles has simply remained itself, as it has done for three thousand years. It does not miss opportunities, it does not abandon ambitions, no, it is content with the story that it has to tell about itself, it is its own urban legend, simply what it is, and you can see that at first glance, pure present, light, colourful and light-hearted. This is the reason why Marseilles is so blood-curdlingly ugly in many places. It despises all pretentiousness – hence the ugly blocks of flats that seem to have been specifically made for arguing in because otherwise nothing at all would happen. It ruins divine bays and creeks on the coast, like Les Goudes, with appalling concrete (a French invention) and ugly plastic. But you can still swim indifferently out among the rocks until, just above the water line, you see a divine view across the bay with

169

the Château d'If in the distance. In short, Marseilles is nothing except what it seems, it has no secrets, and that continues to fascinate us. So much so that a North African writer like Tahar Ben Jelloun, who comes from a culture where cities do have secrets, paradoxically exclaims of Marseilles: Marseilles is a mystery. But this mystery is the absence of an explanation, the impossibility of getting a hold on the dazzling light of the streets, the lack of any single coherent thought: what on earth are they up to here? Planning for today, and just that. For this reason, here and there in Marseilles, the desolate suburban feeling has penetrated deep into the centre itself; after the devastation of the Second World War, the town council plonked down streets of apartment blocks, whose very construction, as it were, already contained the decline of human respect for the lives of other people. Architects – and particularly the untalented city architects with lifelong contracts – draw at their bare drawing boards the lot of people in chilly corridors, bleak landings, degrading lifts, cramped entrance halls and poky rooms, desolate balconies with desolate views and boredom in the hollow echo of reinforced concrete. Their psychological and moral responsibility, or lack of this feeling, is often greater than is suspected.

Take the F and the N of Le Pen's party out of *La France* and you know what they mean, writes *Libération*. But this typical Parisian newspaper with its rather too forced 'we are hip' style that takes its front page and the following three pages to commemorate the twentieth anniversary of the death of Elvis, is read only infrequently in Marseilles. 'Libé n'est pas Français' – a jibe with a very cynical undertone. The alternative is the paper, *La Provence*, right-wing, populist and shamelessly focused on its own navel. The progressive paper, *La Marseillaise*, sometimes has surprisingly similar points of view. The populism is a crucible in which the right and left wing have in the last decades melted into an explosive kind of energy, which for the time being no one knows how to handle.

Urban legends? Hard facts? Tityrus under his oak has already nodded off again.

While my father was messing around with French tanks in 1940, another boy was born in the working-class districts of Marseilles. His father had fled in the 1930s from Barcelona from Franco and fascism, had crossed the Pyrenees on foot and had had to explain to the French customs officers what his business was (that was more or less the same period in which the German Jewish philosopher Walter Benjamin, a little way south of Perpignan, became so desperate with fear of the Vichy régime, that he took poison because the same customs men detained him for a whole day). What was his business? This was not completely clear to Monsieur Carlos himself; he knew mainly what his business was *not*: to die. After much talking to and fro, he was allowed across the border and given a provisional French passport. The duty customs officer spelt his Spanish surname – Carlos – wrongly and turned it into Carlus. In the difficult years after the war, his son will save virtually his whole family from starvation by standing on the quay every morning at six o'clock with a wicker basket in his arms and a grin on his dark arrogant face, directed at the newly-arrived fishermen tipping their catch into great containers on the quay. Every day they will throw him one or two fish from the thrashing mass and shout something to him as the first sun glimmers over the quay. The boy will return every day with a full basket of fish to the gloomy street where he lives and the whole family will eat from his miraculous catch of fishes. He tells me this story laughing, now he has become a universally famed purveyor of bouillabaisse, a frank and noisy pastis-drinker and charmer, a feared player of boules, a game that Marseillais and Belgians usually call pétanque, and of which he one day tells me the story.

Pétanque, I could of course hear that already, is a typical word from Marseilles, it has the sound of *calanque* (the small bays in the sea) and the story originated somewhere there too.

One day a man who had grown old and lonely (malicious tongues maintain that he came from Lyons, but that is not proven) and could no longer get out of his chair, sat gloomily throwing a number of balls at a stone and trying to hit it. A friend who came to visit him every few days, played with him a few times to console him and threw the balls in the direction of the stone. But the old man protested; it was much more difficult for people who had *les pieds tanqués*, that is, who had their feet rooted to the ground. Players had to stand with their feet rooted to one spot like the old man. So the whole game of the *pieds tanqués* resides in the subtleties, arguments and differences of opinion about how and where to place the feet. By now, however, there are so many variants of the game that there are cases where the true master is only allowed to throw the ball after taking three large strides, after which he jumps and has to throw the ball while still in the air, with his legs wide apart and approximately 30 centimetres above the ground. In order to judge the correctness of the leap, photos are sometimes taken during matches, mainly to avoid disputes that get out of hand. As Giono says, regarding another topic: this will not be so immediately clear to the Greenlander, the Dutchman or the Belgian. We remember the image of the Greek historians: that of the savage peoples to the north of Brittany. The barbarian holiday-maker who wants to play the game stupidly enough pays attention only to the balls – typical northern functionalism – and not to the feet. But it's not just about throwing, says Carlus as he pours me a tenth pastis smiling, his eyes sparkling, but the ballet, with the feet on the spot, *les pieds tanqués*.

You won't find the word *tanqué* in any dictionary, though; it is a dialect word, used for someone who runs into a glass door and for a moment sticks to it in perplexity (*il avait la gueule tanqué dans la vitre*), a car which because of its Marseillais speed falls into the ditch (*sa bagnole était tanqué dans la boue*). It may be a popular Marseillais derivation of *tangage*, which in turn means something like the pounding of a ship. Pétanque, as we could already guess, is therefore nothing but the helpless

172

swaying when a ship is grounded, a terrible image of the old man's nostalgia for walking, who therefore – who knows – wanted to walk over the water to join the fishermen of his youth, who disappear over the horizon every day; a Christ-like longing for the infinity of the sea. And the pétanque players, who long for the infinite by standing swaying with a ball tucked behind their hands in order to hit an object they have just thrown away, well, it's clear they long unknowingly for the quiet peace of death rocking them in its wide embrace. What Marseillais would not like to die like that, peacefully rocking and making their way over the water until they dissolve on the horizon in the light of the Other Side, which they both abhor and love? They throw their last ball with great precision and behold, they strike Nothingness with a cracking dry impact. They have won.

The man who arose from death and could walk again, Lazarus, traditionally came to Massilia and lived happily ever after. He was accompanied by three Biblical women, all of whom were called Maria, and he landed in, you guessed, Les Saintes Maries de la Mer.

According to Jean Giono, the slightly better-off residents of Marseilles live with their backs to the sea and all those stories about the south; they take their holidays in the mountains in the north, go to the Alpe d'Huez or rent a little old house in a village high in the hills to escape the oppressive summer heat, and are quite prepared to leave the stories about the Mediterranean to the tourist, to literature, the *cafard* of the Maghrébin and the postcard industry.

France is fond of calling itself *L'Hexagone*. This hexagon is more or less studded by six points, each of them cities: Lille, Brest, Bordeaux, Marseilles, Grenoble and Strasbourg. If you juxtapose and compare these six cities, you see the mosaic of French imagination, the multicoloured assembly of cultural variations that makes the heart of the true nationalist beat faster when it booms through the countless loud speakers of the country, whether it is uttered by de Gaulle in his London exile, by the Pharaoh-like old Mitterrand, by the vulgar, pragmatic Chirac or by the much more vulgar pit-bull terrier Le Pen: 'Fran . . . çais! Fran . . . çaises!'

It resonates as far as the smallest Bar Tabac in the quiet valleys and hills, in the cool cellars of Burgundy and Limousin, on the plateaux of the Touraine and the Landes, in the ozone-rich hills of the Dordogne, in the hot silence between Narbonne and Perpignan, in the desolate countryside north of Arras, the country of Yourcenar, in the eastern forests and in the petit-bourgeois towns captured from Germany, in the sophisticated places and the dreariness of Annécy, in a narrow street in pre-tentious Montpellier, in the poor loud speakers in countless muzak-filled toilets in the equally numerous desolate petrol stations along the endless motorways; in the lorry of the trucker driving towards the skyline of Brest with gusts of light and plumes of black diesel oil in his wake, who has never heard of Jean Genet; in the Paris metro stations, in the neatly ensconced villas of rich pensioners in the Bois de Sologne south of Orléans; and thinking of this last city, I remember an old song by Crosby, Stills, Nash and Young, over twenty years ago, boom-ing with homesickness, some names of French towns sung in an American accent. It began with Orléans and ended with Vendôme. Even then it evoked for me the consciousness-expanding feeling of being *on the road*, a feeling that in France with its millions of kilometres of winding roads, is cherished with great reverence; and as I steer the car round hairpin bends above an idyllic valley, I hear the crackling gangster's voice of Chirac coming from the radio: 'Fran . . . çais! Fran . . . çaises!' The hitch-hiker whom I have picked up looks at me with eyes glowing and says 'Ah! Les Belles Françaises!' And he puts a cassette into the dashboard with music by the French cult group *Nique ta mère* ('Fuck your mother').

Of course, and this is very important, there are at least two kinds of Africans in Marseilles, who have little to do with each other: on the one hand, the 'blacks', the Africans from Central Africa who exude melancholy, self-respect and silent homesickness. They hawk fake wooden statues, earrings and bracelets, and people have been wondering for decades who ever actually buys such things – and on the other hand, the Maghrébins with their complex love–hate relationship with everything that calls itself French culture, and equally with their paradoxical attitude to Islam. The 'black' African quietly despises the neurotic attitude of the nervous Algerian, he sits smoking in the shade and looks the other way when all the bustle gets too much for him. But the average emancipated Muslim from North Africa has a difficult time. He is between 20 and 40, hangs out in the discotheques, is obsessed by blonde girls, and once he has got one talking – irrespective of how she looks, only the crude semiotics of the type has him in its grasp – he starts complaining about the decadence of the West and the nobility of his lost culture, his Muslim seriousness comes to the fore and he loses what he wanted; or, even worse and more irritating, he despises the girl when she gives herself to him because once again it was too easy, and he dreams of the dark girl from the neighbourhood where he grew up in a small dusty village, while he is on his way to the next discotheque and gets into an argument in the metro. In the fullest sense of the word, he finds himself in a cleft of history which is translated into a flashing, desperate eroticism and is so intense because the ground beneath it is miasmic and dark, a question of long-interrupted traditions of love, homelessness, longing and homesickness, spiced with new sensations, kicks, attitudes and mannerisms, fast money and fast sex. As if these people can only experience history as bad theatre that they are obliged, reluctantly, to act out. And they play it with such intensity because the rules are not explicit. The magic of this game is the impossibility of finding the *reason* for the rules.

And if you look at this game with its exhausting and

inexhaustible misunderstandings for very long, you understand in a trice why all over the world women live longer than men.

Walter Benjamin said surprisingly little of interest about this city. He makes a comparison in which Marseilles becomes a tarted-up woman and the sea forms the ring of jewels around her neck and in her ears. He says something about the whores, the local colour, notices the picturesque rather than the demographic, visits the Notre Dame de la Garde on the hill. He visits the mussel and oyster stalls, he talks of the supposed randiness of the fishermen and the down-and-out immigrant. The average modern tourist does better. But then he approaches the suburbs and immediately his vision is sharp and analytical:

> The further away we get from the centre, the more political the atmosphere becomes . . . suburbs are the state of emergency of the town, the theatre in which the great decisive battle between the town and countryside rages without a break. Nowhere is this so grim as between Marseilles and the Provençal interior. It is a hand-to-hand combat of telegraph poles against agaves . . . The long Rue de Lyon is the explosives tunnel, which Marseilles has dug into the landscape, in order to make it explode in Saint-Lazare, Saint-Antoine, Arenc and Septèmes. And bury it under grenade fragments of all the local and commercial languages . . .

When I arrive in Septèmes via the old Route Départementale through the little town of Calas, completely stripped of its atmosphere, I seem to be driving through a lunar landscape. The woods have only just burned to the ground, smoking black stumps and kilometres of grey ash line the road. Here and there, as if by a miracle, a small elm or an olive tree has been spared; in its haste, the fire has leapt over them, it was eager to cross the asphalt road, gulping in space and air and in this greed, here and there something fell out of its hot maw. A spindly pink tree stands shivering behind a signpost and behind its thin trunk, we see only black scorched earth, apocalypse, then before we realize it, we are on the last section of wide motorway that takes us into Marseilles. The great arc towards the west past the recently renovated stacked houses, the couple of ocean-going ships gleaming in the dock in the light, and the stream of traffic take us as if automatically to the point where the journey should end, but where, unnaturally, since the building of the motorway, it has begun: to the sea.

Travellers calling in at this city in the past arrived by train at the atmospheric station of Saint-Charles further north, and were unexpectedly plunged into the heart of the multicultural pandemonium, the traces of nightlife and violence, before finding the Canebière and after walking for an hour finding themselves to their surprise by the sea, as a crowning point in their journey, at a square of water around which life tarts itself up for the tourist. This must have happened to Stendhal, who arrives in the old harbour, on the one hand dazzled, on the other hand choked by the stench: it is the sewer of Marseilles, he says, and one can almost detect love in this comment.

When the Nazis occupied Marseilles, they dynamited the bridge at the end of the Vieux Port, because the Marseillais had blocked the harbour. Colourful details have found their way into the urban legend of this heroic act. People will tell you that Marseilles blocked its harbour *avec des sardines*, a surrealistic-sounding act of war. But finally it turned out they were simply referring to a sturdy ship called *La Sardine*.

In order to vent their stubbornness and rage at this wilful destruction of their old bridge, the Marseillais immediately established a ferry service, simply from one side of the harbour to the other. The ferry service is still there and in its fairly use-less record it has only one thing to say for itself: resistance to anyone who wants to lay a finger on the city. And when I think of this besieged city and from there of the maquis during the war, I again feel the astonishment which can take hold of me in Bulgaria, Greece or wherever under the southern sun: what business did those German bastards have here, with their shad-owy forest romanticism and their bloody hands? Immediately afterwards, I realize with a jolt that this city is prey to a hatred of Arabs which flares up as high as anti-Semitism in a Polish harbour or in a former GDR provincial backwater. Adorno was right: enlightenment, or civilization; or whatever we want to call our collection of illusions of tolerance and morality, can obviously do absolutely nothing about the fate of individual people.

The extremely affable German on the terrace of La Samaritaine asks the waiter in broken French for another beer. The waiter pretends not to have heard him.

At the end of the Vieux Port, where the Pharo stands and the sea opens with a quarter turn between the reinforced banks, scores of small dark-brown boys dive incessantly into the waves, right next to the ships sailing by, and when they climb back on shore they pull themselves up on the sign which says it is strictly forbidden to swim there. They remind me of a quay on the Neva, in Petersburg, where the same kinds of boys gather on hot days and dive in and out of the water in the same way, like living scum, like human sardines round the gaping maw of the water.

There is no more breathtaking description of Marseilles to be found than that of René de Chateaubriand who, in his *Mémoires d'outre-tombe*, tries to paint a picture of the last great plague epidemic in Europe. According to the usual story, a skipper sails into the harbour of Marseilles in 1720. He has two cases of plague on board, presumably brought from Arabia, but fails to report this to the harbour authorities, for fear of jeopardizing his economic situation if the whole of his cargo is destroyed for safety reasons. A few days later, suppurating death has penetrated deep into the city, the ravaged citizens close shutters and doors, all the dazzling and multicoloured life is stilled and the southern port city holds its diseased terminally ill breath. 'Now and then amid the silence one heard a window open and a body fall out,' writes Chateaubriand.

Bodies have been brought for three weeks to the esplanade of La Tourette, by the sea, which exposed to the sunlight and melted by its rays, formed a great rotting lake. On this expanse of dissolving flesh only the worms left an impression of movement in the fleeting, undefinable forms, which may once have been human faces.

The man to whom the Cours Belsunce is dedicated, Bishop Belsunce, cautiously emerges from his palace after a few weeks and, like a minor pope, hastily blesses the city *urbi et orbi*. 'What hand could have called the blessings of heaven down more bravely and with more purity on so much misfortune?' Chateaubriand wonders, and it is impossible for the modern reader to read this other than as a sarcastic comment.

In their commentary on the outbreak of this last epidemic of European plague, Julie Agostini and Yannick Forno, the compilers of the book *Les Ecrivains et Marseilles*, immediately add the comment that the irresponsible ship's captain reminds them of a more recent case of the same lack of moral responsibility: the French doctors who, out of economic considerations, allowed blood infected with HIV to be used for transfusions.

Much to the chagrin of the envious, the Rue Canebière can only be translated as Spliff Street: the Greeks stored their supplies of cannabis there.

A regular marijuana smoker, the poet Arthur Rimbaud, arrived in this city after his much-vaunted wanderings and feats of arms in the Arab world. By then he was a wreck, his left leg was completely crippled by arthritis and dropsy, he wrote plaintive letters, he couldn't get about any more; life had become impossible, 'and I, impotent and unhappy, I can't find anything, any dog in the street can tell you that . . . Tell me,' he writes to the harbourmaster, 'when I can be taken on board . . .' A little later he is dead. The longing for the coast, on which Alain Corbin has written such an impressive book, here manifests itself in its ultimate form: carry me away from here, only the water can bring me release. As if he wanted to carry his diseased body out of the city again to recover at sea. Thus, the dying poet, with his one frail sick body, turned the story of the plague imported from the sea on its head, like a small, weeping, failed Christ, suffering in no one's place or name, stoned and dead tired and with only one leg, like a leper, like Lazarus who wants to go back to sea, with a longing to go home: 'Tell me when I can go aboard because I want to go home . . .'

But what does home mean?

The boy, in 1940, took more than a year to get home and then immediately went underground to escape the inevitable consequences.

Never Run Away from a Kiss

Of all the ideas that were formed in the generation to which I belong about the nature of modern cities, those of Walter Benjamin have become the most widespread – and hence the most petrified into a cliché. The symbolism of the indoor shopping arcade, the attitude of the intellectual *flâneur* who, like Baudelaire, is absorbed in the 'non-auratic' appearance of the merchandise, the reflection of the intellectual bohemian who is conscious of being stared at like a witness lost in a reflection – all this has been aired extensively, particularly during the 1970s and 1980s.

Talking about cities means always using a kind of metaphor. And as I recently read somewhere, petrified metaphors are dogmas. European culture is scattered in cities, each of which argues against the unambiguous definition of the word culture. Present-day European culture is formed by the negation of a fixed culture. This is why it is absurd to play off cities one against the other, as Régis Debray does in his book *Against Venice*.

And yet the image of the modern city as it grew in Benjamin in the *Passagenwerk*, a massive uncompleted tome that can be regarded as a fragmentary modernist variant of the eighteenth-century encyclopaedia, is infused with an image that again and again manages to bloom in his nostalgic poetry: that of glass-covered shopping malls, the dream of an intimate city where anonymity and eroticism reinforce each other. Although it is of course true that as a dialectical materialist and philosopher, Benjamin was not exactly aiming for this vulgarized intellectual effect of the 1970s and 1980s – this fashion is also abhorrent to his strictest interpreters – and such an analysis of the city would have done better to concentrate on the rapid development of the masses in London. Nevertheless, there is in this metaphor, this talking of cities as covered spaces in which the semiotics of desire and hidden cross-connections glow beneath the surface, something that is constantly groping beyond the boundaries of analysis and trying to become experience again. It is something that occurs to you when, for example, you have a coffee on the terrace of the Mokafé in the Galerie du Roi in Brussels. For we are aware of how this image of Benjamin's, this metaphor of the nineteenth-century modernity of the big city – the arcade – became the basic model for a large part of our critical thinking about contemporary complexes like City 2, the Galeries Lafayette or Harrods.

Just as Bologna becomes unforgettable when you walk from one street or alley to another under the arcades in light rain, or as Ostend only really shows itself when you have learned to connect the Thermen and the pier with the image of provincial life in the town, or as the shady arches of the Plaza Mayor in Madrid conjure up history in a single image, in the same way, Benjamin has characterized the modernistic Paris of before the First World War in an image – an image of what has gone, a Paris that we can scarcely find any longer in today's streets. Because La Défense and the Trocadero, the bubbling district of Oberkampf (sic) show a contemporary Paris trying to project itself far forward into a different age and century from the so-called modern: that of a utopian globalism.

On 5 August 1935, Adorno writes, in a letter, of Benjamin's attempt to see historiography as the awakening from the dream of time, that things only become charged with all kinds of hidden meanings when they lose their utilitarian value; subjectivity begins to smother them with emotions of anxiety and dreams; thus, these objects acquire a kind of aura of what has been lost and what is infinite. Benjamin includes this passage in a chapter of the *Passagenwerk*, in which he tries to establish the epistemological foundation of his great undertaking and adds the following sentence: 'Dialectical images are constellations of alienated things and carefully circumscribed meanings.'

Things from which we have become alienated, but from which a precise semantic charge has somehow remained in the language – something like the arcade, that is, something old-fashioned with its air of aloofness that nevertheless gives us the feeling that it is familiar and close by. This interaction between the familiar and the alienated forms the basis of that specific, pleasant feeling of expanded consciousness when we first arrive in a foreign city.

The books of W. G. Sebald, the melancholic traveller around England of Bavarian origin, are always bathed in the deep glow of the incomprehensible atmosphere that can radiate from places. No one has understood better the interaction between the alienated and the accurately described than this man, who is able to lose his way systematically in order to get precisely where he wanted to be. Walking through Somerleyton Hall in East Anglia, a country house that has defied the centuries and in the course of centuries has come into the possession of related families, he thinks of the gas lighting that was used in the past for the huge series of conservatories, which leads him to reflect on the 67 airfields in the area that were used to carpet-bomb German cities. The gardener of the estate, William Hazel, interrupts the atmosphere of Sebald's peaceful reflections on this estate of Somerleyton with a vision that hangs deep in the imagination, like a possible doom, over all cities:

> Every evening I watched the bomber squadrons heading out over Somerleyton, and night after night, before I went to sleep, I pictured in my mind's eye the German cities going up in flames, the firestorms setting the heavens alight, and the survivors rooting about in the ruins. (from *The Rings of Saturn*)

This William Hazel, who had never heard of the German Jew, Victor Klemperer, had definitely seen Klemperer and his fellow sufferers in his anxious imagination; and the bombed Jew from Dresden, who felt condemned by the fury of the Royal Air Force, did not know that he had existed in the head of someone else – and an Englishman at that – albeit as a possibility, an image of all the others. Thus, reading a book by a Bavarian about England, I found myself in Dresden again, which I couldn't forget because I did not understand what I had seen.

In the night, one's thoughts go from city to city, from one place to another, and the air is full of incomprehensible signs, while the street-walkers and the pushers, the bourgeois opera-goers, the couch potatoes chewing on their toothpicks and the losers in the suburban pubs dream of another life in each other's place. In the night, we walk aimlessly through cities, having lost ourselves a little, and the image of the city effortlessly transcends the streets through which we are walking. What are you going in search of, sleepless, towards morning, in streets where crunching, loose sand has taken over from the life that still glowed there a few hours before? I regularly dream that I am walking through narrow alleyways, pursued, I jump on the back of a motorbike, we race off, and I look up and see a signpost in the dark sky above me. They are fragments of a life that I once lived. And I think of the impossible book, the book on the City of God of the patriarch Augustine, I feel the pathetic longing to go under in a city without limits, and the sewers gurgle, oil drips from the spluttering engine, the wind forces vicious grains of sand through a gate that during the day had looked so innocent. My lover is standing weeping against a wall, her knees grazed and a patch of blood on one cheek. And I awake with a start, embrace the sleeping body next to me, wake the drowsily grumbling woman with kisses and listen with her to the noises in the night-time street.

One Sunday afternoon, strolling through Ljubljana, I saw nothing at all of what I had expected, but because of that I was confronted with the traces of my own imagination. The small film crew had cordoned off a few Baroque streets and got a group of clumsily acting figures in historical costumes with parasols to parade behind a peasant cart. It was like one of those dreary Flemish films depicting the Good Old Days. We had expected a glimpse of the Slovenian cult group, Laibach, something of a heavy scene, but we saw only houses that seemed to be made of sugar, bourgeois, clean, free of even the tiniest tag or graffiti. Initially this was disappointing, we found ourselves guilty of a cheap longing for sensation as we walked through the silent streets. But slowly, in this emptiness, in this emptiness and within our memory, the protesting, hectically driven voice of the philosopher who dominated this city, Slavoj Žižek, something began to dawn on us. Something of this crushing provincialism was undoubtedly necessary to be able to think up a group like Laibach at all. Their sarcastic parodies from the 1980s, in which all forms of rhetoric were ridiculed indiscriminately, undoubtedly had something of the crude provincialism that lurks in every anarchic revolt, feeling one-self not bound by any nuance at all, just by an all-penetrating rejection. Rather like Vienna in miniature. Laibach, with their biting caricatures that target both East and West, both Stalin and Hitler, any hopeful humanism or contemporary fascism, the bombast of Freddie Mercury as well as that of Wagner, both the pathos of rock and that of the political speech, the terror tactics of the cross-examination or that of the commercial show – this cult band suddenly seemed to be a bunch of peasant lads making a terrific noise from an Arcadian country with silent hills and remote farms. We thought of New York, where in the 1980s, Laibach was almost a cult band, we walked through this Baroque and silent décor and we finally burst out laughing – perhaps at ourselves.

At the end of the 1980s, in the Turkish district of Skopje, the exciting and, at the same time, oppressively provincial capital of Macedonia, among the filth, the noise and the exciting sexual atmosphere of a sloping street where the tension could almost be cut with a knife, I felt I understood for the first time some-thing about the Balkans at the end of the communist era – but again it was that mixture of the alienated and the finely described meanings in my imaginative world, which gave me a shock and yet also the feeling of being for a moment in a timeless space – a space that was full of historical signs. A man with a blue-black beard was talking at me with bubbles of spittle coming from his mouth and assuring me that everyone in the West would go to the devil, decadent as we were, and that they would be in Paris in a few years: his culture was fresh and vital, ours was ancient. He looked at me contemptuously because I refused to take a knife before we went into town. It was scarcely a year before the craziness in Yugoslavia began.

At the end of the 1970s, detained in Sofia in Bulgaria because my transit ticket turned out not to be valid, I walked through the park and saw there a kind of parody of 50s couples, all the same, in the sultry air after a shower at seven in the evening. The girls were all carrying an identical, red rose grown by the state nurseries in their hands, all identically packed in a wafer-thin sheet of chalky paper, given them by the timid-looking boys with their gypsy-like fiery looks. I was immediately apprehended by four policemen: I was forbidden to walk around the city. But because of those ten minutes, the rusty tram that screeched as it turned the corner and the smell of gravel paths sprinkled with lukewarm water have forever stayed in my memory as an image of another life in another world, which I search for anew in every city. Not by looking for it systematically but by getting lost without direction.

In Moscow in Gorky Park, also on a Sunday afternoon, sometime at the beginning of the 1980s, still completely under the post-Stalinist paranoia of the old grizzly bear Brezhnev, I saw a man reading a thick book, on an old bench, under the light green of a lime tree, and next to him was a pram. The baby was asleep, the man's left hand rocked the pram by pushing it repeatedly, without thinking, because all his attention was focused on the book. I longed to be that man, to live there and then in that image, under a dictatorship that forbade me to chase so hectically after the satisfaction of my desires, as I did in those days. Shamefully sentimental, I admit, but also an essential feeling of anonymity that makes us aware of the things, the smells and the history of Musil's world of possibilities. That Sunday I would have liked to stay in Moscow forever. Later that same day, I saw an unkempt, muddy path between two blocks of flats and it took me to a clumsily hidden Orthodox church. I went inside and was overcome by something that took my breath away: behind the iconostasis, the gold partition that divides the space in the church into two, I heard the alternating deep basses of the men and above them the pure, high soaring of a soprano. This was perhaps the most overpowering musical moment in my whole life; deeply moved, I was reminded of the Russian songs that the young Stravinsky wrote about his home village of Ustilug. But this was purer, closer to the source of something that I could not name – the alienated – that you recognize nevertheless. On this side of the iconostasis, people were lying with their faces on the cold lapis lazuli floor. A young woman lay sobbing deeply. I saw curly hair fanning out around her head, the legs in the thick, dark, knitted stockings protruding from a grey skirt. She looked like a warm doll thrown on the ground. Religion, pursued by the contrast with the enforced profane inhospitable ethos outside. I tumbled back into something that reminded me of the Sunday mornings from my childhood: the emotion, the ritual, the singing. I stood, as a homeless person, staring at something that I knew so well yet no longer understood. The music was divine, the desolation of these people fathomless and overpowering. The blue church with the onion-shaped tower lay like a toy behind the threatening concrete walls of huge buildings in the vicinity of the Kosmos Hotel. Through a dull window, with yellow stained glass motifs, I saw the black branch of a lime tree that had almost finished blossoming like a hand against the window.

In Frankfurt, near the grass covered bank beneath the high apartment blocks, there is still an old tram rail that allows one to imagine everything that was once bombed to the ground: a city where Goethe once lived and which in the last few decades has disguised itself as a German New York. There, walking in the dusk, I saw a man moving along the famous pedestrian bridge across the Main. The bridge was closed at that moment because of restoration works, the surface was largely dug up. The man had some difficulty in jumping over the great gaping openings. After 30 metres or so he stopped, wobbled for a moment on the few remaining planks above the fast flowing water of the wide river, looked around and then clambered as nimbly as a monkey up the great iron arch, until he was right at the top and was looking out over the middle of the river, perhaps twenty metres above the normal pedestrian level of the narrow bridge, in precarious equilibrium. Because more and more people were stopping to watch, the police finally turned up. The man was exhorted to come down. He remained sitting motionless. After about ten minutes, a policeman ventured onto the planks over the water, held desperately onto the iron railing, much more desperately than the man had done. He made slow and obviously reluctant progress. What's more, he was being laughed at by the bystanders; this made him furious and powerless, so he began shouting upwards and uttering curses. The other man, who had meanwhile adopted more or less the attitude of Rodin's *Thinker*, sat motionless. It became dark, his figure faded. The policeman withdrew, cursing, and joined his watching colleagues. One of them put their van search-light on and set the siren screaming. A second van stopped by the now dew-laden grass in the dusk. The man on top of the bridge remained sitting. When it became completely dark, the fire brigade also arrived. The air smelled of chill, water, late autumn. I could smell the hair of the woman who was watching and laughing just in front of me. A large lorry pushed a long ladder towards the man, laboriously, carefully. At the same time, a fireman was manoeuvred on a long pneumatic arm to the highest point of the bridge. When the fireman had almost reached him, the man on the bridge slid nimbly down, crawled

like a rat across the separated planks, leapt over gaping openings and disappeared in the direction of the far bank, where
the hash-smoking Eastern European dealers cheered him. In the
grass too, by the old tramline on our side, there was laughter,
whistling and clapping. The walkers resumed their slow
strolling; in the avenues you heard the wail of another siren.
The sound echoed from the gleaming tall towers and slid away
across the water of the Main.

In Langres, the small town in central France that lies neatly
with its circular ramparts above the rather dreary plain, I suddenly had a glimpse of the everyday experience that Denis
Diderot must have had in mind when he explained the meaning
of the circle and knowledge encompassed by the concept of the
encyclopaedia (because etymologically the word encyclopaedia
means something like teaching people who are sitting around
you in a circle: en means in, kuklos circle, and paideo to teach;
you can in fact also interpret it as 'knowledge in a circle').

I saw, as it were spatially, how he had wanted to bring everything literally into a circle and assign it its fixed place; this
provincial town with its feeling of enclosure was actually the
basic pattern for his longing for order. In his youth, he had
undoubtedly walked up and down the town ramparts countless times and experienced the order between the enclosed
and the unknown at first hand. Since then, the notion of the
encyclopaedia has been linked for me with the ground plan of
this small town, its sombre Catholic church and the profane
summer light outside, the large gate, the silence round the
Hôtel de la Poste, the small square with its coffee bar, the newsagent's and a few old men with their first glass of the day.
Central France, its endless variety in countless villages and
towns, the fall of the light in great old corridors, the dung heap
near a large village fountain in old slate, the fishermen on the
edge of the city by the pond of some gradually run-down park
or other. There is something infinite in its anonymous details.
But then he came, the man who wanted to enclose everything

in a circle, gave it a place and, in so doing, imbued it with a new meaning; it was the familiar, ordinary circle of the town ramparts around his native town, where he had walked countless times as a boy. The space of his daily experience had given shape to the space of his theoretical imagination. Perhaps this is the only thing that really counts: recognizing the city as the possible spiritual experiential space of others, however abstract the traces may have become. For every theory is the delayed record of experience. It was no accident that, as a result, the city became the arena of people without a territory, as Andy Warhol once said of Baudelaire.

Often it was only through distance, through leaving a city again, that I understood what had happened to me; as if the constantly oppressive presence of the image of the city itself had got in the way of the experience that I was having. When I had just arrived in the port of Piraeus, alone on a seedy terrace and looking at the lazily gliding boat that was to take me to Iraklion, I understood what had happened to me in Athens: a shock which had made me lose my personality, whatever that may be, for a few days, and had caused me to wander, terribly drunk, be robbed of all my luggage, sleep with an Italian girl in the city park, come close to being run over scores of times, there in the neighbourhood near Omonia, the stink of asphalt and stench pipes, mixed with the scent of blooming oleanders that swayed in a few front gardens in the heat and the dust.

The next morning, I arrived in Iraklion, after a night of swaying on a boat in stinking rooms, walking on deck and shivering and sitting down again and hugging my body. The town was bathed in the yellow light of six in the morning. A shattering silence lay over the ancient high walls. It was as though we had travelled back centuries in time. It was before the great tourist devastation of the island had begun. A number of large birds were circling above the town, which I did not yet know. I walked through some streets near to the centre, sat on a terrace in front of a bar that was still closed, tried to get a little warm

in the early sunshine. Then a girl came out through a low doorway in a side wall. In her hand, she held the nozzle of a garden
hose and pointed it at me. In front of me, the reflection of the
sea glistened in the glowing light and, when the first drops
landed on my hair and my neck, I heard her laugh.

In Adelaide, an almost provincially quiet city on the south coast
of Australia, I had a delayed bout of jet lag, was sitting on a
floor in a Hilton Hotel and saw the slowly swaying American
jalopies in an empty, wide street. I had just got off an internal
flight from Sydney, was given a hotel room on a floor above the
inaccessible thirteenth, felt the air conditioning with relief as I
threw my bags down at the foot of the bed. It was February and
40 degrees. I looked outside through the full-sized smoked-
glass window across the empty concrete, suicidal balcony: an
abandoned fruit market, scorching tarmac, not a soul in the
street, empty, vague buildings and above them, a mercilessly
still sky, meltingly grey-blue. It took my breath away. I could
not cope with this, this emptiness without a sense of time or a
feeling of space to give a meaningful framework to what I saw.
I could not stand this looking at a constellation that refused to
form without a semiotic compass, because it appeared like an
abyss in myself. There too it was Sunday afternoon, about four
o'clock, and I thought that something would snap in my head
and start bleeding and make me crazy forever, so confused and
empty and without meaning did I feel. It was fear of the emptiness of the absence of meaning in the empty fruit market to my
right, the complete desolation of a provincial city in the new
world: no sanctuary for the eternally snuffling meaning that
shields us from the piercing meaninglessness of the sun! And
on the other side, the line of a distant beach, the airport to the
left of me, the vague wooden structures in an arbitrary pattern,
an absolute absence of history and meaning, a vague afternoon
light as far as the horizon, where the flat water of the southern
ocean began, something that ends only at Antarctica. I saw
the unbearable meaninglessness lying there in front of me,

shameless, obscene as if it had been caught unawares, sunk in its own perversity: the emptiness of human existence, things and animals, the nothingness in the light; shop fronts, a single car, the heat. I had to lie down on the floor to recover from what I'd seen – rather like looking into the famous abyss from which, according to the philosopher Martin Heidegger, the true nature of existence should glow, dazzling and disconcerting. However, the banal truth turned out to be simply unbearable because there was nothing to distract me.

I was short of breath and hot, and didn't know how to defend myself against the obscene spectacle outside and then suddenly felt cold from the air conditioning. I scrambled to my feet again in disbelief, again looked into the depths, but it was still there, it was clearly there sleeping because it was convinced that no one was looking: the great horrific nothing-ness of everything that exists, snoring like a stray hell-hound, one afternoon in the heat. It remained lying there, for an hour, perhaps two hours. And then I couldn't bear it any more, I could feel something in my head tighten, tighten as if to kill me, as if the wires in my head would snap and everything would explode. I ran out of the hotel, leapt onto the rickety old tram with its old-fashioned Victorian atmosphere, its cool, pale, gum-chewing adolescents standing with their surf boards by the old wooden open windows, and I went to the desolate, British-looking seaside resort about ten kilometres away. The beach itself was marvellous, the silver line broke against a pier, behind which in the far distance the dolphins leaping up and down were visible as flashes and arcs of light. There I wanted to calm down, but a storm was just getting up; I leapt into the splashing waves and then realized that I'd put on my swimming trunks inside out, behind me two girls who were watching screamed with mirth; I took off the swimming trunks in the water, the waves lifted me up, the swimming trunks disappeared in a swirl of foam and seaweed, the wind became even fiercer, the day darkened. I stumbled naked out of the water after a quarter of an hour's struggle to get back onto dry land. By now the beach was deserted, and the wind whistled over the embankment, through the crowns of a few palm trees, over the flapping shutters and the piled up wooden chairs. Salt spray and sand burned deep into my skin. I got dressed, strengthened by this absurd non-existence, this almost tragi-comic flight from something that couldn't be called anything but nothing. As though I were doomed to repeat the joke of the failed Greek hero in the cave near the home of the Cyclops, who saved his life by saying that he was called No One: it is Nothing that torments me, it is Nothingness that has driven me crazy, that made me flee, tumble and almost drown – it is Nothingness. I took the tram back, walked completely aimlessly through the streets, sat down in a restaurant and started drinking ice-cold white wine in great gulps. The image faded only slowly. Later in the evening, I sat smoking on a terrace near the park on the river, and for a moment I was liberated from everything that I was. After the storm, thin trickles of water rose up from the great lawns, a couple of black swans on the bank of the Torrens surveyed the smoking stranger who was looking at them and I suddenly thought, I didn't know why, of a small terrace on the small, slow-moving Flemish Lys, where I once saw an elderly man sitting in the grass verge crying next to a young woman who could not console him.

At night, when I returned to my room, cautiously, like someone who keeps a dangerous pet at home, I went hesitantly to the window, saw that It had disappeared, cleared off, packed up and gone elsewhere, perhaps to go and lie next to a couple of wooden shacks in the suburbs, in a metro station, or elsewhere by a stretch of grass where the tarmac stops and barbed wire hangs from an old eucalyptus tree over which an ant colony is moving. The Great Nothingness had gone, I got my breath back with relief and began my stay by sleeping fitfully, getting up again, drinking water, zapping the TV. But on television I suddenly saw images that struck me as surreal: on a motorway in my unsightly homeland, two hundred cars had crashed in the winter morning fog. Images of a foggy morning in winter on the other side of the planet, while I sat puffing away in the summer night. A huge mound of hissing, twisted and dented metal, inextricably entwined with bruised limbs, motionless heads, invisible horror in a huge indifferent light leered at me, amid a landscape that I knew in detail – just by an exit road where I knew a friend lived. *Crash*, but on a massive scale, theatrical, apocalyptic in the pale winter sunshine. It seemed to me a mythical suicidal ritual of runaway metal lemmings. My heart missed a beat, but in fact it was all unreal and incomprehensible. So that's where Nothingness went when it left me, and it pounced, amid something that was familiar to me; it had just lain sleeping off its hangover before striking there so close to home but twenty thousand kilometres from where I was. There too I looked again at the completely absurd stopping and beginning of things, situations, lives, landscapes, histories. On the screen, the sun came slowly through the fog, an apocalypse that went on for miles showed itself in an unmanageable number of horrific stories, which disintegrated in the absurd silence of the frosty meadows and fields. Hissing engines, trucks lying sighing and puffing, high-pitched voices that were vaguely like those of small animals in their death throes. Outside I could hear laughing people coming out of a nearby discotheque, crossing the street, shouting something in the darkness of the empty hot street. From that moment on, the awareness has never left me: while, on one side of the planet, people walk through a foggy winter's night with their collars turned up against the polluted mist, others are lying laughing at the edge of a wood in the late summer, with the smell of ripening fruit and dry grass in their noses. Everything takes place at exactly the same time – at each breeze, at each dusk, of everything that I saw I could just as well think the reverse. It no longer made any difference. OK, clichés, planetary visions, nothing new, *vieux jeux*, they were already in fashion at the beginning of the century, those kinds of stories (the Dutch critic, ter Braak, already made fun of them). But the things you know are not the things you experience. There is a gaping chasm between understanding and experiencing.

All my memories of London are muddled up – images of the first time, a guest house in Kensington Gardens, I see the naked body of my lover against the light of an old town garden and I know that, after making love, we were rather disgruntled about something, but I can still see the reflection of that light on her skin. Years later, with another woman, I see the small gloomy room to which we are shown by a Greek, I am lying on my back and she is lying on top of me and watching; it's raining outside and later we will drift from one strange situation to the other until late at night, a little fatalistic and indifferent, as people are after they have been deeply satisfied by each other. I see faces in the underground which will be with me for ever; a man with a slash right across his face, an old woman in her newspaper stand who calls everyone *honey* and *sugar* with a cynical grin, the boy lying delirious under a bush somewhere on the edge of Hyde Park, a face that I believe I recognize over ten years later in a New York street scene in Paul Auster's *Smoke*.

Having just crossed Checkpoint Charlie in Berlin with a lot of fuss – we had provoked the Vopo by putting the car radio on at full volume, Bowie: 'We are the goon squad and we are coming to town, beep beep'– we walk at five in the afternoon in the direction of Alexanderplatz, still completely set up by the days in the West, and see rabbits sitting playing in the grass, the centre of the city, while on the other side of the wall, the exhaust fumes billow and the endless lines of cars glitter in the light – you can see that from the high tower in the East. A little later, my girlfriend gets the giggles about something that we remember together; a few silly remarks later, I get them too and before we know it, we're standing there screaming about almost nothing and a few seconds later, two men, taken straight out of a strip cartoon by Enki Bilal, are staring at us and asking if everything is all right, after which we are asked to show our passports. We stiffen, obediently hesitating, the gentlemen look us up and down, then examine the photos seriously, look straight through us, hand back the passports and say that we must move on. We are taken aback, feel like typical Western idiots. The subtlety of a malevolent, omnipresent surveillance descends on us. We succeed in not laughing for the following few hours. But that very same evening, walking through a desolate street through the dusky distance, we smell the aroma of sprouts, mixed with the wet hemp of empty coal sacks on a hand cart, and I realize that this is definitely my *madeleine*: just as Proust saw his whole youth open up in front of him by re-tasting that cake, so this combination of smells turned the complex combination lock of my memories, a shock which opened the door onto a lost experience, an experience which landed me somewhere in the middle of the 1950s, in the back garden of a grubby old neighbour who, holding her long black shiny skirts together with one hand, stood weeding in the dusk of her garden. This old woman, I suddenly remembered, was called Prudence – a name that now seemed suddenly full of meaning, but about which I could say nothing. Shocks, things that are alienated colliding with a precisely circumscribed meaning; things that are lost yielding themselves up for a moment. Caution. It is, I think, 1980, and all my later visits to Berlin have been coloured by that one moment.

An empty perspective, a street without life, just before dusk, a side street of the long Moskva Prospekt in St Petersburg, which then, in 1982, was still called Leningrad – reminds me constantly of a combination of my childhood and my memories of Berlin. Remembering a memory, this is how memory builds layer upon layer into a very complex and malleable whole, which can be manipulated by nothing and is felt most intensely when you're not ready for it, only available for the moment. It can reside in the way the light changes, in the shape of a cloud, in a window that is open and allows you to intuit what you cannot see.

On a long avenue, on the extravagantly wide pavements, masses of people were strolling in the sultry, damp evening (outside the city there are great marshes) and when you tried to catch someone's eye, no one looked back. That rapid, almost virtuoso evasive casting-down of the eyes, I found it again in the marvellous Moscow underground stations built by Stalin, where train carriages stopped with rows and rows of people in them, all sitting in identical positions, reading some thick book or other. I couldn't decipher the titles, but I'd never seen such a silent, withdrawn mass of commuters, people who all appeared the same and cast a look in the same way, with their eyes downcast, with countless identical thick old-fashioned books with thick grey covers, carriages and carriages in succession, and on benches on the platforms. And the rustling of pages in endless subway tunnels, innumerable pages that had replaced possible speech, came years later into my memory, as a compensation for the meaning that I had not been able to find, and it would not let go of me. Since then I have dreamed that scene countless times and always started awake with the rustling of those pages in my head.

From Budapest I remember the sunbathing women under the tall bridge near Margareta Island; as the traffic roars past you see the lazy, warmly gleaming bodies in their old-fashioned bikinis there under the bridge, in a small strip along the Danube. I had had the smell of dust and oil in my nose and everything in me seemed to be a memory of something that I had not experienced. So many images of a possible intimacy, a way of beginning your life anew from one moment to the next and consequently something impenetrable, etched indelibly in your mind. In the evening, I went with a friend from Buda to Pest and the girls, suddenly no longer attractive, were sitting in a desolate lounge of an old military complex that had now been turned into a hotel, their cheeks plastered with stale-smelling Rimmel make-up; they assured us that it was not at all expensive and very safe. We simply walked around the block and were astonished at the smell of grass in a bleak, industrial suburb, the exotically overhanging trees in poor gardens, the smell of the hills in a small street, the eyes of a girl of about ten. She offered us wild flowers at a stall that stank of peppers, oil and fried fish.

However, in Prague I bought one of those cheap silver rings for my new lover, in the middle of winter at twelve degrees below; it was at the beginning of the 1990s, it smelled of brown coal in the steel cauldrons on the square, the Baroque gables sank slowly into an ice-cold mist. We came out of the Jewish synagogue and were completely silent. I looked in astonishment at this evaporation of an old world while I paid the boy on the stall, and so missed the kiss that my lover was trying to give me – and so she kissed, laughing and with her lips pouted, the cold Prague air. And the boy called after us, as we embraced each other because of that missed kiss: 'Never run away from a kiss,' in broken English that will always have an exotic beauty about it. Up on the hill, on the Hradshin, I again smelled the scent of brown coal. It was bitterly cold and cloudy, the frost lay on the roofs beneath us. Smoke curled over the roofs of the city like an image from the late Middle Ages. Half-frozen and pale, the Moldau lay around the city and, for the first time, standing under the high gateway through which Kafka must have walked countless times to the Jewish ghetto, I understood what he meant by the Gate of the Law. It was here that he had thought of it, with the city like a timeless Breughel picture down below, those houses with their dark roofs and pale yellow gables, in this timeless cold. It was here that the Model was created. Again the city, in its concrete form, had been the basis of an abstraction to which he had adhered all his life.

And I stood for an instant, just for a moment, in the city of cities and I closed my eyes, because I was being kissed.

Clouds. Home

*My dilemma was this: was I doing participatory anthropology or was I
going to just observe and keep my distance?*
H. C. TEN BERGE

In *Surprises,* a witty essay on being at home – 'a place to be fed
up in' – Patricia de Martelaere undermines, in her characteristic way, the idyllic images that people usually fashion of their
home and being at home: a place where you're supposed to be
able to materially read their identity – at least so they hope, or
fear, depending. But home is usually something completely different, often more alien than abroad: it's a place where things
become invisible, where we stop using our senses to explore the
world. At home we put our powers of observation into neutral.
Home is the place where the world around us becomes invisible;
that gives us the peace that we need to be able to think about
things that are further away. At home, things hide beneath their
familiarity. Everything disappears and becomes neutral, things
and perspectives seem to be asleep, no astonishment can arouse
them, we walk unimpeded straight through things and are alone.

That is what we call home, it's the place where we can be
alone with ourselves undisturbed, not because we are somewhere, but because we are nowhere. The place and things
become so invisible that we have time to create a space in our
heads. Thoughts, reflections, broodings or imaginings, but also
self-reproach, anticipatory embarrassment, the necessary
complications of a brain that is not distracted and weaves its
own fantasies. In moments of peace, thoughts become a closed
infinite vault, with countless staircases, landings and rooms
that open up slowly with a perspective that surprises us – a

world like that of Piranesi. (Specialists like Daniel C. Dennett have pointed out often enough that the spatial metaphor for the brain does not hold water: nothing there is located in specific places, there is only activity, energy, impulses flashing to and fro in an organization that is constantly shifting; so that, in our more realistic moods, we are forced to conclude that the brain of the solipsist sitting thinking at home most closely resembles that of a large busy city.)

Home is the paradoxical place where we travel through the world without moving. This was the subject of the famous book by the eighteenth-century French writer Xavier de Maistre, *Voyage autour ma chambre*. De Maistre describes in an inimitable ironic way a number of objects in his room but, in fact, he is at the same time mainly talking about what carries him far from these things, namely the associations that they evoke in him. Besides the spirit that resides in him, there is unmistakably a beast that lodges within and that emerges from material things.

So de Maistre thinks and writes because he supposedly sees the things around him very clearly and absorbs them. But anyone who expects to find a precise description of his room, is in for a disappointment. The room does not become at all visible or clear because everything that he finds immediately takes him towards texts, myths, worlds outside. A journey round the world in 80 minutes, a travelogue with such large inserts that the background becomes invisible. This means no more or less than that de Maistre was really at home: he could say nothing concrete about it. Just as with the young, somewhat neurotic Berlin poet, Gottfried Benn, whom I discuss below, everything was immediately an excuse for a trip to eternity.

We can only really think properly when there is nothing to distract us because the specific quality of the space has long eluded us, because the décor exudes a neutrality that allows us to design unimpeded someone who is not determined from outside – our self. Hence the recklessness of people travelling through their own head: they design a virtual parody of the blood, sweat and tears of the explorer, they punish not their bodies but their heads, and it sometimes gives them a very schizophrenic feeling.

Even the Dutch writer, Hans ten Berge, who, as is well known, has done a lot of travelling, begins his book with its telling title – *The Stay-at-Home Traveller* – with this provocative statement:

> A confession to start with: I've never been anywhere. All my journeys have been invented. Greenland, Poland, Mexico – I have never been there. Adventures at first hand, forget it . . . I have an immense fear of travel, which prevents me from crossing the Dutch border.

What follows is a virtuoso piece of prose, at once a pretence and a journey to New York. There are even a number of photos attached, printed alongside the text, which could not be more explicit: the narrator has certainly travelled, somewhere he has even seen women squeezing a breast out of their saris to squirt a splash of mother's milk over the food of Savimbi's soldiers; and he really has seen a huge striptease artist throwing her right leg in the air while a shoulder strap of her lace bodice has already slid from her large left breast . . . Except, the photos are a little suspect. In fact they look very like photos that have been cut from a newspaper. After a number of weeks of wild scenes in America, the traveller comes home; he announces that he has been cured of his fear of travel. The last sentence reads: 'Some day I wanted to see everything that I'd experienced with my own eyes . . .'

The converse of this game of virtual travelling can be easily guessed: anyone who actually does travel, regularly observes that because of the new things around him, he is constantly reminded of things that he thought he had left behind. We could just as well say that anyone who travels, in fact always in some sense stays at home (perhaps the thing to do when travelling is to stay 'virtually' at home as little as possible: otherwise we are like the kind of tourists who go abroad only to continue their own petty habits in an almost neurotic way, to protect them and even to demand them in a whining voice).

Not being home is therefore perhaps nothing but a state of mind, an attitude, a form of detachment from the world, or shall we say: from one's own small world. Not being home means that in your own little room you are amazed at things that you had long since ceased to notice. Anybody who finds a memory hidden under a layer of dust years later, pretends not to be home when there is a ring at the door.

Only people who are *not* at home see things, because they are astonished; people who are astonished are brought up short by the oddness that they always believe they see in what is unknown, they look, observe and do not take things at face value. But people who walk through the city where they live, who are at home in the streets on the squares, at a monument covered in sprayed graffiti or at a tall office building in a run-down street behind an old station, on the sunlit cracked asphalt behind which looms up an old gable that they have not looked at for years although they pass it every day – those people are home.

> Home is the place where you sleep best, and deepest. Nowhere else does bed feel like it feels at home. The truth is that bed at home doesn't feel at all any more, one quite simply doesn't feel it . . . (Patricia de Martelaere)

In a poem that has become famous, Gottfried Benn has described the attitude of the stay-at-home as that of the man who is constantly designing himself; only the stay-at-home, in principle, was capable of becoming a 'radar' thinker, someone who in his mind could extend his antennae to the furthest horizons and remain cold at the prospect. A negative attitude towards, even indeed a deep contempt for the excitement that the world has to offer, was a basic condition for this: the stay-at-home radar thinker lived on stasis in order to be able to imagine all the better the all-embracing movement of life. The lonely Benn sitting in his sober Berlin rooms did not feel cut off from the world. On the contrary, again and again, dynamic shreds of the world that he arrogantly rejected appear in his poems. Benn's urban solitude was not a fruit of the age-old tradition of withdrawal of the ascetics (except perhaps in one sense: that he, like St Anthony, was punished with visions of the countless copulations, murders and deaths that take place every moment). Nor was his static existence related to the infamous mediaeval *acedia*, that supposed idleness in which the devil found work for idle hands, the idleness through which bad thoughts come (although on occasion he expressly alluded to this: in his poems there is talk of snorting cocaine and of *'dunkle, süsse Onanie'*).

> Taking up positions,
> acting,
> coming and going
> is the sign of a world
> that doesn't see clearly
> (from *Static Poems*)

The poem 'Travelling' says:

> Oh, in vain all the travelling!
> Only late do you learn what you are:
> stay and quietly cherish
> the I that encloses itself.

And in a poem entitled 'How Awful', the fifth verse reads:

> Awful: being invited,
> while the rooms at home are quieter,
> the coffee better
> and no conversation's required.

In one of his early prose fragments, Benn describes his literary alter ego, the young doctor Rönne, who would like to go from Brussels (where Benn was stationed as a military doctor during the First World War) to Antwerp, but never gets to the point. Ironically enough, the piece is called 'The Journey': 'Rönne

203

wanted to go to Antwerp, but how could he do that without going to pieces completely?'

So he simply imagines what it would be like: himself in the train, people at the table who would be talking about him and gossiping about him. He breaks out in a cold sweat: 'Had he gone mad, trying to break the mould that bore him?'

The anxious, indeed neurotic question being posed here is of great importance. It shows the deepest depths of the fear that some people feel when they leave their familiar home: that they will lose their identity – this amalgam of unreflected ego neuroses that one has to give up outdoors because one is frightened of being stared at.

And since Rönne finally does not go to Antwerp (of course not), he travels in his imagination and fear travels with him: 'Who is so terribly addicted as I am to the connection between things . . .' Finally, he decides nevertheless to get out of the stifling enclosure of his room, goes outside and walks to the park:

> Again it loomed up darkly, cloudy and trembling, from the feeling of sleep in which one was submerged, without allowing any excitement about it, having died in misery, only existing as a kind of intersection; but he still walked on through the spring and created himself as he walked past the bright anemones and the grass; he leant against a Hermes column, derelict and pale, eternally of marble, here and there disintegrated, but originating from the stone quarries where the southern sea never faded.

Thus, Rönne – who is not travelling to Antwerp after all – arrives in Hölderlin's 'blessed Greece' in the park round the corner . . . in order to group himself together fleetingly as an ethereal and elusive I. Hence a typical large city-dweller of his time, if only reluctantly: someone who can see in every spot in his neighbourhood, a reference to something that is far away and yet at the same time very close, namely in the head. Usually he sees nothing at all of his surroundings, except the inside of that head.

But, in turn, that nothingness in the head is equally a place where the whole world appears in imagination – something like the infamous Aleph from the story of the same name by Jorge Luis Borges. Perhaps we must conclude that all of us have an Aleph like that – an imaginary ball glowing in the dark where we see the whole world simultaneously writhing and moving – in our own cellar.

The 'radar' thinker, the person who receives vague signals from the world buzzing around his quiet spot and listens to the silence of the house, who sets himself up as a mini-observatory for radiation which can seep through anywhere and charge the silence with its imperceptible tensions, listens to the silence of the things that have long escaped him. Only because of this is he a self-designer, because there's nothing more that can frustrate him; he is the absolute ruler because the things sleep at his feet like dogs; he is calm and sovereign because the world no longer intrudes on him with its always strange and unexpected surprises. Exhaustion, the inconvenience and the pain have been reduced to a minimum. That is why being at home is like being in the womb and constantly carries the danger of regression. It leads back to a world where we float weightlessly and with eyes open, while we need to see scarcely anything, and the sounds of reality penetrate only vaguely as if through a wall, a world which protects and shades us. In the womb of home, we live regressively but we are brooding there on the strength that we shall need tomorrow when the front door opens and we hastily take a taxi to the airport, or the tram to the station.

The fact that in that city park in Brussels with its Hermes column, Benn dreamt of a southern sea, is of course intimately connected with the fact that he was still something of a tourist in that city: things still hit him with surprising force. If that column had been on his daily route to his office, the magic would long since have disappeared. No Belgian commuters dream of recognizing that column as a metaphorical object of Greek civilization. And if they did so, they are bound to have difficulties in the office because of lack of concentration.

As soon as we start to feel at home in a foreign city, that city also starts working on its disappearance. After three days, we no longer look at the stops on the underground or tram as they slide past; after ten days we walk down the main streets with our eyes closed because the goal appears instead of the trajectory; after two months, the whole city has become buried under its naturalness, the links between the streets no longer evoke associations but simply their own dreary selves and, through this being-themselves, they disappear from view, though not necessarily from our consciousness.

This strange, unobtrusive 'being-themselves' quality of things that we know so well disappearing from our conscious field of vision, becomes for the first time a real reference. They refer to the symbolic system in our head and no longer to the image that they, purely by themselves, still represent when we walk past them hastily and with an absent-minded look. They have stopped making themselves up to be looked at, tarting themselves up with a morning glow or a sharp shadow by a broad turn, and they withdraw into something like a town plan in the memory; they allow us to go our own way, they make room, they leave us more than ever alone. But, at the same time, they take their place in the system, they slumber like a pinpoint, a bit of information.

It's probably not strange that we have a slightly paradoxical attitude to being abandoned in this way: when we sense that our surroundings are disappearing into the background, we escape our feeling of loneliness and start feeling at home. When we have just arrived in a city, surrounded by all the strangeness that is constantly assailing us, we feel more lonely than ever (at least if we are not travelling in company) but when things and perspectives start leaving us and we are really abandoned by the appearance of the world, we start feeling 'at home' and our feeling of loneliness disappears because we can again be by ourselves undisturbed, and no longer be reminded of the fact that we really understand nothing about the world, no longer reminded of the absurdities of history and geography, of the lives around us that we shall never penetrate, no longer dismayed by the absence of any kind of meaning in an abandoned park, a seedy back street or an empty car park at three in the morning.

All my life I have been at home in a medium-sized Flemish provincial town. That means that I am nowhere, particularly while I'm sitting absent-mindedly in the tram or rushing to the baker's through the rain. The specificity of other cities affects me like a tonic: through the constant operation of the 'as if', those cities tear me away from the place where I am. I compare, decipher, look at a street plan and far away from myself have experienced that as liberating. And yet it constantly chains me to an agenda that is not mine; the world around me determines my actions to a greater extent than usual. At home, I have nothing to do because my eyes are not surprised by anything; and therefore I'm always busy with things that make me forget my surroundings. At home, the hidden agenda comes to the surface, the secret priorities of which we're often not completely unaware of ourselves. The naturalness with which we do things is shocking, it saves energy but neither asks nor gives at any moment an explanation for our actions.

At home, the ego sleeps in its display case of curiosities, which it passes off as self-evident.

Recently I was asked to say something at a symposium about the identity of my home town to which, despite a number of intermediate stop-overs of years in other places, I have always returned (with the danger of putting down provincial roots on the one hand but, on the other hand, my identity is too arbitrary, I have been elsewhere too often, and I lived too little integrated in the local people's mentality to put down roots). I said no, no to something that I experienced as impossible. I see no identity where I am so at home that I no longer understand anything; where every distracting astonishment is missing but where life has attained a transparency that guarantees me the paradise of the empty day, the calm of no longer having to see it. Its ultimate identity is located in this elusiveness. Suddenly, after doing one's work, one nevertheless catches a glimpse of the familiar as something very strange and immediately gives a name to what appears: beauty, beauty of an old wall, a path behind three bushes, a jetty by the stinking water of the town, a view from a window onto an old industrial complex, the emptiness of an alleyway – all these hidden things that should pass as identity. Home is the place where I am no one, although the opposite pushes itself forward as something obvious.

Of course it is here, in this impossibility of saying who I obviously am at home, that the illusive meaning of identity resides: it presents itself as the famous blind spot, the focus which we ourselves cannot see, the place where we disappear from ourselves but where we exist most typically. My experience of this city is like the truths from psychoanalysis: they are removed from my field of vision because they concern me most intimately. They are my home to such an extent that they become invisible.

When they're at home, people labour, often unconsciously, at orchestrating an impossible and secret project: the successful day. That means: ordering all the details that the subjects who know themselves too well encounter every day until there is not the least resistance that could inhibit the neutral happiness of the perfectly ordinary day – 'Oh, paradisial forgetting on ordinary days, be praised'.

I once heard a young woman, who lived in a splendid house and who was on the point of leaving her adventurous and energetic boyfriend, sigh: I long for every day to be the same as the day before. This is the secret, slightly mystically coloured utopia of the stay-at-home. Every day one banishes things to the periphery, sits still and thinks and, through motionlessness, tries to understand what eludes one. To do this, one does not need to be sitting reading or writing; the young woman who found her life too adventurous and too restless may have perhaps wanted to silently sit and look at the things around her. Her longing to obtain something of an old state of mind is completely out of fashion: in fact, she was longing for a domestic form of asceticism.

In his 'Essay on the Successful Day', Peter Handke has described such a day: the demons of solitary domestic happiness which Benn is concerned with, and because of which he regards the traveller with contempt, are for Handke a constant challenge, an invitation to try to exist. And where the stay-at-home Benn becomes as arrogant and unworldly as a Buddha, Handke becomes attentive, almost clairvoyant and childlike, he fights with the humiliation of everyday things. The sticking of the saw in the recalcitrant block of wood, for example; the fact that the block of wood then also falls from the bench onto his foot so that he hurts himself and that whole longing for a lucid, silent action ends in a minor débacle followed by tragi-comic self-humiliation. This impossibility of being completely happy, recurring every day, is something of which we should be ironically aware so that being at home becomes a quasi-heroic game with one's own trivial shortcomings and the blot of ink on the blotter spreads into a continent, full of self-reproach and longing for something better. This conflict, says Handke, must ultimately give one the insight that the day is perfect, successful just as it is. Perhaps this is the feeling that my Viennese friend was looking for when he opened his eyes wide and, with an ironic twinkle, spoke of the great 'letting go' in his life.

When you're at home, you try to be happy while you are shopping or waiting at the check-out, collecting a paper, walking down the last dreary street before you turn the corner and put a key in the lock when you're absent-mindedly thinking of something else. But home is also the place where the average person also gives in to his own precious shortcomings: scratching, picking his nose, dozing off, sitting on his own hand, belching, counting stairs, picking at his earlobes as he reads, muttering angrily at an imaginary enemy, suddenly talking aloud to himself (calling out 'That's what *you* think!' as he stands ironing a shirt), punishing a falling spoon severely for

209

obstinately giving in to the laws of gravity or slamming a door with a sudden scream welling up: 'So what, sucker?' and grinning because no one heard it except the door which slammed shut in fright.

Home is the place of unbridled egocentrism, the overtaking-manoeuvre point of humanitarian society where we can air all our bad qualities in a mini-circus of small vanities. That is also why home can so easily be the place of terror for people who live too close together: when there's no room for the paradises of isolation and banal peace.

In the essay 'On Thinking, Building, Living', Heidegger says that we live 'to the extent that we rescue the earth'. It's the introduction to the famous speech in which he actually launches the ecological form of building. For Heidegger, the building is not the literal building of a new house – a kind of living of which I have always had an instinctive dislike – the egocentric grasping of the last piece of greenery that one destroys as one grasps it, while there are houses standing and decaying that have a history, an atmosphere, a choice selection of old materials that deserve better than to be indifferently allowed to rot. No, building is in fact living itself, for Heidegger it contains a kind of passivity, something of 'letting go', letting things go their own way: 'We do not live because we have built, but we build and have built to the extent that we live, that is to say to the extent that we are *livers*.' This means that living is something like building your own life. Every day you lay a stone, rather thoughtlessly and, before you know it, you have an arbitrary structure like the famous French Facteur Cheval. According to the theory of the first great existentialist, we only live to the extent that we respect the place, 'we leave it to itself'; that we, as he says so splendidly 'do nothing to what has been preserved'. In this way, Heidegger creates a link between living and being-in-the-world, living becomes almost a metaphor of existence and our way of living and furnishing, an indication of the way in which we view ourselves in the world.

Home – it is the farewell to the last damp smells in an old wall, not putting on the lights in the stairwell in order to see the night-time gloom waving against the high walls in the restless shadow of a solitary urban tree against the background of an orange street lamp; it is sitting on a stair, listening to the almost imperceptible moving of a roof beam in the night.

Elfriede Jelinek, who makes fun of the jargon of Heidegger's authenticity in her characteristic, mercilessly peevish way in a book with the title *Clouds. Home*, throws this ball back to him. Sneering at the *In-our-country-everything-is-better* feeling of the Germans, she vents her bile on the *Gemütlichkeit* of belonging together, of finding one's own viaducts, street signs, all the uglinesses that we call home, marvellous. She opposes the jingoism that consists of being relieved when we see our ugly home country again – an ambivalent feeling that is particularly familiar to Belgians and Dutch. This collective being at home, this feeling, as Jelinek says with her unparalleled dislike, of 'just when we were thinking that we don't belong anywhere, suddenly we're in the middle', this getting sentimental at the sight of a car number-plate from our own country, is in fact a last form of nationalism in which we try to act out our suppressed infantile passions. (A young Dutch woman to her husband, in a street in Trieste: 'Don't you agree darling, that we've got the nicest number plates in the whole world?' and he, growling with a low male voice that starts in a high-pitched way: 'Yes, and definitely the nicest money too'– this is the extent to which the infantile feeling of being at home can take over people when they think that no one around them can understand them.)

No, this collective feeling-at-home is not what I mean. I'm not at home in my home town for the sake of other people, but despite other people. In the small coffee bar where I revel in a dialect that for foreigners must seem like a kind of Swedish gobbledygook, I see the everyday theatre of *laissez-faire*, the coming and going of the shop assistants and sales girls who order coffee with a dollop of whipped cream. They smell of excessively and clumsily applied perfume, the air is thick with cigarette smoke, the landlord stands there openly and noisily interpreting the latest news in broad dialect, accompanied by the spouting steam of his espresso machine like a geyser. In this emptiness, where signs are no longer signs but inverted commas, where the world disappears to allow me to exist completely by myself, I catch a glimpse of being at home about which nothing further can be said, except that it distracts us from where we are, and that it is a luxury feeling, a feeling for home, for the moments when the other cares cease to exist, and we have time which is revealed to us by a space that has disappeared from consciousness, the time to labour at a self which will only reveal itself when we are no longer there, in that place which is home and nowhere.

So I can't write about my city; it is not much more than *clouds. home.* Yet I can see it from the window where I am writing, lying there like a faded postcard, but life-size, so that the postcard becomes the world: the blunt tower of Sint-Michiels, which was never given a spire because in the fifteenth century the finances of the feverishly competing parishes had become exhausted; the ramparts of the eleventh-century citadel, the Gravensteen, beyond the plain grey roofs of a renovated former monastery; the steep roof of a chapel built in 1607, close by, and when I've reached the highest point in the house: behind it the three tall towers, which are supposed to be so characteristic that they are praised in American tourist brochures as a 'mediaeval Manhattan'– so nothing but history, the flags of Ghent, Flanders and Belgium, meaningless and at half-mast on a rainy day, above the Gravensteen, in the wind and weather, against the clouds, against home.

Bart Verschaffel has written what I consider to be a marvellous essay on this city ('Ghent, the Centre as a Fault Line', in *Figures/Essays*) in which he illustrates the impossibility of characterizing Ghent as an historical place, indeed a spatial one. It is, he says, a town that has not grown from fullness, from being full, but from an empty space – initially perhaps the space where the two rivers Scheldt and Lys converge – centuries later the over-ample area within the new town walls. Verschaffel observes, with the acute eye of someone who is not at home here but has come here to be amazed and observe the extent to which this city is a succession of empty places, how the connection is actually only a hanging together, a succession, which does not admit centralization, and from which the indifferent tolerance of the average native of Ghent seems to derive.

Just as Belgium is a country that produces relativizing inhabitants who only half identify with their state, Ghent has produced citizens for whom relativism is obviously even more in their blood (I of course mean the latter not as an innate quality, but as an acquired habit, a cultural climate, an attitude that has arisen through living together in a particular place).

Ghent has always been a bilingual town, the better classes spoke French and Ghent dialect. Later, from about 1930 onwards, Ghent dialect was replaced among the better-off citizens with 'standard Flemish' which, to their dismay, still remained incomprehensible to the Dutch; and later, in the 1960s, by 'General Educated Dutch', which because of the dreadful rasping and gurgling accent that the average native of Ghent produces in Dutch, was still to their dismay called dialect in the northern Netherlands. Even today, the secondary-school children of Ghent pride themselves on an absolutely unbearable kind of jargon, a mixture of 'fragmented Flemish' and Ghent dialect, deliberate and fashionable precious mannerisms and pep talk, of which the pleasure in use increases with the irritation that it can provoke. For this reason, Ghent people always remain somewhat like naturalists of the old school, their 'dialect' is their certificate of rebellion, their signal to the world that they will still not submit – what was previously perhaps a heroic attitude and still the unmistakable sign of provincialism, this passionate hobby of people who at the end of the twentieth century feel that borders are blurring everywhere and who are afraid that the differences which gave them an identity are rapidly disappearing.

When the famous symbolist Ghent poet, Karel van de Woestijne, was observed by a couple of his literary admirers on a terrace in Blankenberge sometime in the 1920s, to their dismay he ordered his beer in French. Van de Woestijne was a typical example of the better-off classes in Ghent: he spoke only Ghent dialect and French. He would not have dreamed of speaking correct Dutch: that did not interest him. Van de Woestijne, who sought his literary affinities with international symbolists, knew very well that the specific, Stefan George-like exultation of his stately poetry would have immediately been infected by allowing the Dutch of his age to trickle into it. In this way, the language in his poems became what it is, an impossible looking, fascinating neo-Gothic building. But when this same van de Woestijne, in an epistolary novel that he wrote jointly with Herman Teirlinck, the *Towers of Clay*, starts telling stories about 'his' town, we hear the naturalistic writer with all his *couleur locale*, with his both quaint and colourful dialect expressions. The dichotomy in this Ghent poet, at the same time an intellectual symbolist and a full-blooded naturalist, seems typical of the average native of Ghent, who is more likely to seek a link with things abroad than go to Antwerp for the day and, because of the fact that he cuts himself off rather haughtily from what happens elsewhere in the country, he also continues to think in local terms. The result is a mixture of flair and deliberate coarseness. Perhaps Benn's Rönne was a stray native of Ghent.

In this city, which like most other historical towns has sold out fairly shamelessly at the political level to the newest commercial operations, these two worlds orbit and brush past each other: the awkward, waddling suburban families from Holland in the shopping streets that now scream with vulgar commerce take up the whole pavement at one demographic extreme while the slightly withdrawn snobbish super-rich families from the western part of the city, who elegantly and self-consciously avoid the centre, in some cases still send their children to the formerly French-speaking school, the Institut de Gand; extreme proletarian smugness and extreme smug reserve are juxtaposed. In many of the small-town bourgeois families, those two extreme character traits have produced a specific attitude and a middle way, a third, historically developed bourgeois variant, in which reserve and irony have merged in a moderate blend; an attitude to life which was present not only in van de Woestijne, but also in the only Nobel Prize winner whom the inhabitants of Ghent have proudly entered on their roll of honour, the Frenchlanguage writer Maurice Maeterlinck. It is also an attitude that I recognize in the work of the poet Christine D'Haen who grew up on the edge of Ghent. The result is an elusive mixture of earnestness and irony.

At first sight, the natives of Ghent have a penchant for secretiveness that contrasts sharply with their apparent boastful sincerity. The Ghent author, Jean Ray, who also writes in French and whose *Oeuvres Complètes* appeared in Paris in the 1960s, wrote an internationally famous novel, *Malpertuis*, in which the moribund and ghostly remnants of the Greek gods terrorize and taunt the inhabitants of a typically gloomy mansion of the kind still found in Ghent. Such a house with dark nooks and crannies, with secrets that only emerge slowly from behind the flaking stucco walls, seems the appropriate environment for citizens who have learned to link sociability and secretiveness. But it is also the recognizable context of the symbolist era. It is perhaps not coincidental that it was in that period that the city had a great literary heyday.

Perhaps the tendency to reserve is more understandable in a city that developed its identity in the Gothic period than in a city that rose during the Baroque era. The extrovert nature of Antwerp is reflected in its Baroque heritage, in its façades and wide, straight avenues. The reserve of Ghent is reflected to the same extent in the labyrinthine town plan and the close, intimate atmosphere of the old districts, which were created in the fifteenth and sixteenth centuries. What the Baroque was subsequently able to do with the spirit of a Gothic town becomes

215

clear to anyone standing inside St Bavo Cathedral: the old, stylish and sober Flemish Gothic was in later centuries buried under exuberant masses of marble, which were intended to show the emancipation and assertiveness of the citizens from the beginning of the modern era. Wedged in between historical reserve and emancipating bragadoccio, there is an indefinable area, in which provincialism and a certain sophisticated disdain for the outside world go hand in hand.

> Ghent has had difficulties with all forms of domination: with kings and emperors, with Catholicism, with Belgian nationalism, capitalism. Perhaps the rebellious reflex has more to do with a suspicious, stubborn resistance to what is open and strange than with pride and the urge to freedom. (Bart Verschaffel)

One of the put-downs about Ghent says that it is not only literally, but also figuratively, halfway between Bruges and Antwerp: a Gothic city, with here and there small historical interventions from the Baroque era. But it has no town plan that has torn open streets, and in the historic core there are no spectacular road-widenings or great nineteenth-century building projects to be seen like those of Haussmann in Paris or Emperor Franz Josef in Vienna, nor has a confident main street been built as in Antwerp; there is only this withdrawn continuation of life in an unmanageable, historically grown street plan without any logic, anathema for touring the city by car and a dubious protection for the inhabitants now that the cars are gradually starting to give up racing through the narrowest streets as if they were driving along a wide city boulevard. The mediaeval town plan is open for all to see. Now it is suddenly presented by tourism as a fetish: the marvellous sixteenth and seventeenth-century properties, a few eighteenth-century mansions that have remained intact, the spacious nineteenth-century houses, deceptively discreet from the outside, but also the typical 'hovels' of the proletarian textile workers that have survived the demolitions, the unsightly squares in the bend of a linking street. Now that it has been completely restored, the

Gothic enclosure of the narrow streets of the late-mediaeval Patershol has been stripped of all historical individuality by contemporary self-orchestration – by the smell of frying that rises from the ridiculous concentration of restaurants and bistros, a hectic grasping of what can be taken from the chance passing tourists as if this were a remote spot where they had to hoard up for winter. In this district, where the alternative lifestyle is gradually becoming financially secure, perhaps the only exoticism is now to be found among the better-integrated immigrants. Unlike in larger cities, the immigrant population has not found itself in a ghetto but, to a certain extent, it has integrated in small commerce – the carpet trade, the hotel and catering sector, the small independent construction firms. That is perhaps the only way of confronting the ever threatening presence of extremist groups like the Grey Wolves. Immigrants often have an easily recognized identity, they usually speak excellent broad Flemish and make jokes at the expense of the slightly awkward natives of the city who go into their shops for the first time.

In a Moroccan greengrocer's, I saw a Ghent woman screaming at her two-year-old child and hitting it. The Moroccan assistant, a confident woman who wore elegant North African clothes and a chador, intervened and pointed out in perfectly articulated Flemish that 'you couldn't achieve much like that and that a little diplomacy worked better'. She smiled broadly and amiably at the astonished working-class woman who could only speak broad dialect, not the 'higher Flemish' spoken by this confident Moroccan woman. At a Tunisian butcher's, I heard another old Ghent bourgeoise complain because the assistant in the shop addressed her in Dutch. 'C'est encore plus bizarre ça, il parle flamand,' she cried indignantly. When I answered her politely in French that the boy was simply well-integrated and was speaking the local language and that, moreover, the local language was Dutch and not Flemish, I got both barrels: 'Vous êtes quand même tous des gens fanatiques vous.' The Tunisian butcher winked at me and smiled. But I don't know if this man realized

217

that there were two natives of Ghent standing in front of him, one of whom felt that she did not belong to the same culture as the other.

The few wide avenues that were built on the edge of the city in the nineteenth century have been swallowed up by the inner city as a result of the crude functionalism of the 1960s. The elegant 'bourgeois' houses – for someone from Ghent something different than a mansion, namely one category smaller although still equipped with marble mantelpieces and beautiful wooden floors – have stood there, orphaned and dust-laden because of the devastating grip of the car on the city, for a whole generation. The tall lines of trees in front of the houses of the skippers on the Vlaamse Kaai or the picturesque peace of the former Heirnislaan with its double row of trees have been absorbed into a kind of urban motorway, all the greenery has disappeared and the asphalt has been made as wide as possible – in many places it is now being made as narrow as possible. Architectural objects stood there out of context for decades with dirty windows and dark sooty fronts. These houses have been rescued in the last few decades owing to the fact that Ghent is a university town: many of the graduates from the provinces who have stayed in the city after completing their studies have opted for cheap accommodation in these half-derelict properties. Now that these students have become affluent, they are restoring the houses on the Coupure (dug at the time of Napoleon), on the great avenues by the town park, in the vicinity of the station and in the quiet streets in the centre, and are fitting them out with the grammar of their own desires: southern washed walls, sober Italian furniture, planed floorboards and renovated plaster-work. It was this enterprising alternative and fashionable lifestyle which has provided a viable answer to nineteenth-century life in these rooms that are too large, the light in the courtyards, the echo in the coachhouse behind a front that one has walked casually past. These large houses experienced their most difficult period in the decades after the Second World War, when the capital to maintain them was lacking and the functionalism of the 1960s contemptuously passed such architecture by. It was not just Eastern Europe that, in the 1960s, abused its patrimony because of the dogmas of functionalism. This is how part of the urban memory of the Ghent bourgeois mentality is being unexpectedly restored by the contemporary 'lifestyle' citizen. Living with an historical awareness, living by 'allowing things their dignity', as Heidegger said, is of course also an indication that a particular world has vanished.

The penchant for the typical, the modesty of the hidden mansions behind unprepossessing fronts, the workshops of the freemasons' lodges and the temples that the layman finds impossible to locate, the sometimes horrific emptiness of the churches and squares when there are no tourists to give the town some semblance of importance; the way in which the almost stagnant water cuts through the city – all this is occasionally reminiscent for a moment of Bruges on winter days – but one simple cultural event is sufficient to awaken Ghent a little from its provincial lethargy and make it seem, if only for a moment, like a big city.

The nervousness of local politics is fired by this unstable self-image since every event, however local or banal, can suddenly get out of hand and acquire an importance that transcends local politics. When looking for a solution, the vision, courage or critical spirit are usually missing. The critical spirit of provincial towns has a tendency to lose itself in subtleties, not in coherent visions. This is why Ghent has often treated its historical infrastructure frivolously, and urbanization is mostly characterized by a high *à la carte* content. Politicians who have realized that the protection of step gables brings touristic rewards, are not necessarily also convinced that industrial buildings from the 1930s also deserve protection, that open spaces with an historical significance do not necessarily have to be filled up, that demographic networks are more subtle than the plans of municipal architects, that the forever protesting, immorally egocentric shop-keeping class must not hold the debates on urbanization to ransom: the buildings that now appear worthless may perhaps be of great sociological value in twenty years, and areas that were given up by politicians can develop, a decade later, a demographic fabric that no one could have foreseen. When provincial urbanization and the vanity of a medium-sized old cultural town go hand in hand it almost always produces the wrong compromises, with which no one is satisfied. The plan, drawn by an uncultured architect, to squeeze the valuable old fish market between a huge post-modern box full of artificial light and coming too long after its time, is the umpteenth sad example of this. Fortunately such plans are becoming increasingly challenged by campaigns organized by residents who still have some historical awareness.

Urban town planners with sinecures usually have no interest in subtle shifts in demography or in the urban fabric, they pick the signals up too late and immediately translate them into functionalist terms, so that significance and 'magic' disappear the moment they try to 'organize' something. Civil servants trying to get a grip on urbanization are like children catching butterflies: usually they're left with a meagre piece of colour on their fingers. Where people do try to develop a vision, the projects decline into misplaced megalomania, like the shopping centre in south Ghent that has been dubbed Ceauşescu Palace by the local population. No one wanted this project except the project developers and the politicians.

At the same time, it has to be said that Ghent is the first town in the country that has seen a big construction project for an under-ground car park in the historical centre rejected, in a popular referendum that was forced by large-scale petitions. And that did not happen simply, as the press suggested, on the basis of a hard core of ecological and left-wing groups. I saw them that day, heading for the polling stations in their best clothes. The elderly, eccentric people of Ghent came with their heads held high to cast their votes, declaring to anyone who was prepared to listen that 'those people over there in the town hall mustn't think that they are going to tear our town to pieces'. It was 'no' and 'no' was the result: the referendum gained the required number of votes and the town council could shelve its ambitious project, for which planning permission had already been given.

Ghent's former covered cattle market, known popularly by the older name – animal market – was a pearl of a specific kind of architecture, whose significance was not realized. The complex abandoned by the livestock sector offered the opportunity to create a kind of miniature Covent Garden where the surrounding districts could have built a splendid meeting place in surroundings that had developed organically. It was mercilessly demolished and replaced by apartment blocks showing an offensive and complete lack of imagination, just next to the roaring traffic of the ring road. There is no indication whatsoever that reflections on quality of life or the urban fabric played a part in this plan, which largely robbed a district of its centre of gravity and significance. Where once there was a place that is etched deeply into my memory, with its ominous smell of blood and the unforgettable eyes of the waiting cattle by the red-smeared posts under the succession of low roofs – but also with its whole entourage of working-class bars and liveliness around the halls – the umpteenth no-man's land has been created, a contemporary concrete desert over which coming generations will shake their heads in indignation, just as we now do with so many abominations from the 1960s, those last tasteless repetitions of the totalitarian Bauhaus dream. Here too the emptiness behind the apartment blocks is strikingly meaningless, it creates a desolate feeling, a lack of direction, as though they've tried to create space for a kind of creature that they don't themselves understand. Having an eye for a town means not only protecting the picturesque centre, but also seeing the tightly-woven urban fabric that has or had developed in the periphery. This has nothing to do with nostalgia. On the contrary, it is part of efficient urban policy to allow people to be at home in historically developed centres – that specific nowhere where we feel ourselves to be somewhere.

Meanwhile, the non-conformist section of the young

population has moved to other parts of the periphery, the harbour with its docks, large old houses and cheap lofts. And so there too, the town-planning vision will undoubtedly come up with ideas which are already being put into practice, with all simplicity and through the common sense of the residents themselves, albeit without money and the politics of show.

It is also there in the enchantment of the emptiness and the desolation on a Sunday afternoon, that I sometimes seem to catch a scent, a fleeting shred or a flash out of the corner of my eye that reminds me of long ago. Not that this is something valuable in itself, but it is something that can confer value on the most insignificant thing that was once forgotten.

So have I said something after all about this town? I have the firm impression that I haven't said anything at all, simply noted something fleetingly. I must have felt very at home.

> It is a late Sunday afternoon, with the shadows of the statues already long on the squares in the centre, and abandoned suburban streets, where the cambered asphalt has a bronze glow. (Peter Handke, *The Absence*)

Ultima Thule

One afternoon, not so very long ago, I visited an exhibition featuring photos of the old part of town where I live. This district, of which the first foundations go back to mediaeval settlements, had a fairly tough reputation in my childhood: run-down little houses in narrow alleyways, noisy bars where knives were drawn daily, where whores and troublemakers crowded together, thugs and drunkards, where children with grubby snotty noses and grazed knees, with sooty black faces and rags on their bodies, simply wandered around through the streets till late at night; but also an infectious and irrepressible gaiety of people who did not have two pennies to rub together – the whole mish-mash that had here made the textile-working proletariat flower like a field full of wildly blooming thistles and stinging nettles, reproducing itself exuberantly in a part of the city that was lying fallow, a labyrinth of narrow alleyways and mediaeval streets where the average citizen did not venture. When my grandfather used to walk through them, he took me firmly by the hand, dragged me along over the bumpy cobblestones, warned me to look straight ahead and put his hand round the large pebble that he had picked up before entering the district. As a passer-by, the chance of getting a bucket of dishwater thrown over you from a window on an upper floor somewhere was quite great. Later, as a student, I frequented a small bar there, and one night, in the small hours, I saw my English lecturer being mugged just in front of the open window. It was said that he had been chasing the impetuous lover of one of the residents. He landed hard on the stones, but a few hours later he stood imperturbably in his lecture room orating about the similarities between David Bowie and John Donne (in his haste, though, he had tied a second tie over the first, and his right eye was closed, something that made him grin with ominous fierceness). If you were at home in this district, you would easily take it all in your stride, that much was clear.

When I came to live here – almost twenty years ago now – rats, in the evenings, still ran in and out of the old gates, hanging off their hinges, and a metre in front of you they would quite calmly disappear into a sewer or a crack in a dark wall. The district, which is actually in the shadow of an old eleventh-century castle, fired the imagination in those days. It was used as a location in the making of the film based on the book *Malpertuis* by Jean Ray. The large old monastery grounds meanwhile housed odd birds of all kinds and in the cloisters there hung the smell of freshly cut home-grown grass.

I had only been living here for a few years when the great eviction took place. People were turned out on the street with all their possessions. Playful and less playful campaigns ensued, but to no avail. The town council was determined to clean up this area, which boiled down to the systematic smoking out of the poor native population and the then constantly spliff-smoking residents. In the emptied corridors there was a large banner with the one hackneyed line by Rilke: 'He who has no house will no longer build one.' Part of the monastery was restored and opened for residential use, the small scale of the houses around the central courtyard was retained, the town council made great financial efforts to restore the old chapel in an exemplary way with an eye to a concert hall. It has all become splendid, in many places the Patershol looks a great deal more elegant than twenty years ago. But since the area has become commercially profitable, its small scale is being exploited on a large scale by the hotel and catering sector. Restaurant alongside bistro, a greedy pseudo-alternative commerce designed to give weekend visitors the feeling that they are doing something 'alternative'. What remains of this town within a town is just the street plan, and here and there a glimpse of the old cynical spirit. The resistance against the barbaric urbanization of the 1970s, when people wanted to turn this old district into a large car park and to demolish all buildings from the six-teenth to the eighteenth century, was sufficient to secure the continued existence of the area, but – owing to a paradox of the success of the generation of 1968 which is difficult to define – the very genie that people wanted to protect has escaped from the bottle: the dark fascination of a district that had a mental threshold, a kind of old-fashioned secret that was hard to fathom and which in fact had a much greater anarchistic power than the rather childish anarchy of the hippies.

On the grainy photos from the beginning of the century, which were displayed in the exhibition, the unfathomability was suddenly there again in all its power. I stared at the lost images of the town and grinned when I recognized a semi-ruin, an overgrown access gate, the half-collapsed glass and mirror factory in the street where I lived ('Biseautage-Glace Gand'), the old shutters on houses that had now disappeared. There is something gratuitous about being fascinated by the past; you look at the image you want to see. But suddenly I was standing in front of a photo that I couldn't place: a row of houses on a wide canal, and the light seemed not to be the light from here, rather something from the south early in the morning. I looked at the caption to the photo and to my astonishment read the name of the street where I live. Here, where I seem to recognize the back of the plain grey houses, there had been water running until after the Second World War, a cool, deep connecting canal with a wide quay and then that vague light over it, sweeping across the water with the thin mist of the winter's morning. It had something Venetian about it, as it sat there glowing in the morning light, in peaceful decay at the beginning of the twen-tieth century, a century that has now ended. What I had always dreamed, had once been true: the old iron gate with its pointed black rails at the back of my garden, where wisteria badly affected by air pollution grew, had once given access to the water. Once people had got into boats there and sailed up the Lys, in a place where now only a few dropouts sit getting drunk and arguing under the waving crowns of a few tall birches. I stood there looking rather bewildered. So little was definitive in cities. Where now the trees swayed in the afternoon sun of a late September day, in a rather seedy town park, a few decades ago there had been barges at anchor. When I later made enquiries, I heard the stories: there was supposed to be a big boat still sunk in the ground, the water was filled in after the war because of a plague of rats, and below street level there is still a steel bridge. You can feel it swaying when big lorries drive into the town. The ground in this district is loose, now and then there is subsidence because of it, and when there is any digging, old cloisters of mediaeval brick are exposed. I walked home, thought about what I had seen and heard, sat down and started reading.

That evening around half past ten, the whole house suddenly started rattling. I thought that, as a result of a mild earthquake, all the books on the upper floor had come down at once and leapt up the stairs three steps at a time. But since everything was untouched and neatly in its place, I opened the window and looked outside. There a few people were standing looking up in concern, others were just coming out and everyone was hastening towards the same spot, just under my window, it seemed. From the broken windows of the sixteenth-century step-gable house just next door, a thick dust cloud was drifting up. People pushed each other away from the creaking gable. The police came, the fire brigade, a couple of town planners were drummed up from their houses and stood there rather indecisively. The historically precious property that, because of the absurd tug-of-war over the restoration had been standing decaying for decades, was sighing and groaning in the night like a dying man, and no one could do a thing. I could feel the vibrations of the tugging mass of stone through the walls pushing against the stairwell, searching for a support to prop itself up for a few more hours. Houses die on their feet. And as I wrote the last pages of a book that was intended to teach me to clarify something about my place in the world, the old house creaked, it scraped with its snapped ancient roof beam across the sliding attic floor like a horse with hopeless hoofs, it wheeled through the air with a few spindly planks and vomited another cloud of old dust. On the other side of the wall, I could hear chunks of stone banging and bumping their way down as if they were asking me to let them in. I could hear the grit subsiding like earth and stone after an explosion. The whole stairwell was filled with the drama on the other side.

When you read this, the last house in this district that had remained unchanged and unoccupied since the Second World War, the last witness of everything that I was keen to know, but can no longer be traced, will have long since vanished. Tomorrow the demolition firm is coming, tomorrow early, the crowd barriers with flashing lights are already closing off the street, a friendly kind of commotion has begun, people who have never spoken to each other fraternize, bringing out a bottle of beer into this narrow street and enjoying the nocturnal spectacle.

I once wrote a story in which I had this house free itself from its cellars, and drift in the direction of Thule, the point to which the liar, Pytheas, is supposed to have journeyed, Ultima Thule, and suddenly land amid the ice floes:

> I read for a whole summer on the veranda, filled with seagulls' cries, a distant splashing of blue water, polyps and iodine, the euphoria of swimmers and the drowned. The house sometimes swayed and seaweed attached itself to the southern walls, the top part of which dried in the sun . . . the glycine saturated with salt water and wind, carried sea grapes and swelled till it was higher than the roof.

But lo and behold, before it gets to that point, before the imagination can catch up with this house, it collapses. Each pile of rubble has its dream. I am already dreaming of the swaying catalpas, the white poplars and the abundant pollen of jasmine on the gradually rotting rubble.

And I think of the vanished canal filled in after the war,

and the possibility, just behind my own, my very own little town garden, of getting on a boat, sailing away and arriving at Botany Bay, the other end of the world, a bay with swaying white ships by a park with ibises and a huge dog, as there once used to be in my childhood dreams.

Some day I want to see everything that I have experienced with my own eyes.

Check-Out

Aesthetics of travel. In a theme issue on the aesthetics of travel, the German art magazine, *Kunstforum*, discusses all possible aspects of present day travel – the clichés, the brain-waves, the caprices and the paradoxes.

Car. According to Peter Sloterdijk, a womb on wheels. The important thing about driving a car is not the functionality but the thrill with which the womb-like seclusion is combined with the open view of the world gliding past. Ineradicable, eternal pleasure. Deep, deep eternity. Reason is powerless against this archetypal pleasure. Hence fighting the car with ecological arguments is doomed to failure. Freud gets closer to the problem (see *Overtaking*).

Catalyst. According to Sloterdijk the nappy of the excremental car ritual (see *Overtaking*).

Chronic non-specific respiratory diseases (for example, asthma and bronchitis). Sufferers are advised to 'get a change of air' as often as possible. This is supposed to lighten the psychosomatic pressure on the respiratory system. '*Il faut respirer*' say the French when they go on a journey.

Crash. 'Machines do sex for us – hoses, tubes and bars, eternally up and down and in and out; all we have to do is fly,' autobiographical writings of Boris B., the inventor of the perpetuum mobile. From the story 'To Forget the Blackbirds', in *The Limits of Deserts*, 1989.

Emotion/motion. Emotion, says *Kunstforum*, means literally movement away from something, motion away from (e or ex in Latin). E-motion: moving your position.

Far. Perhaps the rather astonished writer, Robert Walser, was 'further away from home' with every walk he took than the Camel Trophy traveller in his khaki world picture.

Francesco's Paradox. On the morning of 26 April 1336, Petrarch climbs Mont Ventoux, with his brother who is three years older. He arrives at the summit after a fairly strenuous ascent, sees the Rhône and Provence, has what we today would call an epiphany, sees as it were the project of his life down below like a landscape spread out in front of him. He is stubbornly silent during the descent, completely absorbed in his thoughts. Having arrived in Malaucène, at the foot of Mont Ventoux (where the bikes are now set out ready), he sits down before supper and writes his frank letter, which has become famous, to Dionigi, an Augustine monk: 'You must change your life.' Because there is no place that does not see you (Rilke).

Geo. Trendy abbreviation for everything connected with planetary consciousness. 'The ego displaces the geo.' – Paolo Bianchi in *Aesthetics of Travel*.

Goal-orientation without a goal. For most travellers with a philosophical cast of mind the only path to truth, which for that matter can only be found in being *en route*. Belongs to the domain of intellectual clichés. Dilemma of the man who at a crossroads is frightened of having a fatal accident if he turns left and so goes right, and a kilometre further on in, in a relaxed frame of mind, crashes to his death.

God. The City of God. Book by St Augustine, which is actually about the whole of world history. The city as the promise of heaven. At the same time, a condemnation of earthly city life.

The city as heaven and hell. Sodom and Gomorrah, but also the heavenly Jerusalem. According to some sources, Petrarch had this book with him on the day that he climbed Mont Ventoux (a huge tome weighing more than a kilo in his knapsack). (In fact he read Augustine's *Confessions*.)

Homesickness. The longing *not* to be at home, to travel or be elsewhere, is also sometimes homesickness. 'Homesickness for far horizons' is a linguistic paradox, because there is no sickness for home. Or is home where the heart is?

Hot air balloon. Somewhere in a book I have a photo of Jorge Luis Borges who, with a broad smile on his face, is standing swaying in one of those baskets under a hot air balloon, next to his girlfriend Maria Kodama. *Felicity*, says Borges, I cannot explain it to someone who doesn't know the experience (he means the buzz of gliding soundlessly above the world). The mythical creatures known as Selenites flew into space in such balloons. According to tradition they reached the interior of the moon. Celestial travel that would now crash into cosmic waste.

Imaginary space. The front windscreen of the car as a television screen. *Crash* as the longing to turn off the screen. The driver driving the wrong way up the motorway is longing for the ultimate, orphic zap.

Jardin. Since every journey is supposed to lead us to ourselves, the end of any trip must be: '*Il faut cultiver notre jardin.*'
– *Kunstforum*.

Mass. The tailback as a post-modern mass. Everyone hates everyone else, hates the thought of being part of a mass. Mass and impotence.

Mobility/mobilization. When everything has been in motion, it is immediately still again. The tailback as a paradox, worthy of

Zeno. Most heroic scenes, the summer tailbacks, the great intersections (the autostrada beyond Bologna, for example). People get out of their cars, picnic, breast-feed children, fraternize, even become sentimental. Say elaborate farewells when the queue moves on a little after an hour, jump half in and half out of cars which again they push three yards further on, 'Andiamo! Andiamo! Allora ciào Alfredo! Ciào Fausta!' The queue stops again. 'Madre Madonna Puta!'

Movement. 'When technology means: complete control of the channelling of movement flows, then there is only one progressive function left for us: to brake!' – Peter Sloterdijk.

Nest. 'The nest is good, but the world is wider.' The line by the almost forgotten poet, Hendrik Marsman, abused for generations as the title for school essays. One must agree with the pronouncement, but preferably very diplomatically.

Net. By moving around, one links up to the road network, a gigantic extension of the World Wide Web, with loops, infinite journeys, cul-de-sacs, sites and sights. Click here!

Nomad/normal. Travel was the normal *modus vivendi* of the first human beings. Staying put is abnormal and more recent (exhaustion of the soil, of the here and now, the blurring of sensations).

Nomadology. Trendy word from the eighth decade of the twentieth century. Actually means: I'm sitting in my room on my lazy backside and thinking about how good it is to be at home and thinking of elsewhere and how stupid other people are not to realize. They can jump in the lake! (See *radar thinker,* see also *Xavier*).

Ouagadougou. A place that is very big in maps. Handy as an alternative for places like moon or hell, word to indicate that you/it/one would like to be *anywhere*, if necessary in Ouagadougou!

Overtaking. See Sloterdijk on the car. The anal pleasure is satisfied in a fantastic way: 'Farting, we leave the other drivers in our wake, as though we were expelling them by passing them. The motorway is a gigantic toilet for human movement' (see *Movement*). Regularly constipated (see *Mobility*).

Poetry. According to *Aesthetics of Travel* an effect of distance and remoteness. '*In der Ferne tritt sofort Poesie in Erscheinung.*' – Michael Rutschky on driving.

Radar thinking. Being at home and trying to think of the whole world at once. Gottfried Benn's famous poetic prose, with the title *Der Radardenker*. Berlin variant of *nomadology* (qv).

Room. For example: 'In my room the world remains closed to me. But if I walk around, I realise that it consists of three to four hills and a cloud.' – Wallace Stevens. See also *Xavier*.

Sedentari. Meaning, seated. The *homo sedens* travels round the world while sitting. 'A long sit.' (Brussels–Sydney, for example. Sitting down for 24 hours until you find yourself at the other end). Variant of *nomadology* (qv).

Slauerhoff. Dutch poet. Journey to one's own obsessions. Rather pathologically nomadological. Unforgettable for the adolescent heart.

Suburbs. Or hinterlands? See *Zone*.

Syntax. 'It will pass, but for the moment syntax is the most important thing.' – Gottfried Benn. Knitting roads and places together until a significance emerges. The motorway and the railway, the escape route and the path, the flight and the tunnel. Sense and nonsense. Grammatical rules for an endless construction of spatial sentences. Every journey has its main clause and subordinate clauses.

Tectonic boogie. Popular expression in Los Angeles, where the city 'survives' from day to day with the fear of great tectonic shifts. Or: when the earth itself goes on a dancing journey. Heard during a performance of an American avant-garde artiste: 'Do the tectonic boogie!'

Tourist. 'The tourist as idiot' – the title of a book by the French sociologist, Jean-Didier Urban. According to this man, the tourist is not an idiot at all, but a modern cultural hero. Thanks to the interest of tourists, the natives rediscover the value of their own culture. Or: the tourist as compensator for the colonialist. Dream or Murder?

Travel. 'Journeying always brings new journeys with it.' – Paolo Bianchi.

U. Letter used in Germany to indicate the underground. You are invited to go underground. An apocalyptic act each time. Confirms religious schemes by technological expertise (see *Black Ponds*).

Water meadows. Former state of the suburbs. Still found in poetry from the inter-war period. For example in Marsman: 'And in the water meadows/the horses gallop, with waving tails, through the grass'; could be rewritten for the postmodern era as: 'And in the suburbs, the cars glide, with cloudy speed, through the gas'.

Xavier de Maistre. Wrote *Voyage autour de ma chambre* in 1794. Was the first to indulge in wandering around rooms. Very clever of him in the first years after the French Revolution. The first virtual traveller. Regarded his room as a kind of CD-Rom with a predetermined circuit. Also wrote books about crystals, called *Voyage autour de la chambre-d'oeil*. My old-fashioned encyclopaedia calls this 'witty'.

Yperite. A name with which a Flemish town became internationally famous in a sad way. Ypres was the first town where the Germans used mustard gas in their attacks (12 July 1917). Yperite. Associations of the genre, Dresden-fire, Pompeii-lava, Sodom-pillar of salt, New York–King Kong, Los Angeles–*tectonic boogie.*

Zone. 'You enter the city via the suburbs. The expression of suburbs is complaint, you don't live anywhere any more, neither outside, nor inside. The complaint of being orphaned was heard back in the time of Villon through the districts of the classical city. It spreads into the heart of the modern metropolises. The urchin, the fallen woman, the children of the suburb, come and sing their nonsensical songs on Sunday in the centre. They recite prose poems. They derail poetry. They're called Baudelaire, Verlaine, Rimbaud. 'You read their brochures, the guides, the posters that sing loudly / That is the poetry this morning and for prose there are the papers': Apollinaire begins *Alcools* with 'Zone'. That means belt in Greek, neither land, nor city, but a different kind of place which is not found in the register of place names.' From Jean-François Lyotard, *Post-Modern Fables.*

Zwarte Vijvers/ Etangs Noirs (Black Ponds). Stop on the Brussels metro. Apocalypse of the rush hour (see *U*). Vision of the City of God at five in the afternoon. A girl reading is pestered. Escalator out of action. Orpheus as a busker. Does not look round as he runs upstairs, towards the light. Fleeting visions of doom in seeing masses of people rushing through the narrow corridors. *Purgatorio. Et in Arcadia ego. Sortie.*

Exit.